T0304134

Capitalist Development in India's Informal Economy

This book explores the economy and society of Provincial India in the post-Green Revolution period. It argues that the low 'quality' of capital development in India's villages and small towns is the joint outcome of the informal economic organisation, that is strongly biased in favour of capital, and of the complex stratification of the workforce along class and caste lines.

Focusing on the processes of growth induced by the introduction of the high-yield varieties in agriculture, the book demonstrates that a low-road pattern of capitalist development has been emerging in Provincial India: firms compete over price and not over efficiency, with a constant pressure to reduce costs, in particular labour costs. The book shows that low-skilled employment prevails and low wages and poor working conditions are widespread.

Based on original empirical research, the book makes a valuable contribution to the debate on varieties of capitalism, in particular of the Global South. It is of interest to academics working in the fields of Development Studies, Political Economy and South Asian Studies.

Elisabetta Basile is Professor of Applied Economics in the Faculty of Economics at the University of Rome, Italy. She is co-convenor of the Europe-Asia Working Group of the European Association of Development and Training Institutions (EADI), and has worked extensively on capitalist change in Europe and in India.

Routledge contemporary South Asia series

1 **Pakistan**
Social and cultural transformations
in a Muslim nation
Mohammad A. Qadeer

2 **Labor, Democratization and
Development in India and
Pakistan**
Christopher Candland

3 **China–India Relations**
Contemporary dynamics
Amardeep Athwal

4 **Madrasas in South Asia**
Teaching terror?
Jamal Malik

5 **Labor, Globalization and the
State**
Workers, women and migrants
confront neoliberalism
*Edited by Debdas Banerjee and
Michael Goldfield*

6 **Indian Literature and Popular
Cinema**
Recasting classics
Edited by Heidi R.M. Pauwels

7 **Islamist Militancy in Bangladesh**
A complex web
Ali Riaz

8 **Regionalism in South Asia**
Negotiating cooperation,
institutional structures
Kishore C. Dash

9 **Federalism, Nationalism and
Development**
India and the Punjab economy
Pritam Singh

10 **Human Development and Social
Power**
Perspectives from South Asia
Ananya Mukherjee Reed

11 **The South Asian Diaspora**
Transnational networks and
changing identities
*Edited by Rajesh Rai and
Peter Reeves*

12 **Pakistan–Japan Relations**
Continuity and change in
economic relations and security
interests
Ahmad Rashid Malik

13 **Himalayan Frontiers of
India**
Historical, geo-political and
strategic perspectives
K. Warikoo

14 **India's Open-Economy Policy**
Globalism, rivalry, continuity
Jalal Alamgir

15 **The Separatist Conflict in Sri Lanka**
Terrorism, ethnicity, political economy
Asoka Bandarage

16 **India's Energy Security**
Edited by Ligia Noronha and Anant Sudarshan

17 **Globalization and the Middle Classes in India**
The social and cultural impact of neoliberal reforms
Ruchira Ganguly-Scrase and Timothy J. Scrase

18 **Water Policy Processes in India**
Discourses of power and resistance
Vandana Asthana

19 **Minority Governments in India**
The puzzle of elusive majorities
Csaba Nikolenyi

20 **The Maoist Insurgency in Nepal**
Revolution in the twenty-first century
Edited by Mahendra Lawoti and Anup K. Pahari

21 **Global Capital and Peripheral Labour**
The history and political economy of plantation workers in India
K. Ravi Raman

22 **Maoism in India**
Reincarnation of ultra-left wing extremism in the 21st century
Bidyut Chakrabarty and Rajat Kujur

23 **Economic and Human Development in Contemporary India**
Cronyism and fragility
Debdas Banerjee

24 **Culture and the Environment in the Himalaya**
Arjun Guneratne

25 **The Rise of Ethnic Politics in Nepal**
Democracy in the margins
Susan I. Hangen

26 **The Multiplex in India**
A cultural economy of urban leisure
Adrian Athique and Douglas Hill

27 **Tsunami Recovery in Sri Lanka**
Ethnic and regional dimensions
Dennis B. McGilvray and Michele R. Gamburd

28 **Development, Democracy and the State**
Critiquing the Kerala model of development
K. Ravi Raman

29 **Mohajir Militancy in Pakistan**
Violence and transformation in the Karachi conflict
Nichola Khan

30 **Nationbuilding, Gender and War Crimes in South Asia**
Bina D'Costa

31 **The State in India after Liberalization**
Interdisciplinary perspectives
Edited by Akhil Gupta and K. Sivaramakrishnan

32 **National Identities in Pakistan**
The 1971 war in contemporary Pakistani fiction
Cara Cilano

33 **Political Islam and Governance in Bangladesh**
Edited by Ali Riaz and C. Christine Fair

34 **Bengali Cinema**
'An Other Nation'
Sharmistha Gooptu

35 **NGOs in India**
The challenges of women's empowerment and accountability
Patrick Kilby

36 **The Labour Movement in the Global South**
Trade unions in Sri Lanka
S. Janaka Biyanwila

37 **Building Bangalore**
Architecture and urban transformation in India's Silicon Valley
John C. Stallmeyer

38 **Conflict and Peacebuilding in Sri Lanka**
Caught in the peace trap?
Edited by Jonathan Goodhand, Jonathan Spencer and Benedict Korf

39 **Microcredit and Women's Empowerment**
A case study of Bangladesh
Amunui Faraizi, Jim McAllister and Taskinur Rahman

40 **South Asia in the New World Order**
The role of regional cooperation
Shahid Javed Burki

41 **Explaining Pakistan's Foreign Policy**
Escaping India
Aparna Pande

42 **Development–induced Displacement, Rehabilitation and Resettlement in India**
Current issues and challenges
Edited by Sakarama Somayaji and Smrithi Talwar

43 **The Politics of Belonging in India**
Becoming adivasi
Edited by Daniel J. Rycroft and Sangeeta Dasgupta

44 **Re-Orientalism and South Asian Identity Politics**
The oriental other within
Edited by Lisa Lau and Ana Cristina Mendes

45 **Islamic Revival in Nepal**
Religion and a new nation
Megan Adamson Sijapati

46 **Education and Inequality in India**
A classroom view
Manabi Majumdar and Jos Mooij

47 **The Culturalization of Caste in India**
Identity and inequality in a multicultural age
Balmurli Natrajan

48 **Corporate Social Responsibility in India**
Bidyut Chakrabarty

49 **Pakistan's Stability Paradox**
Domestic, regional and international dimensions
Edited by Ashutosh Misra and Michael E. Clarke

50 **Transforming Urban Water Supplies in India**
The role of reform and partnerships in globalization
Govind Gopakumar

51 **South Asian Security**
21st century discourses
Sagarika Dutt and Alok Bansal

52 **Non-discrimination and Equality in India**
Contesting boundaries of social justice
Vidhu Verma

53 **Being Middle-class in India**
A way of life
Henrike Donner

54 **Kashmir's Right to Secede**
A critical examination of contemporary theories of secession
Matthew J. Webb

55 **Bollywood Travels**
Culture, diaspora and border crossings in popular Hindi cinema
Rajinder Dudrah

56 **Nation, Territory, and Globalization in Pakistan**
Traversing the margins
Chad Haines

57 **The Politics of Ethnicity in Pakistan**
The Baloch, Sindhi and Mohajir Ethnic Movements
Farhan Hanif Siddiqi

58 **Nationalism and Ethnic Conflict**
Identities and mobilization after 1990
Edited by Mahendra Lawoti and Susan Hangen

59 **Islam and Higher Education**
Concepts, challenges and opportunities
Marodsilton Muborakshoeva

60 **Religious Freedom in India**
Sovereignty and (anti) conversion
Goldie Osuri

61 **Everyday Ethnicity in Sri Lanka**
Up-country Tamil identity politics
Daniel Bass

62 **Ritual and Recovery in Post-Conflict Sri Lanka**
Eloquent bodies
Jane Derges

63 **Bollywood and Globalisation**
The global power of popular Hindi cinema
Edited by David J. Schaefer and Kavita Karan

64 **Regional Economic Integration in South Asia**
Trapped in conflict?
Amita Batra

65 **Architecture and Nationalism in Sri Lanka**
The trouser under the cloth
Anoma Pieris

66 **Civil Society and Democratization in India**
Institutions, ideologies and interests
Sarbeswar Sahoo

67 **Contemporary Pakistani Fiction in English**
Idea, nation, state
Cara N. Cilano

68 **Transitional Justice in South Asia**
A study of Afghanistan and Nepal
Tazreena Sajjad

69 **Displacement and Resettlement in India**
The human cost of development
Hari Mohan Mathur

70 **Water, Democracy and Neoliberalism in India**
The power to reform
Vicky Walters

71 **Capitalist Development in India's Informal Economy**
Elisabetta Basile

72 **Nation, Constitutionalism and Buddhism in Sri Lanka**
Roshan de Silva Wijeyeratne

Capitalist Development in India's Informal Economy

Elisabetta Basile

Routledge
Taylor & Francis Group

LONDON AND NEW YORK

First published 2013
by Routledge
2 Park Square, Milton Park, Abingdon, Oxon OX14 4RN

Simultaneously published in the USA and Canada
by Routledge
711 Third Avenue, New York, NY 10017

Routledge is an imprint of the Taylor & Francis Group, an informa business

British Library Cataloguing in Publication Data
A catalogue record for this book is available from the British Library

Library of Congress Cataloging in Publication Data
Basile, Elisabetta.
Capitalist development in India's informal economy / Elisabetta Basile.
  pages cm. – (Routledge contemporary South Asia series ; 71)
  Includes bibliographical references and index.
  1. Rural development–India. 2. Informal sector (Economics)–India.
  3. Social stratification–India. 4. Marxian economics–India–Case
  studies. I. Title.
  HN49.C6.B375 2013
  307.1'4120954–dc23   2012049012

ISBN: 978-0-415-64268-2 (hbk)
ISBN: 978-0-203-77714-5 (ebk)

Typeset in Times New Roman
by Wearset Ltd, Boldon, Tyne and Wear

In loving memory of my mother Bina

Contents

List of illustrations   xiv
Acknowledgements   xvii

1   **The complexity of capitalist development in Provincial India**   1
    1 A variety of capitalism 1
    2 Economic theory and empirical analysis 2
    3 Purpose and plan of the book 3

PART I
Analysing non-farm capitalism in Provincial India   9

2   **A Marxist/Institutionalist framework for the analysis of**
    contemporary capitalism   11
    1 Introduction 11
    2 The main traits of capitalism according to Marx's theory 11
    3 Evolutionary Institutionalism and the agency/structure
      problem 20
    4 The Marxist/Institutionalist dialogue 26
    5 The Marxist/Institutionalist analytical framework 28
    6 The eclectic framework, the analysis of capitalism, and
      Provincial India 33

3   **Introducing non-farm capitalism in Provincial India**   36
    1 Introduction 36
    2 The historical context 36
    3 Economic diversification 40
    4 Informal development 54
    5 The distinguishing traits of India's provincial economy 71

4   Exploring class structure in Provincial India   75
  1 Introduction 75
  2 The debate on class structure 75
  3 A Marxist/Institutionalist class analysis 81
  4 Capital and labour redefined 88

**5   Caste-based interest representation and the hegemony of
    capital in India's civil society**   90
  1 Introduction 90
  2 Interest representation in civil society 90
  3 Caste as an institution and an ideology 95
  *4 A Gramscian hypothesis on the role of caste in Provincial
    India 100*
  5 Caste, civil society, political society 102

**PART II
A Marxist/Institutionalist analysis of capitalism in Arni**   105

6   Long-term change in Arni's economy   107
  1 Introduction 107
  2 The empirical research on Arni 107
  3 Arni's long-term change 114
  4 On Arni's variety of capitalism 138

**7   Institutional and spatial embeddedness in Arni's silk
    economy**   146
  1 Introduction 146
  2 Arni's industrial district for silk handloom saris 147
  3 Social production relations 151
  4 On the performance of Arni's silk economy 159

8   Capital's hegemony in Arni's corporatist civil society   161
  1 Introduction 161
  2 The survey of Arni's civil society 161
  3 Arni's civil society 163
  4 Class relations in Arni's civil society 180
  5 Arni's societal corporatism 183
  *6 Arni's societal corporatism and India's capitalist
    development 184*

9   The low road of capitalism   188
    1 The necessity of being eclectic 188
    2 The distinguishing traits of capitalism in Provincial India 189
    3 Social downgrading 195

    Notes   198
    References   208
    Index   227

Illustrations

Figures

6.1   Growth and change in Arni's business economy (1973–1993)   120
8.1   Castes hierarchies in Arni   177

Tables

3.1   Sectoral composition of rural employment   43
3.2   Non-farm workers as percentage of the rural workforce in
        2009–2010   44
3.3   RNF workers (u.s.) by state and broad industry division
        (NIC 2004) (% of total RNFL)   46–47
3.4   Rural workers (u.s.) by employment status, sex and state in
        rural India (% of total RNFL)   48–49
3.5   Workers in the *informal sector*: proportion of workers (u.s.)
        employed in p&p enterprises, 2004–2005 and 2009–2010
        (% of total workers in AGEGC and non-agricultural
        activities)   59
3.6   Workers in the *informal sector*: proportion of workers (u.s.)
        in p&p enterprises for different employment statuses in
        employment, 2009–2010 (% of total workers in AGEGC
        and non-agricultural activities)   60–61
3.7   Workers in the *informal sector*: proportion of workers (u.s.)
        in p&p enterprises for different employment statuses in
        employment, 2004–2005 (% of total workers in AGEGC
        and non-agricultural activities)   62–63
3.8   Workers in the *informal sector*: proportion of workers (u.s.)
        employed in p&p enterprises by status of employment and
        by sex (% of total workers in AGEGC and non-agricultural
        activities)   64
3.9   Workers in the *informal sector*: proportion of workers (u.s.)
        in p&p enterprises by industry group, 2009–2010 (% of
        total workers)   65

3.10   Workers in the *informal sector*: proportion of workers (u.s.)
       in p&p enterprises in AGEGC and non-agriculture activities
       (% of total workers)   65
3.11   Informal sector contribution to gross value added (GVA) by
       industry group (%)   67
3.12   Growth rate (GDP at 1999–2000 constant prices) for the
       informal sector and for the economy by industry group
       (1999–2000/2004–2005; %)   68
6.1   Size of the Arni samples   116
6.2   Private firms in Arni   117
6.3   Total gross output in the Arni samples   118
6.4   Total sample average gross output (prices 1993, '000 Rs)   119
6.5   Types of firm (number of firms)   122–123
6.6   Diversification of economic activity (small and big
       businesses according to their investment behaviour, %)   124–125
6.7   Origin of raw materials (small businesses) (% distribution
       of average quantities in Rs 1993)   126
6.8   Destination of goods (small businesses) (% distribution of
       average quantities in Rs 1993)   127
6.9   Origin of raw materials (big businesses) (% distribution of
       average quantities in Rs 1993)   129
6.10   Destination of goods (big businesses) (% distribution of
       average quantities in Rs 1993)   130
6.11   Origin of capital (% distribution of answers by locality and
       type of financing)   131
6.12   Home location of regular workers (number of workers)   132
6.13   Businesses according to ownership (number)   133–134
6.14   Caste codes according to Arni caste hierarchy   135
6.15a Small businesses: % distribution of gross output by caste
       group   136
6.15b Diversification of economic activities by caste (%
       distribution of gross output for small businesses)   137
6.16a Big businesses: % distribution of gross output by caste
       group   139
6.16b Diversification of economic activities by caste (%
       distribution of gross output for big businesses)   140
6.17   Average units of labour (number)   141
7.1   Silk sari production in Arni town (1993) (number of firms)   147
8.1   Associations in Arni by sphere of action (economic
       activities)   164–165
8.2   Associations in Arni by sphere of action (non-economic
       activities)   166
8.3   Associations and informal groups in Arni by membership
       and by influence on phases of production and typologies of
       socio-economic relation (economic activities)   168–170

8.4   Associations and informal groups in Arni by membership
      and by influence on phases of production and typologies of
      socio-economic relations (non-economic activities)   171
8.5   Registered and unregistered associations in Arni by
      membership and by impact on social stability   172
8.6   Registered and unregistered associations by membership
      and impact on economic growth   173

Acknowledgements

The writing of this book has been a long-lasting adventure in which I have been supported by friends and colleagues. First of all Barbara Harriss-White from Oxford University. Barbara has given me her support, friendship and solidarity for many years and has provided me with invaluable guidance in my learning about India and Arni. She has also been so wonderfully generous in sharing with me the precious information and data she has collected in more than 30 years of field research.

Then Claudio Cecchi, husband and colleague at the University of Rome *La Sapienza*. Claudio has supported me for so many years and in so many ways I cannot even describe. Without his firm and constant encouragement this book would never have been completed. My son Michele Angelo has known about this book since he was a small child and, as a child, has accompanied me to India any time it was necessary.

During my fieldwork in Arni I have had the privilege to work with the late P.J. Krishnamurthy, who has accompanied me – as if I were his 'sister', as he used to say – in my learning about the society and economy of rural India, and of Arni in particular. I hope that what I have learned from PJK can be found, at least in part, in this book.

Special thanks are due to Judith Heyer from Oxford University and to Jens Lerche from SOAS. This book has been much improved by their suggestions. I thank also the two anonymous referees who have read with attention a previous version of this book, suggesting important changes.

Special thanks are due also to Kaveri Qureshi (Harriss) and Elinor Harriss Bastin who helped me with the data on Arni, deciphering the field notes of their parents. I could not have done the long-term analysis on Arni change without their help. My assistants Mr Paul Pandian and Mr Jothi, both from the Madras Institute of Development Studies in Chennai, helped me with the interviews and in solving many difficulties, so creating a favourable environment for me to work during my fieldwork in Arni. I thank them both very much. Finally, I thank Luca Scialanga, Ph.D. student at *La Sapienza*, who has helped me with the tables.

1 The complexity of capitalist development in Provincial India

This book is about capitalism in India's small towns and villages. This part of the country – which might be referred to as Provincial (or Mofussil) India or simply as rural India – is interesting for a number of reasons. The vast majority of India's population lives and works in this socio-economic space.[1] Moreover, absolute poverty and deprivation reach their peak in numbers here.[2] Finally, the introduction of the Green Revolution in agriculture has induced a major socio-spatial restructuring in this part of India, exerting a deep impact on the economy and society, which is still largely unexplored.[3]

This process of change is analysed in this book with a specific focus on the non-farm section of India's provincial economy. The overall aim is the assessment of the 'quality' of capitalist development. This aim is pursued at two complementary levels: (i) by pointing out the structures and relations that have been supporting rural non-farm growth since the Green Revolution; and (ii) by exploring the impact of growth on working conditions and living standards.

1 A variety of capitalism

Provincial India markedly differs from Metropolitan India – i.e. from India's metropolises and large towns. Major differences are shown in the endowment of infrastructures, in the structure and organisation of the economy, and in living standards. While lagging well behind Metropolitan India in relation to infrastructures for health, education, transport and communication, Provincial India is also much dependent on agriculture. Despite its decline and its lower rate of growth (in comparison to the other sectors of India's economy), the primary sector continues to be a major source of employment and income in rural areas, and the emergence and growth of rural non-farm activities essentially rely on the human and financial resources extracted from it.[4] Jointly, the lack of infrastructures and the dependence on agriculture largely account for the low rate of growth of India's provincial economy, for the increasing income and employment gaps with India's metropolises and for the differences in living standards and lifestyles (Pande, 2011).

In comparison to Metropolitan India, Provincial India is often seen as an 'inferior' space – marked by 'slowness' and by the 'absence of the new and recent' (Kumar, 2006: 397) – in which a backward socio-economic organisation seems to prevail. In this space, the transition to capitalism is still ongoing, while non-market institutions and structures – such as family, caste, gender, and ethnicity – regulate economic transactions, showing that market is not the prevailing organising principle – as it occurs in capitalist countries (Basile and Harriss-White, 2010).

In this book, I challenge this view at two levels. First, I argue that the idea of Provincial India as a static economy and society is wrong and misleading. This is largely due to the change induced by the Green Revolution, which has given birth to a new type of socio-economic system. This new socio-economic system strongly differs from the pre-Green Revolution situation for a new pattern of intersectoral relations and a new and complex social structure. Second, I argue that India's provincial economy clearly shows the main traits of capitalism – i.e. the commoditisation of the workforce and capital/labour conflicts – and that the persistence of social regulation should not be taken as a signal of an incomplete capitalist transition. On the contrary, its non-market features are an outcome of the interplay between capitalist production relations and the institutions and structures that India has inherited from her colonial and post-colonial past. They represent a major aspect of India's historical and cultural specificity.

Jointly, the new production organisation and the emerging social structure, together with social regulation, identify a 'variety' of capitalism that is specific to Provincial India in the current phase of capitalist development. My aim in this book is to assess how this variety of capitalism is organised and how it works.

2 Economic theory and empirical analysis

The analysis of contemporary capitalism is a difficult task. The 'purely' capitalist economy in which all social relations are money relations and individuals are rational and optimising beings is only found in mainstream textbooks. Moreover, despite predictions about institutional and economic convergence, real world economies do not converge toward a unique model.

Income distribution among and within countries has been deteriorating since the first Industrial Revolution (Bourguignon and Morrisson, 2002; Milanovic, 2006, 2010), and globalisation has had a worsening impact on economic inequality (Wade, 2004; Milanovic, 2011). Besides, against any predictions, power structures and institutions inherited from the pre-capitalist past are not being dissolved by capitalism and intertwine with capitalist production relations, giving birth to multiple modes of inequality – class, gender, religion, and ethnicity – which add to economic inequality, and to a variety of socio-economic organisations and patterns of change. As a result, capitalist societies and economies are highly diversified and conflicting (World Bank, 2006), and show a great variety of production structures, socio-economic relations, and patterns of spatial distribution of resources (Hodgson *et al.*, 2001; Hall and Soskice, 2001; Boyer, 2005; Jackson and Deeg, 2006; Baumol *et al.*, 2007).

The co-existence of class and non-class modes of inequality and a notable variety of social relations and structures are also found in India. Income inequality is a major distinguishing feature, but so too are urban/rural inequality and inequalities between genders, and among religious and ethnic groups (Corbridge and Harriss, 2000; Bagchi, 2002; Deaton and Drèze, 2002; Chakrabarti and Cullenberg, 2003; Sen, 2005, 2006; Rani and Unni, 2009). In any context, a multiplicity of relations supports the organisation of economy and society, creating an institutional mosaic (Sen and Drèze, 1997, 2002; Baru, 2000; Bagchi, 2002; Harriss-White, 2003a).

Economic theory is not fit to address the complexity of contemporary capitalism. The evidence of the varieties of capitalism undermines the concepts of uniformity and convergence and, with them, also the interpretative power of mainstream economic theory. Marxism and institutionalism – taken in a broad sense as theoretical approaches rather than specific analytical frameworks – might appear as suitable candidates. Yet, each considered individually, they could not account, simultaneously, for the variety of capitalisms and for the increasing inequalities among individuals and countries. On the one side, Marx's theory contributes to the understanding of capitalism, pointing to the commoditisation of labour and capital/labour conflicts as its main traits; yet, the abstract concept of capitalist economy, in which pre-capitalist residuals are cancelled out by the growth of productive forces and individuals share the same pattern of behaviour, cannot explain the variety of socio-economic systems. On the other side, Institutionalism proposes an agency theory that accounts for the influence of country-specific and history-specific institutions on individual behaviour, and therefore also for the emergence of a variety of socio-economic systems; yet, it misses the key role of labour commoditisation and capital/labour conflicts in shaping capitalist development.

In this book I argue that innovative theoretical tools are needed to address growth and change in 'real world' economies; and I propose an eclectic combination of Marxist and Institutionalist conceptual categories and propositions, within a single framework, as a guide for empirical analysis. This proposal is intended to be a methodological – rather than a theoretical – contribution to the debate on capitalism. Combining Marxist and Institutionalist propositions to represent the relationships among agents and the interplay between agents and society, the framework does not propose a *new view* of how real economies and societies are organised and work. Instead, its originality lies in the ways in which the basic concepts and propositions are causally related to explain capitalist growth and change.

3 Purpose and plan of the book

This book explores non-farm capitalism in Provincial India by means of the Marxist/Institutionalist framework with the aim of providing an interpretation of post-Green Revolution change and of assessing the impact of change on the organisation of the economy and on social and class structure. It contributes to the debate on contemporary capitalism in Provincial India at two levels. The first contribution is methodological and is found in the proposal of an eclectic framework as a theoretical support for the analysis of capitalism. The second contribution is in the sphere of applied political economy and directly follows from the methodological contribution: the use of Marxist/Institutional categories makes it possible to assess production relations in Provincial India taking into account all forms of social stratification and the influence of country-specific institutions and structures on individual and social behaviour.

The book is organised in two parts. In the first part (Chapters 2–5), I introduce the Marxist/Institutionalist framework and I employ it to point out the main distinguishing traits of non-farm capitalism in Provincial India and to explore its working. In the second part (Chapters 6–8), I apply the concepts and propositions of the eclectic framework to the analysis of post-Green Revolution change in Arni, a market town in a semi-arid rice-growing district in northern Tamil Nadu (South India), which I take as an example of India's provincial economy. Chapter 9 draws the main conclusions of the analysis in terms of the quality of capitalist development.

The Marxist-Institutionalist framework

The Marxist-Institutionalist framework – which is introduced in Chapter 2 – is eclectic in many senses. On the Marxist side, it is built on Marx's analysis of capitalism integrated and amended of dogmatism and determinism by the contributions of Critical Marxism. The 'contamination' of Classical Marxism with Critical Marxism produces a theoretical approach which may account for the 'unpredicted' (by Marx) developments of capitalism in the twentieth century, and in particular for the persistence of capitalism and the weakness of its working class. On the Institutionalist side, it relies on Evolutionary Institutionalism, i.e. the branch of institutionalism that, building on Thorstein Veblen's agency theory, rejects the concept of maximising rationality as unrealistic and inadequate, focusing instead on the influence on individual behaviour of institutions – broadly defined as formal and informal rules originated in social intercourse.

The combination of the Marxist political economy and Evolutionary Institutionalism shows several advantages for the empirical research on contemporary capitalism: for its Marxist origin and strength, the eclectic framework explains the class origin of inequality and conflicts; for its Evolutionary/Institutionalist hypotheses on human behaviour, it explains the variety of organisational forms and social relations, and their historical specificity and path dependence.

Conceptualising capitalism in Provincial India

I employ the concepts and propositions of the Marxist/Institutionalist framework for an original analysis of non-farm capitalism in Provincial India. My aim is to point out the traits that distinguish it from other varieties of capitalist organisation. Consistent with the Marxist/Institutionalist framework, I explore the organisation of the economy in Chapter 3, and then, in Chapters 4 and 5, I turn to social stratifications and to the institutional framework for socio-economic interaction.

The first step is the definition of the non-farm economy of Provincial India and of its boundaries. This analysis relies on the official information provided by the National Sample Survey Organisation (also known as the National Sample Survey Office). Then, I propose a critical review – through Marxist/Institutionalist lenses – of the literature on India's provincial economy in order to unveil the socio-economic relations that account for its growth and change. The review intends to enlighten class structure, institutional structure and social regulation, and the interplay of economic structure with institutional/ideological superstructure.

In Chapter 3 I show that India's provincial economy is a diversified and informal economic system in which petty production prevails, non-farm activities are increasingly informalised and socially regulated, and the quality of employment is poor. I also show that, while diversification is endemic as a 'distress resort' in agrarian crises, the emergence of *new* non-farm activities largely depends on the availability of local resources and on the delocalisation of industrial and service activities to peripheral areas, and that this process is enhanced by the increasing informalisation of the non-farm economy: supplying cheap labour and inputs to decentralising firms, the emergence of informal non-farm activities provides flexibility to production organisation and facilitates the access to rural resources, bolting them into the global circuits of capital.

The use of Marxist/Institutionalist categories makes possible an innovative analysis of the working of capitalism in Provincial India. The diversified and informal economy of Provincial India is shown to be *institutionally* and *spatially embedded*. Institutional embeddedness originates from social regulation and is revealed by the multiple forms of social stratification and the widespread heterogeneity of employment arrangements. Spatial embeddedness descends from – and is perpetuated by – the use of resources largely drawn from agriculture. While the *quantity* of physical and human resources and their *localisation* circumscribe the scope of provincial (non-farm) economy, the institutional framework shapes the actual pattern of its capitalist development by influencing the *quality* of the available resources and regulating the *access* to them and their *use*.

In Chapter 4, I focus on the intertwining between capitalist production relations with the power relations and social structures that the country has inherited from her colonial and post-colonial past. By means of the Marxist/Institutionalist analysis of the literature I show that two antagonist classes inhabit Provincial India: capitalists and subaltern workers. These classes differ from the classes of the 'purely capitalist economy': while they represent the interests of capital and labour – as it occurs in any capitalist country – the behaviour of their members and their intercourse might take contradictory aspects, being shaped by the institutions and ideologies rooted in India's culture and history.

India's culture and history also account for the *segmentation* of classes: each class of Provincial India's economy is made of segments, which, while sharing economic and political interests and social aspirations, differ for their trajectories of class formation. This implies that, for the construction of class identities and class-consciousness, the homogeneity of political and economic interests and aspirations matters more than it does the homogeneity of the trajectories of class formation and also the homogeneity in the location in production relations.

I analyse the interplay between economic structure and the ideological/institutional framework in Chapter 5. I focus on India's civil society, which is taken as the sphere in which particularistic interests are expressed and represented. My assumption is that the organisation of civil society reveals the working – and also the intertwining – of class and non-class interests and power relations.

Caste is chosen as a privileged key to explore India's civil society. By means of a Marxist/Institutionalist review of literature, I show that caste has not dissolved with capitalism, undergoing instead a cumulative process of institutional change in which new economic and political functions have been emerging. In this process, caste has acquired a twofold characterisation: it is an *ideology* – i.e. a system of values and beliefs rooted in Hindu religion – that, transforming from ideas into social norms, has become an *institution*. Through its twofold role, it defines patterns of civil society organisation – widely accepted in contemporary India – that construct and legitimate social differences.

Arguing that both roles need to be taken into account if the influence of caste on social production relations is to be assessed, I formulate the hypothesis that caste – both as an ideology and an institution – generates a corporatist civil society that supports the hegemony of capital over labour. Relying on Gramsci's theory of hegemony – which emphasises the two-way interplay between economic structure and ideological/institutional superstructure – this hypothesis is consistent with the Marxist/Institutionalist framework.

My preliminary conclusion is that the general assessment of capitalism in Provincial India seems to support the plausibility of the Gramscian hypothesis on the impact of caste on social production relations. Preventing subaltern workers' perception of the conflicting interests of capital and labour, the ideological use of caste values and beliefs seems to play a key role in capitalist development. Yet, the available evidence and analysis, on which this preliminary conclusion relies, cannot provide an assessment of the forms in which class and non-class interests are expressed and represented in civil society and the forms in which capital's hegemony is negotiated. I then propose to explore the Gramscian hypothesis empirically in the case of Arni in the second part of the book.

An eclectic analysis of Arni's capitalist development

Arni provides a major opportunity to explore capitalism in Provincial India. The town has been repeatedly surveyed since the introduction of the high-yielding varieties. Initially the aim was to assess rural–urban linkages as a result of the new agricultural techniques and, then, to measure their impact on the local economy. Besides, several subsequent research projects have been conducted on other socio-economic aspects of the town. Then, a large amount of information and data (covering four decades) is available that can be employed for long-term analysis.

Arni is an emblematic case of rural industrialisation too. Through the migration of labour and capital, the injection of technical change in agriculture has had a major impact on economy and society. From being a local market town for agricultural goods in the 1960s, Arni has now transformed into the centre of an agro-industrial economy, dominated by small- and medium-size firms specialised in silk production and in the manufacturing and trade of agricultural products, with an increasing endowment of services. This change has been accompanied by the emergence of new classes and new forms of civil society's organisation.

The analysis of Arni's economy and society relies on the available field-evidence, which is analysed by means of Marxist/Institutionalist conceptual categories. It is carried out in three steps. In Chapter 6, Arni's long-term growth is reviewed on the basis of the data from the three major surveys on Arni's business economy (1973, 1983 and 1993). In Chapter 7, economic organisation and social production relations are assessed in the case of Arni's silk sector – an important part of the town's economy widely researched over the last two decades. Finally, in Chapter 8, the Gramscian hypothesis on the impact of caste on social production relations is explored by means of the evidence from a survey on civil society organisations that I carried out at the end of the 1990s.

As the evidence suggests, Arni's economy shares the major features of Provincial India. The intense growth in the post-Green Revolution period did not lead to sectoral specialisation, and diversification is the main trait of the town across the decades. Despite the remarkable development in manufacturing (silk saris) and in the processing of agricultural goods (rice), trade continues to be a major activity in the town, both as retail and wholesale trade. The economy is composed of two broad segments: in the first, production largely relies on local raw materials and sells to its hinterland and to other centres in Tamil Nadu; in the second segment, production uses raw materials from distant sources and sells to distant markets. The economic and spatial integration of the town with its local areas is enhanced by the change that occurred in the surrounding villages after the introduction of high-yielding varieties in the local agriculture.

The features and working of Arni's local system are explored in the case of silk handloom weaving, a strategic sector in Provincial India, which has persistently played a prominent role in the town.

By means of a Marxist/Institutionalist reading of the available information and data, I show that silk handloom weaving relies on self-employment and small-scale family-based units, and is organised on a putting-out system, involving a segmented class of capitalists – master-weavers and *maligais* (traders) – and a segmented class of subaltern workers – wage-workers and family labour. Jointly, the putting-out system and social segmentation ensure the flexibility of production organisation. Capitalists control production techniques, production quality and quantity, and marketing, while the segmented class structure limits upward social mobility and ensures a prompt reaction to market signals. The use of unpaid family labour is enhanced by caste stratification, increasing the marginalisation of groups of subaltern workers.

Yet, caste does influence production relations also by creating an institutional framework in which capital's hegemony is negotiated and workers' 'spontaneous' consensus on it is gained. Building on the Marxist/Institutionalist reading of caste, I take caste as an institution and an ideology that imprints the organisation of civil society. With the support of the evidence from the survey of Arni's civil society organisations, I show that an associational corporatist order exists in the town, in which caste-based associations act as *representatives* and *intermediaries* of class interests in political interaction with the State, enhancing the hegemony of capital and systematically under-representing the interests of labour.

My general conclusion is that the assessment of Arni's capitalism confirms the main features of Provincial India pointed out in the first part of the book. India's provincial economy is diversified and informally organised, and relies on petty production, largely employing subaltern workers. Civil society is organised on the basis of particularistic interests and socio-economic intercourse is regulated by institutions and ideologies rooted in culture and history, among which caste plays a key role, undermining class-consciousness and enhancing the hegemony of the capitalist class. Caste cannot be seen as a 'pre-capitalist residual' to be dissolved by capitalist development. It is instead a major support for the development of a specific 'variety' of capitalism.

Chapter 9 concludes the book. It points out how the eclectic approach has enhanced the understanding of capitalist development in Provincial India. Starting from the profound process of change that has involved economy and society after the Green Revolution, it reviews the distinguishing traits of the economy and society, showing that the change has not led to an improvement of working and living standards. By contrast, capitalist development has relied on the downgrading of subaltern workers, which has been made possible by the use of ideological and institutional constructions supported by India's culture and history. The main conclusion is that India's provincial capitalism is moving along the low road of capitalism in which change and growth rely on workers' exploitation.

Part I

Analysing non-farm capitalism in Provincial India

2   A Marxist/Institutionalist framework for the analysis of contemporary capitalism

1 Introduction

In this chapter I introduce the conceptual framework for the analysis of capitalism in Provincial India and in Arni. I build on the assumption that economic theory lacks suitable tools to address the complexity of contemporary capitalism and that this is largely due to the inadequacy of neoclassical economics to explore variety and conflicts for its focus on equilibrium and uniformity, and to the fact that other theoretical approaches which explicitly address conflict and change – such as Marxism and Institutionalism – only provide partial explanations. To overcome this theoretical impasse, I propose the combination of Marxist and Institutionalist propositions in a single framework.

My aim in this chapter is to show that the eclectic combination is feasible and enhances the understanding of contemporary capitalism, addressing, simultaneously, inequalities and conflicts, different patterns of individual behaviour and the varieties of organisational forms.

The chapter is organised as follows. Section 2 deals with Marxism. First, it summarises Marx's contribution to the conceptualisation of capitalism; and, then, it turns to the integrations and amendments to Marx's theory that have improved the understanding of capitalism facing the unpredicted developments in the twentieth century. Section 3 deals with Evolutionary Institutionalism. My aim is to show that, with its emphasis on change and growth, this branch of Institutionalism provides a far-reaching theory of capitalism that can enter into a dialogue with Marxism. Section 4 reviews the debate on the dialogue between Marxism and Institutionalism, pointing out the major discrepancies between the approaches. It also suggests adaptations that might assist the dialogue. Section 5 presents the proposition of the Marxist-Institutionalist framework. Finally, Section 6 concludes, underlining the contribution of the eclectic framework to the analysis of capitalism in Provincial India.

2 The main traits of capitalism according to Marx's theory

Marx analyses the capitalist economy by means of a theoretical approach known as 'historical materialism' that is presented in the most coherent form in the

Preface to *A Contribution to the Critique of Political Economy* (1859). Following Burawoy (1990: 780), Marx's historical materialism can be summarised in seven 'postulates' from which Marx's view of the capitalist society clearly emerges.

Relying on the postulates, Marx's view can be summarised as follows: (1) human beings enter into relations of production that are 'indispensable and independent of their will' and that correspond to a 'definite stage of the development of the productive forces' (i.e. technologies and institutions necessary to produce the means of existence); (2) these relations of production constitute the 'economic structure of society' and give birth to the superstructure; (3) the interaction between the forces of production and the relations of production determines the development of the mode of production; yet, in the course of development, productive forces come into conflict with production relations, and the latter become 'fetters', giving origin to a period of social revolution; (4) when the structure changes, also the superstructure changes; (5) the end of a mode of production requires the full development of productive forces – a new mode of production appears when new productive forces emerge; (6) the capitalist mode of production emerges after the Asiatic, ancient, and feudal modes of production; (7) capitalism is the social formation that ends 'the prehistory of human society', creating the condition for the emergence of communism.[1]

Relying on this theoretical background, Marx builds his conceptualisation of capitalism, exploring class structure and the commoditisation of the labour force, capital accumulation and the introduction of technical change, and the laws of motion of capitalism.

The capitalist economy is inhabited by three major classes identified on the basis of their control of the means of production and their revenue: 'owners of labour power, owners of capital, and land-owners, whose respective sources of income are wages, profit and ground-rent' (Marx, 1894: 302). The capitalist class structure also includes an intermediate class – the 'petty bourgeoisie' – seen as a *transitory* class that is to be dissolved by the spreading of capitalism. Petty bourgeoisie fights for its survival by assisting the capitalist class as a 'supplementary part of the bourgeois society' (Marx and Engels, 1848: 63).

Class antagonism in capitalist society occurs between capitalists and workers. Marx analyses capitalists and workers in abstract terms, and not as individuals, but as 'personifications of economic categories, embodiments of particular class-relations and class-interests' (Marx, 1890: 18). Class antagonism requires class-consciousness, i.e. that the members of each class become conscious of their class interests and pursue their class interests collectively. In turn, this requires a process of class formation: the transformation of 'class-in-itself' (a class of individuals who share class membership but are unconscious of their common status and their common interests) into 'class-for-itself' (a class of individuals who are conscious of their common status and join together to fight for their common interests).

In the capitalist economy labour power is a commodity that its possessor – the wage-worker – sells to the capitalist. The buying and selling of labour power

– i.e. the *commoditisation* of labour power – is only possible when two basic conditions are fulfilled: (i) the owner of labour power 'offers it for sale or sells it, as a commodity', a situation that requires that the worker considers it 'his own property, his own commodity'; and (ii) the owner of labour power is obliged to sell the labour power in order to live (Marx, 1890, Part 1: 184–186). As a commodity, labour power has a value, which is determined by the quantity of labour that is embodied in it, i.e. by the quantity of labour socially necessary for its production.

Production is the result of the combination of means of production and labour power. Both are bought in the market by capitalists, who directly control the work of the labour force and appropriate the produced goods. Their purpose is to produce goods that can be sold as commodities with a *higher* value than the value of resources employed in production.

Capitalists exploit workers by producing and appropriating surplus value: the difference between the quantity of the labour-time socially necessary to produce the commodities and the quantity of the labour-time socially necessary to produce the means of subsistence for the workers engaged in production. Then, the surplus value comes from unpaid labour-time.

The surplus value is converted into capital – i.e. it is employed not for consumption but for the purchase of other means of production and labour force, enlarging the scale of production. Capital accumulation increases the physical basis of production leading to the growth of productive forces. In performing this function the major support comes from technology, i.e. the systematic application of 'science' to production. Technology increases the *quantity* and the *quality* of the means of production, by reducing the 'working-time required in the production of a commodity' (Marx, 1890, Part 1: 107). Technology is then the main factor of capitalist change.

The role of technical change is enhanced by competition among capitalists. As innovations increase the quantity of appropriable surplus value, they rapidly spread among capitalists, leading to the mechanisation of the economy and, then, to the further development of productive forces. In this sense, the development of productive forces should be taken as the joint outcome of technical change *and* of competition among capitalists, and has the final objective of increasing the level of workers' exploitation.

Owing to the compulsion of capitalists to extract surplus and accumulate, and to technical change (introduced in order to cut costs), the amount of necessary work decreases per unit of product, bringing about a decrease of the average rate of profit. This determines the tendency of the organic composition of capital to increase, leading to the secular decline in the rate of profit.[2]

This internal contradiction also accounts for other tendencies of the capitalist economy. Owing to the systematic introduction of technical change and to the failure of small capitalists to survive in a competitive environment, the competition among capitalists creates the conditions for technical revolutions and for the concentration and centralisation of capital – i.e. the enlargement of the quantity of capital employed in production and the reduction in the number of competitors. Simultaneously, in an attempt to limit the decrease in the rate of profit, capitalists increase the exploitation of workers by increasing the length of the working day. Together with the displacement of workers due to technical change, this leads to class struggle.

These tendencies constitute the 'laws of motion' of capitalism. They lead to the final collapse of capitalism that appears to Marx to be inevitable, being a consequence of the conflict between forces of production and relations of production exacerbated by technical change and the increasing exploitation.

From Marx's conceptualisation, capitalism emerges as a 'world of commodities' (Khalil, 1992: 23), which relies on the commoditisation of the labour force and is driven by the conflict between capital and labour. Not only is the labour force a 'thing', but – more importantly – it is a thing whose 'value' is determined through exchange. Capitalism is, then, a dehumanised world, in which 'social relations masquerade as things or relation between things' (Kolakowski, 2005: 227).

The commoditisation of the labour force is a stringent necessity for production and accumulation. The labour force is commoditised by the capitalist class, which organises production in order to maximise the extraction of surplus value. This accounts for the conflicting interests of capital and labour that become manifest in the different phases of the productive process, influencing the introduction of technical change, and therefore the development of productive forces. Technical change is never class-neutral and the actual introduction of the new techniques depends on the balance of power between capital and labour. So, while capitalist change depends on technology, the introduction of technical change depends on class relations.

Capital/labour conflicts lead to the dissolution of the capitalist mode of production. This is the outcome of the inherent conflict between production forces and production relations, which determines a 'revolutionary' change in the material conditions of production and living. As the development of productive forces is determined by technical change – which depends on the balance of power between capital and labour – also the conflict between production forces and production relations can ultimately be reduced to class conflicts.

Class conflict is the ultimate fate of capitalism. This fate is a consequence of individual choices and actions. Workers are 'free' wage labourers that dispose of their labour force to sell in the market, capitalist appropriate super-values and transform it into capital. Class struggle is a 'necessary' behaviour for workers, as it is accumulation for capitalists.

2.1 Understanding the unpredicted developments of capitalism

As Hodgson *et al.* (2001: 6–7) argue, Marx conceptualises the 'purely capitalist society': an abstract model of society where all pre-capitalist residuals are cancelled out by the growth of productive forces and classes are made of individuals sharing the same pattern of behaviour (which is consistent with their class status). The basic features of the 'purely capitalist society' are to be observed in every historical and geographical context, and, as Marx asserts in *Capital*, 'the country that is more developed industrially only shows, to the less developed, the image of its own future' (1830, Part 1: 16).

History has provided a critical test for this position. Marx's predictions about universal laws of motion and the inevitable collapse of capitalism have been invalidated by twentieth century history, which has produced a number of 'anomalies' not accounted for (Gouldner, 1980: 14). As Burawoy (1990: 781 et seq.) shows, the development of capitalism and the Russian Revolution 'falsified' the postulates of historical materialism. In advanced economies, the expansion of the forces of production was not being 'fettered' by relations of production, and the concentration and centralisation of capital were not leading to the end of capitalism, while a weak class struggle was unable to lead the transition from capitalism to socialism and pre-capitalist 'residuals' were persisting in co-existence with advanced forms of capitalism. By contrast, the revolution occurred in Russia, a backward country in which the 'material conditions' for the existence of capitalism had not yet emerged from feudal production relations.

Denying the primacy of structure over superstructure

Antonio Gramsci (1891–1937) is the first Marxist to challenge explicitly Marx's view of capitalism, laying the basis for the revision that is necessary to enhance the interpretative power of Marxism in front of the 'anomalies' of twentieth century capitalism (Resnick and Wolff, 1987: 75–76; Boggs, 2002: 58 et seq.). In contrast with Marx's historical materialism, he moves from a historical relativist approach, maintaining that the ideas and concepts on which individuals rely for their activity are an outcome of social relations (Kolakowski, 2005: 963 et seq.).

Gramsci's view of history is first introduced in 'La rivoluzione contro *Il Capitale*', an article published in the socialist newspaper *Avanti!* in 1917.[3] Commenting on the fact that Russia was not 'ready' for the Bolshevik Revolution – and that therefore the evidence of Russian Revolution was against the postulates of historical materialism – Gramsci argues that the revolution is the outcome of an historical process in which both structure and superstructure change, and that change is not induced by abstract 'universal laws', but by 'collective, social will' which becomes 'the driving force of the economy and moulds objective reality'.

This revisionist view of history provides the theoretical basis for Gramsci's theory of hegemony. By means of this theory, elaborated and presented in *Quaderni del carcere* (1975), Gramsci analyses the relations between ruling classes and dominated classes in a context in which – like Fascist Italy – the working class is not revolutionary and supports a right-wing regime. Here, Gramsci explicitly challenges the primacy of structure over superstructure and denies that history is moved by historical laws exclusively rooted in production relations.

Gramsci assumes – with Marx – that the power of the ruling classes has an economic basis (i.e. the control over the means of production); yet, he also associates this supremacy with other forms of political, moral and intellectual dominance. For Gramsci, the ruling classes keep their leadership over subordinated classes by ensuring their consensus by means of shared ideas and values. The subordinated classes accept the leadership of the ruling classes by accepting their moral and cultural values, and not as a consequence of the use of force.[4] To describe this form of cultural and moral leadership, Gramsci introduces the term 'hegemony', while he calls the dominant classes 'hegemonic' and the dominated ones 'subaltern'.

Hegemony requires a complex process of construction of political and ideological consensus that does not necessarily imply the use of coercion (though coercion is not always excluded) but is based on 'ideology': a system of beliefs, values and symbols that are expressions of particularistic interests.

The construction of hegemony by means of ideology requires the assimilation of moral beliefs and values of the hegemonic classes by subaltern classes. It is a sort of 'pedagogical' process in which the subaltern classes are led to absorb dominant values and moral beliefs (Gramsci, 1975: 1331). It is also a process of negotiation and re-negotiation, in which hegemonic classes take into account the needs of minority groups and combine them with their own interests. The merging of interests is carried out by building a network of alliances between subaltern and hegemonic classes that take the form of voluntary associations (i.e. associations in which each individual enters on a voluntary basis) that represent the institutional framework of civil society.

Arguing that ideologies often are more powerful than material forces, Gramsci introduces the concept of the 'historical bloc' to emphasise that the distinction between material forces (structure) and ideology (superstructure) has a mere 'didactic' significance. In the concept of historical bloc he includes both material forces and ideology, stressing that material forces are the 'content' and ideology is the 'form', and that content and form cannot be taken separately (Gramsci, 1975: 869). He also stresses that in each historical moment there is only one historical bloc that governs the economy ensuring social stability: the historical bloc is composed by a specific structure (material forces) and a specific 'ideological system' that is consistent with (and expression of) the structure (Gramsci, 1975: 1051). Ideology and superstructure overlap, while structure and superstructure are 'the reflex of social production relations' (Gramsci, 1975: 1051). As Althusser puts it (1970: 51), with the concept of historical bloc Gramsci unifies 'structure and superstructure'.

Stressing the mutual determination of structure and superstructure, and, then, the impact of ideas and institutions on social production relations, Gramsci deeply influences the development of Marxism in the twentieth century. Due to the uncertain outcome of the interplay of structure and superstructure, the very concept of laws of motion is challenged, while, at the same time, the impact of ideas and institutions on social production relations is acknowledged, undermining the material basis of Marx's concept of class and raising the issue of what determines human agency.

Overcoming class polarisation

As Wright (1985: 6) argues, while his work is 'filled with class analysis', Marx never 'systematically defined and elaborated the concept of class' and never explained what constitutes a class. Moreover, though in his historical writings he describes several categories and social groups, in his abstract representation of class relations he points to a simple polarisation of the capitalist class structure, describing classes in their pure form on the basis of the relation to the means of production.

Building on the evidence of capitalism, in which other variables add to the ownership of the means of production in shaping class structure, Wright challenges class polarisation. He explores classes at two levels: the macro level, exploring class structure – the 'overall organization of class relations within some macro unit of analysis'; and the micro level, assessing the 'location of individuals ... within class relations' (2006: 63).

Wright builds on the key class relation in capitalism that identifies two distinct class locations: capitalists and workers. Yet, he argues that, while capturing the conflicting nature of class structure, this polarised image is misleading. This is due to the complexity of class structure, which depends on: (i) the co-existence and intertwining of a variety of different types of class relations (which are specific to different modes of production that might co-exist); and (ii) the existence of a variety of social institutions and formal/informal rules that influence individual rights and powers over production and exchange. Impacting on the position of individuals in classes, the complexity of class structure gives birth to 'contradictory locations' (2005: 10).

Through the concept of 'contradictory class locations within class relations', Wright conceptualises the position of the middle classes in the capitalist economy. Middle classes consist of individuals with contradictory class locations: they might have different locations according to their functions in the production process – for instance in the case of individuals who, for some activities, occupy a capitalist location and, for others, a working class location – and/or they might be individuals to whom 'certain kinds of skills and credentials' confer 'effective rights and powers over many aspects of their work'. Individuals in these situations do not have a univocal location as they are neither owners nor workers and/or they are 'simultaneously' owners and workers (1985: 125 et seq.).[5,6]

But what is the social function of a class analysis? And how, being Marxist, does a class analysis enhance our understanding of society?

Wright answers these questions by pointing out that 'class counts', in the sense that the distribution of 'rights' and 'powers' over resources has systematic consequences at micro and macro levels. In this analytical framework, two core propositions emphasise the role of class relations (and then the importance of class analysis) (2005: 15): (1) 'What you have determines what you get'; and (2) 'What you have determines what you have to do to get what you get' (2005: 15).

To be Marxist, a class analysis needs to build on the concept of exploitation. In conceptualising exploitation, Wright does not rely on Marx's labour theory of value. By contrast, he defines exploitation as the situation that satisfies three principles (2005: 16):

1   The inverse interdependent welfare principle: the material welfare of exploiters causally depends upon the material deprivations of the exploited.
2   The exclusion principle: this inverse interdependence of the welfare of exploiters and exploited depends upon the exclusion of the exploited from access to certain productive resources.
3   The appropriation principle: exclusion generates material advantage to exploiters because it enables them to appropriate the labour effort of the exploited.

This conceptualisation has many advantages: (i) it allows for a wide perspective on class relations, including both production and exchange; (ii) it identifies the roots of conflicts in the capitalist economy; (iii) it shows that class relations are substantially power relations in which exploiters confront the exploited in order to appropriate rights and powers over production and exchange; (iv) it lays the basis for a theory of the formation of consent: as class relations are power relations in which exploiters appropriate rights and powers over production and exchange, and as this appropriation is costly, then, appropriators can employ ideological mechanisms to reduce the costs for the appropriation; and (v) it facilitates comparative analyses in time and space.

Analysing the complexity of labour power commoditisation

A major aspect of class relations is the commoditisation of the labour power, a foundational process of the capitalist economy occurring as workers exchange their labour for the money that is necessary to re-produce their labour force. While for Marx labour commoditisation occurs when workers are 'free' to sell their labour time in the market and exchange it for a wage, Marxist analysis has recently focused on the multiplicity of forms of labour commoditisation existing in contemporary capitalism.

Marcel van der Linden (2008: 19 et seq.) challenges the two 'questionable ideas' on which Marx's theory of commoditisation of labour power is built: i) that the labour power is sold by the worker 'who is the *carrier* and *possessor* of this labour power' and that the workers who sell their own labour power '*sell nothing else*'. He argues that the distinction between the 'carrier' and the 'possessor' of labour power allows distinguishing between 'autonomous' commoditisation (when the carrier of labour power is also its possessor) and 'heteronomous' commoditisation (when the carrier of labour power is not its possessor). To these, two other forms may be added, considering that 'the carrier's labour power can be offered by the carrier him- or herself or by another person'.

With the support of this conceptualisation, van der Linden concludes that the commoditisation of a free worker selling her/his labour force is only one example, while in the real world commoditisation takes '*many different forms*'. Questioning the very existence of Marx's free wage-worker (22), he outlines many intermediate forms of commoditisation: (i) in between wage labour and slavery; (ii) in between wage labour and self-employment; (iii) in between slavery and self-employment; (iv) in between wage labour/slavery/self-employment and *lumpenproletariat*. These forms of commoditisation need to be analysed, keeping into account key evidence, such as: economic and non-economic linkages between employers and employees; the possibility that labour power is not exchanged for money; and the possibility of multiple employment relations, both for the employer and for the employee.

The complexity of labour force commoditisation requires the boundaries between free wage-workers and other forms of workers to be redefined. It also requires a new conceptualisation of the working class in which different forms of commoditisation may be accommodated. Relying on Cohen's redefinition of the proletarian as the individual who '*must sell his labour power in order to obtain his means of life*' (1978: 72), van der Linden defines the class of subaltern workers (2008: 33 – emphasis in the text):

> *every carrier of labour power whose labour power is sold (or hired out) to another person under economic (or non-economic) compulsion belongs to the class of subaltern workers, regardless of whether the carrier of labour is him- or herself selling or hiring it out and, regardless of whether the carrier him- or herself owns means of production.*

The class of subaltern workers includes all categories that do not have control over their labour power (their body), over their means of production, and over the product of their labour, whose lack of control is due to their socio-economic dependency within the household and within the production process (2008: 34).

2.2 The unsolved problem of agency and structure

The weakness of the working class is a major evidence of twentieth century capitalism – an 'anomaly' that Classical Marxism fails to account for. This draw-back is a consequence of an inadequate analysis of human behaviour and of its influence on social structures.

Marx's theory deals with human agency in methodological collectivist terms. Methodological collectivism is one of the two main approaches to the agency/structure problem, the other being methodological individualism. In methodological collectivism, individual choices and actions are explained in social terms: they are an outcome of social phenomena and structures. Social structures are attributed willingness and deliberation – they are the 'agents' – and their features determine individual aims and desires: individuals are then made puppets (Hodgson, 2007: 100). By contrast, methodological individualism takes deliberate and conscious behaviour as specific of human beings and social phenomena as an outcome of individual choices and actions. Individuals generate social structures, but social structures do not exert influence on them. The features of society are embodied in individuals and society is nothing more than a collection of individuals (Archer, 1995: 251).[7]

Both approaches elude the agency/structure problem: in methodological collectivism, what counts is the social structure that is dominant in any specific situation; in methodological individualism only agents matter. Both fail to provide an answer to foundational questions about the relations of individuals and structures, about the nature of their mutual influence, and about which one of the two entities has the primacy (Archer, 1995: 57 et seq.; Archer, 2000: 66–67; Hodgson, 2007: 96 et seq.).

The postulates of historical materialism clearly point to methodological collectivism (Callinicos, 2004; Hodgson, 2004). They focus on 'mass phenomena' that, obeying 'regular and impersonal' laws, cannot be reduced to the conscious willingness of individuals and to the 'personal motives' behind human agency (Kolakowski, 2005: 280 et seq.). Class is the agent and the motivations of human agency are found in class interests rationally pursued by individuals. Human agency is then explained in determinist terms: individuals enter production relations that are independent from their will, their consciousness is determined by the material conditions of production, and their actions are consistent with their class location.

Denying the supremacy of structure over superstructure, Gramsci challenges this view of human agency, pointing to the influence of non-economic factors on individual behaviour. Yet, after his path-breaking analysis, the issue has been substantially neglected in twentieth century Marxism, the only notable exception being Analytical Marxism.

In a search for rigorous 'micro foundations', and as a solution to the lack of an adequate agency theory, Analytical Marxists – in particular Roemer (1986) and Elster (1986) – introduce the concept of rational optimising behaviour into the basic Marxist framework and apply it to the analysis of Marxist issues, such as class struggle, exploitation and the process of formation of ideas. The outcome of this eclectic combination is an ambiguous form of Marxism, in which social processes are reduced to individual actions, and the methodological individualism of neoclassical economics is substituted for the methodological collectivism of classical Marxism. Marxism is then left without a sound theory of agency to explore the 'source' of individual desires, aims and choices, and fails to explain why individuals behave as they do and what is the outcome of the interplay between them and social structures.

3 Evolutionary Institutionalism and the agency/structure problem

Evolutionary Institutionalism differs from neoclassical Institutionalism for its research programme. For neoclassical Institutionalism, institutions are the product of individual optimising actions and their existence and evolution is described in terms of efficiency in meeting the needs of agents. Since preferences are given (exogenous), institutions may not be used as explanatory tools for individual behaviour. Evolutionary Institutionalism reverses causation. It assumes that institutions influence human agency and are themselves social outcomes, while the aim of its research programme is to explain how institutions and human agency interact, and how this interaction evolves in time and space, generating different economic structures.

3.1 Agency and structure

Veblen's critique of mainstream economics provides the theoretical background for Evolutionary Institutionalism. Veblen (1919) rejects the concept of rational and optimising human behaviour as unrealistic and inadequate for economic analysis. 'Rationality' is simply not possible because individuals live in a situation of structurally limited information. Individuals are not self-contained entities with given aspirations and desires: they are social beings whose preferences and aims are socially determined. Limited information and social relations constrain individuals' aspirations to rationality. The assumption of fixed preferences – the major corollary of rationality – is not adequate for the study of capitalism in which everything, including human beings, changes in an interconnected fashion.

According to Veblen, human behaviour is the outcome of the interplay between constructive and destructive instincts and institutions. Institutions – which Veblen defines as 'settled habits of thought that are common to the generality of men' (1919: 239) – influence individuals' perceptions of reality and preferences, shaping human agency. Individuals are social beings historically situated. Past situations determine present behaviour through a selective process that makes individual preferences endogenous (Hodgson, 1993b: xv). Preferences are constructed on the basis of the interplay between instincts and habits and routines crystallised in the form of institutions. Like preferences, aims are institutionally and socially determined.

Evolutionary Institutionalism builds on Veblen's view of human and social behaviour incorporating important progress in anthropology, biology and psychology (Hodgson, 1988, 2004). Institutions are seen as the 'cognitive framework' to interpret sense data and to transform it into information. The cognitive framework is necessary as sense data may be incomplete (or inadequate) to provide the necessary information and the human brain is not able to process the full amount of information coming from it. Then, filtering and selecting sense data, the cognitive framework supports human agency in a situation of limited information.

Habit is the core conceptual category of Evolutionary Institutionalism and refers to a 'largely non-deliberative and self-actuating propensity to engage in a previously adopted pattern of behaviour ... a form of self-sustaining nonreflective behaviour that arises in repetitive situations' (Hodgson, 1998: 178). Habits are necessary to assist human action because the human brain is limited: they are mechanisms that individuals develop 'for relegating particular ongoing actions from continuous rational assessment' (Hodgson, 1988: 125).

Individuals acquire habits in conscious and unconscious ways: by imitation of others and by learning, and through choices that, being initially conscious, transform into unconscious behaviour by habitual repetition. They are 'congealed' repeated actions, 'removed from the sphere of rational deliberation' (Hodgson, 1988: 127).

Owing to imitative behaviour, habits spread in time and in space and become 'routines' – i.e. accepted rules of behaviour widely shared by individuals in a community – while an integrated set of habits and routines produces an institution (Commons, 1924: 45, quoted by Hodgson, 1998: 180). The function of habits and routines within institutions is to preserve the knowledge necessary for institutions to play the role of cognitive frameworks for human agency.

While institutions influence individual preferences and aims, they do not transform human beings into 'puppets' (Mayhew, 1989). Individual actions are not free from external conditioning but they are not entirely moulded by it. As social products, habits and routines are involved in a continuous process of institutional change and do not impose on individuals a mere automatic behaviour. Actions differ in their level of consciousness and intention: while there is a category of unconscious and non-deliberative behaviour that substantially depends on instincts, other typologies show a variable degree of consciousness and deliberation. Human action maintains some degrees of spontaneity and indeterminacy, even if it can never be fully deliberative. It is then 'partly determined and partly indeterminate: partly predictable and party unforeseeable' (Hodgson, 1993a: 224).

Institutions are 'both "subjective" ideas in the heads of the agents and "objective" structures faced by them' (Hodgson, 1998: 181). In empirical terms, the concept includes: formal organisations (such as firms, banks, state agencies); common patterns of behaviour (such as social conventions and 'ethical codes'); norms and prescriptions (such as formal and informal laws) (Coriat and Dosi, 2002: 98; see also Hodgson, 1998: 179).

For their capability to select and elaborate sense data, individuals depend on institutions that support decision-making when rationality is internally and externally bounded. Yet, being by-products of human society, institutions also depend on individuals. The interaction between agency and structure moves in two directions: the 'downward' direction – institutions influence individuals – and the 'upward' direction – individuals influence institutions. This interaction is 'causative', in the sense that institutions can change individual behaviour, while individual action can change the institutional framework (Hodgson, 2000: 326–327; see also Hodgson, 2001a: 294–296).

Institutions are established and reproduced both to constrain and to enable human behaviour: they perform this twofold function because they embody the cognitive framework necessary to human agency. By means of the cognitive framework embodied in institutions, individuals 'learn' what is accepted behaviour and 'acquire' the habits of thought and action necessary to implement it. The cognitive framework also transmits information about the aims and desires shared by the society; again, individuals absorb this information and adapt their behaviour. Then, embodying habits and routines, institutions 'constitute' and 'reconstitute' individual aims and desires in a continuous interaction (Hodgson, 2004: 177; see also 184–185).

The concept of 'reconstitutive downward causation' allows Evolutionary Institutionalism to explore the impact of power relations on economic processes (Hodgson, 2000: 326). As they 'constitute' and 'reconstitute' individual aims and desires, institutions may be created – or transformed – in order to embody cognitive frameworks that are suitable to established or emerging vested interests.

3.2 The institutional embeddedness of change

Individuals and society cannot be taken for granted. Preferences and aims change under the influence of institutions, while the interplay between individuals and the external environment changes the institutional infrastructure of society. The economy is then an open system under a process of continuous transformation in time.

As institutions influence individuals and individuals influence institutions, it is pointless to ask where the process starts. As Hodgson argues, 'neither individuals nor institutional factors have complete explanatory primacy', while the question to be asked then is not 'which came first?' but 'what processes explain the development of both?' (1998: 184–185). To answer this question, Evolutionary Institutionalism applies Darwinian evolution theory to the analysis of capitalist change, incorporating into the Institutionalist framework the main Darwinian principles and adapting them to the economy.

Nothing in the economy and society is 'given'. Variety is the major trait of the institutional structure and a necessary condition for selection to occur. Institutions behave as 'units of selection': they have a durable nature, and emerge and die according to the needs of society. The 'selection' of institutions is based on their fitness and on their capability to adapt to the context. Social evolution is then a process of selection that involves institutions and individuals in an 'ongoing creation of variety' (Hodgson, 1993a: 44; see also Hodgson, 2003 and Delorme, 1994).

Selection is a 'causal process' – which needs to be explained – and a 'cumulative process' – in which individuals and institutions change continuously and their change is the starting point for further change. As in biology, the selection of institutions implies causality. Institutions endure *because* they are *fit* or adapt to be fit in a specific context. Economic change is then a process of 'cumulative causation' (Hodgson, 1993a: 132–133). There is no room for determinism in this evolutionary view of change: no 'laws of motion' govern the outcomes and change never has a 'final term'.

Institutions are established and reproduced by different categories of social relations that take form because individuals live in society, acquiring habits. Different types of social relations produce different types of habits and routines that, in turn, crystallise into different types of institutions. According to Evolutionary

Institutionalism, the main source of habits is found in culture and in the relations that human beings establish with the environment for their survival.

Individuals are 'encultured' beings that have instincts and material needs (Mayhew, 1989; Rutherford, 1989). They live in a society and their social life generates culture: 'a complex of the habits of life and thought prevalent among the members of a community' (Veblen, 1919: 39). In turn, culture generates institutions. Then, habits of thought are ideas and repeated actions that are 'foundational', both of individual and social behaviour.

Human beings require the means to survive, and they live in a social environment. The search for the means of human survival is a social task that generates two major types of social relations and, then, of institutions. Economic relations give birth to 'provisioning institutions' (Hodgson, 2001a: 284) that are essential to the 'provision and protection' of the means to ensure human survival. They include institutions related to the production and exchange of goods and services necessary to human life, including educational institutions and families. Strictly related to economic activities are legal institutions, such as markets and contracts, that regulate property rights, which are essential for economic transactions.

Then, institutions play a key role in determining individual behaviour and are, at the same time, the outcome of the relations that human beings establish among themselves and with the environment for their survival. This double interplay gives birth to a cumulative process of change that involves both institutions and individuals. This situation may be described as one of *embeddedness* of socio-economic change in institutions – i.e. of *institutional embeddedness*. Change does not progress toward a predetermined outcome, but the outcome itself depends on the ways in which the process of change occurs, which in turn depend on the culture and history embodied in institutions (Hodgson, 2001b: 69). Moreover, as the institutional framework is the outcome of the relations between human beings and the external environment, institutions are specific to any historical and geographical context: change is then path dependent and historically specific.

Institutional embeddedness accounts for the diversity of institutional structures and trajectories of development, and explains the divergence of real-world countries from the model of the 'purely capitalist society' described in Marx's theory. As Hodgson (2001b: 70 et seq.) argues, this divergence is due to 'impurities' – institutions and structures of the previous modes of productions that capitalism does not dissolve. For the 'limits to the extension of the market', the capitalist system cannot be fully commoditised. It includes non-market institutions – the family, for instance – that are regulated by cultural and social norms descending from the past. These impurities are 'necessary' to the working of real-world capitalism and, together with path-dependency, mark the direction of long-term change.

3.3 The inadequate conceptualisation of capitalism

In *The Theory of the Leisure Class* (1899) Veblen presents a 'cultural view' of capitalism, arguing that to understand its nature, it is necessary to explore its 'pecuniary culture' (1899: 7–8). He distinguishes between 'industry' and 'business': while the former refers to the activity of making 'goods', the latter refers to the activity of making 'money'. Accordingly, society is divided into two classes that are defined on the basis of their position in relation to work: the leisure class, made of individuals who receive income but do not have to work for it, and the lower servile class, made of individuals below the leisure class, who need to work in order to have an income. The pecuniary culture – which refers to the situation in which making money becomes an end in itself – is specific to the leisure class. Then, the relation of the leisure class to the economic process is 'a pecuniary relation', i.e. a relation of exploitation (Veblen, 1899: 209).

The leisure class and its pecuniary culture emerge with the beginning of ownership and are reinforced in the course of industrialisation. They concur in building the system of power that for Veblen represented the core of American capitalism at the beginning of the twentieth century.

The cultural view of capitalism proposed by Veblen strongly contrasts with Marx's view, which focuses on the material conditions of production. This contrast is reduced by the recent theoretical developments of Evolutionary Institutionalism, which pay a major attention to production and employment. A significant example is provided by the definition of capitalism recently proposed by Hodgson (2001a: 323, emphasis added):

> [Capitalism] is a social formation in which markets and commodity production are pervasive, including capital markets and labour markets ... [a] generalised commodity production, where most goods and services are destined to become items of trade. Under capitalism, most production takes place in capitalist firms. A capitalist firm is an institution in which products are made for sale and workers are employed under the supervision of the management. *The employment relationship is thus the core relationship of production under capitalism.*

While the emphasis on commoditisation and on the employment relationship greatly facilitates the Marxist/Institutionalist dialogue, this conceptualisation of capitalism does not seem to be fully adequate to the assessment of contemporary capitalism. The main reason is that it misses the specificity of the capitalist mode of production in comparison to the others. While acknowledging that capitalist society is unequal and conflicting, it neglects the role of class as a conceptual category and, as a consequence, it misses the key role played by class inequality and class conflicts in capitalist development.

True, class cannot be taken as a collective agent, and behaviour and action have to be explained in terms of individuals, like Institutionalism does. Yet, class is an institution and, like other institutions, it constitutes and reconstitutes individual behaviour in a continuous interplay. Moreover, while also other institutions count, class deserves a unique place in the capitalist economy for its key influence on inequality and conflicts.

Several modes of inequality cross the capitalist society. Some of them – for instance, inequality within the family and gender inequality – are also found in non-capitalist societies. By contrast, capital/labour inequality is specific to capitalism and deeply impacts on other modes of inequality. As Amartya K. Sen points out (2005: 205–207), class plays a 'very special role in the establishment and in the reach of social inequality' as it makes 'the influence of other sources of disparity ... much sharper'. The influence of class is not 'merely additive' – i.e. 'there is class and then there is also gender..., caste, and so on' – but also 'transformational', as it strengthens the impact of the other modes of inequality.

Moreover, class conflicts – which in the capitalist economy take the form of capital/labour conflicts – directly impact on the core relations of capitalism, such as capital accumulation and technical change. They ultimately determine the development of productive forces and the living standards, defining the trajectory of change.

In Marx's theory, the crucial role of class conflicts is established by means of core concepts such as accumulation, commoditisation of the labour force and exploitation, and, as we have seen, their analytical importance has also been confirmed in the development of Marxism in the twentieth century. By contrast, Evolutionary Institutionalism overlooks the specificity of class interests, including them in the broad category of vested interests of individuals and social groups.

I conclude this section by pointing out that, like Marxism, Evolutionary Institutionalism has advantages and weaknesses for the analysis of contemporary capitalism, and its advantages are found in the areas in which Marxism is weak, and vice versa. This conclusion supports the idea that an eclectic combination of Marxism and Evolutionary Individualism might improve the understanding of capitalism. In the next section I explore the feasibility of this option.

4   The Marxist/Institutionalist dialogue

That a dialogue between Marxism and Institutionalism is possible and that it might improve the understanding of capitalism is not a new idea. Veblen was the first to raise the issue, inaugurating a long-standing debate. As a socialist, he was sympathetic towards Marxism, while being at the same time critical of Marx's philosophical foundations.

For Veblen, Marx's major original contribution, as well as his major theoretical weakness, is found in the combination of 'Materialistic Hegelianism' and 'the English System of Natural Rights' (Veblen, 1906: 409 et seq.). Moving from Hegelian premises, Marx assumes that a natural law exists according to which workers have the right to claim the whole product of their work, and builds his labour theory of value and exploitation on the conviction that the appropriation of surplus deprives the workers of a 'natural' right.

Veblen challenges the very idea of a 'natural' right on the grounds that rights are defined by the institutional framework and that economic analysis should examine how institutional factors separate workers from the means of production, rather than to indulge in 'moral' assessments of workers' natural rights (O'Hara, 2000: 50). Yet, the core of Veblen's critique refers to Marx's view of class-consciousness.

Marx does not find a direct causal connection between material forces and actions, stressing the rationality of human beings and overlooking physiological needs and instincts and, also, the interplay between individuals and structure. By contrast, Veblen maintains, the influence on individual behaviour of instincts and physiological needs is continuously combined with ideological factors and class interests: human agency is not always conscious, nor can it be explained exclusively by class factors. According to Veblen, Marx's determinist conception of class struggle is ultimately grounded in his incapacity to interpret human nature. With an adequate theory of human agency, Marx would have produced a more sound analysis of capitalism, rejecting the notion of conscious class struggle and seeing change as a cumulative process, in which both structure and agency change. Then, history would have appeared as a process of change without goal or final term (Veblen, 2006: 416).

Veblen's critique of Marx's theory starts a debate in which two opposite views confront themselves: the conviction that the Marxist/Institutionalist dialogue is not possible due to the theoretical differences; and the conviction that the dialogue is feasible as the approaches produce a similar substantive analysis of capitalism.

Revisiting the debate about Marxist/Institutionalist relations, Hunt (1979) argues that Marx and Veblen's analyses are not only compatible but also complementary. For Hunt, the discrepancies emphasised by Veblen are the outcome of *misunderstandings* and *mistakes*: the major argument of Veblen's critique is wrong, as Marx is not a dialectical materialist and Marx's view of history is not teleological. The importance of Marx and Veblen's theories lies in their analyses of capitalism. Stressing the historical relativity of capitalism and the role of conflicts and class struggle, they reach results that are either similar or complementary.

Edgell and Townshend (1993) challenge Hunt's conclusion. They argue that there can be few doubts about Marx's teleological view of history, and that the similarities between Marx and Veblen are very much confined to the fact that they both were socialist. Mayhew (1987) shares a similar position: an alliance between Marx and Veblen is not acceptable since Marx is rooted 'in the pre-Darwinian world of natural rights' (984), while Veblen develops a Darwinian approach. Hodgson also takes this position arguing that Marx's theory of change is basically antagonist to the Darwinian concept of evolution (2001a, 2001b).

On the opposite side, Henry (2001) argues that Marx and Veblen are compatible and should be studied in tandem. They share the same view of capitalism – as a transitory form of organisation in which production is organised 'around money' – and a holist approach to economic analysis. While part of Veblen's critique is wrong, the actual discrepancies between Marx and Veblen are very few: Marx's premises are only formally Hegelian, while his analysis is essentially evolutionary. Moreover, political tactics explain Marx's emphasis on economic relations and forces.

Similarly, O'Hara (2000) maintains that similarities prevail over differences. He argues that Veblen had only a partial access to the works of Marx and based his analysis on secondary sources and that this partial and biased access accounts for his wrong interpretation. He also argues that in the third volume of *Capital* Marx moves towards an institutional approach in the analysis of the formation of aggregate social capital. His conclusion is that Marx is a 'softened' Institutionalist and Veblen a 'softened' materialist.

The debate is clearly inconclusive. Despite the daring attempts by Henry and O'Hara, the theoretical discrepancies between Marx's theory and Veblen's Institutionalism cannot be denied. Marx and Veblen lived in different contexts and in different historical periods and these differences are reflected in their theoretical constructions. Yet, to mark this difference does not imply that the Marxist/Institutionalist dialogue is not feasible.

Building on this difference, and with the joint contribution of Marxists and Institutionalists, it has been shown that the dialogue between Marxism and Institutionalism is feasible and improves the understanding of capitalism. With the support of a comparative analysis of capitalism, the Institutionalist William Dugger and the Marxist Howard Sherman (Dugger and Sherman, 1997, 2000) point out how specific discrepancies may be overcome in order to enhance the dialogue.

They point to class analysis and agency theory as major areas of divergence, arguing that other significant differences follow in the analysis of capitalist change, which is seen as a process determined by capital/labour conflicts, on the Marxist side, and as an evolutionary and cumulative process driven by the two-way interplay between individuals and institutions, on the Institutionalist side. This discrepancy requires an adjustment on both sides. On the Marxist side, the existence of more than two classes and the impact of non-class factors on individual behaviour are to be acknowledged; on the Institutionalist side, the primacy of class stratification and class interests is to be accepted. Their conclusion is that, with these adjustments, the dialogue is possible and improves the understanding of capitalism.

Also Cullenberg (1999, 2000) stresses the advantages of the Marxist/Institutionalist cross-pollination, pointing to the 'analytical connections' between non-determinist Marxism and the Institutionalism built on Veblenian roots. Relying on this cross-pollination, it would be possible to account, at the same time, for the impact of class conflicts on change and for the influence of institutions on individual behaviour. The consequence would be an improvement of the understanding of capitalism (2000: 811 et seq.).

5 The Marxist/Institutionalist analytical framework

Sharing the conviction that the Marxist/Institutionalist dialogue improves the understanding of capitalism, I present in this section an eclectic framework based on Marx's theory – integrated and amended to account for the 'anomalies' of twentieth century capitalism – and Evolutionary Institutionalism. Its aim is to provide the conceptual tools to interpret and explain the behaviour and processes leading to growth and change in contemporary 'real world' economies.

The framework proposes a theoretical representation of the main socio-economic relations of the capitalist economy. It consists of 15 propositions for three levels of analysis: the nature of the capitalist economy, its working, and its change. The propositions are presented below. Each group is introduced by a short comment in which the linkages with Marxism and/or Institutionalism are pointed out.

The capitalist economy and society

The view of the capitalist society shown in propositions 1 and 2 broadly relies on Marx's theory (Marx, 1890). However, it is not distant from the view of contemporary capitalism proposed by Hodgson (2001a), which focuses on commodity production and on the employment relationship. Together with the concept of labour force as a commodity (proposition 1) and the idea that labour commoditisation is central to capitalism (proposition 2), which belong to classical Marxism, also the hypothesis of multiple forms of commoditisation has been included, as theorised by van der Linden (2008).

Propositions 3 and 4 are jointly inspired by Marxism and Institutionalism. While the existence of class and non-class inequalities is pointed out, only capital/labour relations and conflicts are taken to be specific to the capitalist economy. The primacy of class conflicts is also acknowledged. Building on Wright's contribution, class conflicts are conceptualised by means of a concept of 'exploitation', in which exploiters and exploited are compared in terms of access to resources and living standards. To assess the nature of middle classes I have employed the concept of 'contradictory class location', which is again borrowed from Wright (2005).

Proposition 1: The capitalist economy and society and the market
Capitalist economy and society is the social formation produced by the capitalist mode of production. Markets and commodity production are pervasive. The vast majority of goods and services are produced for the market (including the labour force).

Proposition 2: Capital accumulation and the commoditisation of the labour force
Capitalist production requires accumulation to enlarge the scale of production and to enhance growth and employment. In turn, accumulation requires the commoditisation of the labour force. Multiple forms of commoditisation of the labour force exist according to the features of employers and employees and to the patterns in which commoditisation occurs.

Proposition 3: Social stratification
The capitalist society is unequal and stratified. Modes of inequality and forms of stratification vary among and within countries. Several modes of inequality co-exist – in relation to wealth and income, gender, religion, ethnicity – producing a complex network of social stratification that takes economic and non-economic forms. Among all modes of inequality, the one between the capitalist class and the working class pertaining to the control of the means of production is specific to the capitalist economy, as class conflicts over the access to resources and over the appropriation of labour effort are specific to capitalism.

Proposition 4: Class relations and class conflicts
Capitalist class structure is complex owing to the persistence of pre-capitalist residuals and the variety of social institutions and formal/informal rules influencing individual rights and powers. The main classes are the capitalist class – which includes the individuals who control the production process and commoditise the workers – and the class of sub-altern workers – which includes the individuals who do not have control over their labour power, over their means of production, and over the product of their labour. Capitalists exploit workers, excluding them from the access to resources and appropriating their labour effort.

Proposition 5: Middle classes
In between the capitalist class and the class of subaltern workers, there are the middle classes. Middle classes exist due to the complexity of class structure. They are made of individuals with contradictory class locations, who are at the same time employees and employers or, alternatively, who are neither employers nor employees.

The working of the capitalist economy and society

The working of the capitalist economy is analysed by means of two different types of propositions. Propositions 6 to 8 focus on individual behaviour and largely rely on Veblen's theory of agency; propositions 10 to 11 deal with social intercourse, which is theorised by means of conceptual categories borrowed from Gramsci's theory of hegemony (1975). Proposition 9 works as a connection between the two levels of analysis.

After the rebuttal of the idea of rational and optimising behaviour in proposition 6, the role of institutions as a cognitive framework for human action is pointed out in proposition 7. Also the two-way 'reconstitutive causation' between individuals and institutions is established (Hodgson, 2004). Proposition 8 points to institutions as a tool to shape power relations. Proposition 9 establishes that, while being made of agents, class is not an agent and then the concept of agency does not apply. The influence of class on agency is mediated through individual class identity, which is jointly influenced by economic and non-economic factors.

Deviating from Classical Marxism and moving on the track opened by Gramsci, proposition 10 establishes the two-way interplay between economic structure and the institutional/ideological superstructure. The impact of this interplay on capitalist development is pointed out in proposition 11.

Proposition 6: Agency
Individuals are not rational optimising beings; rationality is not possible, due to uncertainty and to the limits of the human brain. Individual behaviour is socially determined by means of institutions – formal and informal social rules – in which shared habits of thought are embodied.

Proposition 7: Agency and structure
Institutions provide the cognitive framework for human action. They constrain and enable human behaviour and, being the by-products of human society, are influenced by it. Institutions influence individuals and individuals influence institutions: between them there is a 'reconstitutive causation'.

Proposition 8: Power and institutions
Owing to the reconstitutive causation between individuals and institutions, institutions may constitute and reconstitute individual aims and desires. They may also be created – or transformed – in order to embody specific cognitive frameworks in function of established or emerging interests. Then, they may be used to enhance the power of individuals and groups.

Proposition 9: Agency and class
Class is not an agent, but it is made of agents. Agents in a class might acquire class-consciousness and participate in the process of class formation on the basis of their class identity. Class identity is the outcome of the relationships with the means of production and is articulated on the basis of culture – construed as ethnicity, caste, gender, and religion.

Proposition 10: Structure and superstructure
The capitalist economy and society is made of an economic structure – *i.e. relations of production and forces of production – and a* superstructure *– i.e. ideas and institutions. No primacy is given to economic structure over superstructure: economic structure influences the superstructure and is influenced by it in a two-way causation. So, production relations are*

determined by productive forces, ideas, institutions, and by the past history of production relations, while productive forces are determined by production relations, ideas, institutions, and by the past history of productive forces.

Proposition 11: Ideology and hegemony
The capitalist class exerts a hegemonic – i.e. economic and non-economic – dominance on the subaltern class obtaining its consensus by means of ideology and of an institutional framework in which the hegemony is negotiated between the classes. Production relations and ideology constitute the 'historical bloc' that enforces the hegemony of the dominant class, ensuring social stability.

Change and growth of the capitalist economy and society

The Marxist/Institutionalist synthesis also enables the interpretation of growth and change. Proposition 12 relies on Veblen's view of change. Proposition 13 introduces the core concept of institutional embeddedness of capitalist change. Proposition 14 points out the influence of non-capitalist structures and institutions on the working of the capitalist economy, introducing the concept of 'necessary impurities' (Hodgson, 2001a). Finally, proposition 15 stresses the primacy of class conflicts over non-class conflicts.

Proposition 12: Evolutionary change
Capitalist change is an evolutionary process in which nothing is given and unchangeable. Economy and society change with an adaptive process in which every step may be explained on the basis of the previous one. The fittest institutions and individuals prevail. No laws of motion govern the outcomes and change has never a final term.

Propositions 13: The institutional embeddedness of capitalist change
History and culture matter. As the institutional framework is the outcome of the relations between human beings and the external environment, institutions are specific to any historical and geographical context. Change is then path dependent and historically specific.

Proposition 14: The necessary impurities
Real-world economies diverge from the model of the 'purely' capitalist economy in which all social relations are expressed in market terms. This is due to the persistence of institutions and structures of the previous modes of production that are not dissolved by capitalism. These are 'impurities' that are 'necessary' to the working of the capitalist system.

Proposition 15: Conflicts and change

The capitalist economy and society is crossed by a variety of conflicts determined by different modes of inequality. Among them, class conflicts play a key role in the development of the capitalist economy, both in the short and in the long run. They influence the development of the forces of production, including the introduction of technical change, determining the material conditions for production and the standards of living.

6 The eclectic framework, the analysis of capitalism, and Provincial India

The eclectic framework enhances our understanding of the complexity of contemporary capitalism resulting from the co-existence of a variety of organisational and institutional forms and multiple modes of class and non-class inequality. It describes the capitalist economy as a socio-economic system relying on the commoditisation of the labour force and led by capital/labour conflicts, in which growth and change are embedded in institutions. The institutional embeddedness works at two levels: institutions shape individual preferences and desires, and past culture and institutions influence present institutions, and therefore also individuals. As history and culture matter, change is path dependent and does not progress toward a predetermined outcome.

The framework provides the tools to explore the variety of organisational and institutional forms, accounting for the several modes of inequality that cross the capitalist society: variety is the consequence of the institutional embeddedness of growth and change, while capitalist production relations are at the origin of class inequality, which accompanies non-class modes of inequality, reinforcing them.

The framework constitutes a significant improvement in comparison with other heterodox approaches – such as the Social Structures of Accumulation theory and the Regulation School theory – that have been employed to address the developments of capitalism in the second half of the twentieth century.

The SSA theory analyses capitalism by means of an eclectic framework in which the theories of long waves by Kondratieff and Schumpeter are developed against a background of Marx's political economy and Keynesian economics (Kotz *et al.*, 1994). It is built on the idea that accumulation does not occur in a vacuum but requires a suitable and stable social environment. Yet, stability is structurally undermined by the contradictions of capitalism, i.e. class struggle and competition. Institutions might support accumulation by creating a social structure that ensures the necessary stability. This social structure – which is referred to as the social structure of accumulation – includes all institutions that impact on production and exchange. Crises occur in the case of a contradiction between accumulation and the institutional setting and might be overcome by the emergence of a new institutional setting – a new social structure of accumulation – more favourable to accumulation.

The Regulation School theory develops Marx's political economy by means of the concepts of 'regime of accumulation' and 'mode of regulation' (Aglietta, 1979; Lipietz, 1987; Boyer, 1990). The first refers to the forms in which production, consumption and exchange influence capital accumulation in a particular period of time, and the second refers to the institutional setting in which capital accumulation takes place (from the laws and norms to the institutions that regulate socio-economic intercourse). While the mode of regulation creates a favourable environment for the accumulation regime, crises occur when there is a contradiction between the two. The way out is a change in the institutional setting and, then, in the regime of accumulation.

The two approaches show many similarities, but also important differences (Kotz, 1994; Mavroudeas, 2006). Both stress the influence of non-economic variables on economic processes (through institutions) and both acknowledge the necessity of eclecticism in economic analysis. Yet, the Social Structures of Accumulation theory takes class relations only as a component of social relations. By contrast, the Regulation school theory focuses on the determinants of accumulation and takes class relations as a key factor of change. Both explain the development of capitalism focusing on the relation between accumulation and the institutional environment in which it occurs. Yet, for the first the mover is the change in institutions that undermines stability, while for the second the driving force is the change in the regime of accumulation which requires the adaptation of the mode of regulation.

The two approaches have been successfully employed for research on long-term change at macro-economic level, such as the periodisation of long waves in the USA and in other industrialised countries and the analysis of the Fordist crisis and the post-Fordist transition. Yet, despite this success – which largely accounts for their high reputation in the 1980s and 1990s – they are inadequate for exploring the working of macro dynamics at the micro level as they lack an agency theory to explore the changes in individual behaviour.

The Marxist/Institutionalist framework that I propose as an alternative to the previous approaches has many qualities. First, it relies on Veblen's theory of agency, rejecting the idea of rational optimising behaviour, and solves the agency/structure problem conceptualising the 'reconstitutive causation' between individuals and institutions. Second, it acknowledges the primacy of class and class conflicts as a major driver of growth and change. Third, it rejects all forms of determinism, interpreting change as an evolutionary process influenced by past history and culture.

The Marxist/Institutionalist framework appears to be particularly suitable to the study of capitalism in Provincial India. As we will see in this book, India's provincial economy is 'institutionally embedded'. The institutions and ideologies that the country has inherited from her colonial and pre-colonial past – such as caste, gender, patriarchy and religion – shape individual and social behaviour, originating (and perpetuating) multiple modes of inequality that co-exist and interact with class. The outcome is a stratified society, composed of a set of dynamic subsystems, in which class and non-class relations and interests are intertwined.

Accounting for the institutional embeddedness of capitalist change, the Marxist/Institutionalist framework provides a much more comprehensive interpretation of the nature and working of India's provincial capitalism than Marxism and Evolutionary Institutionalism individually taken. By means of the eclectic framework, the persistence of pre-capitalist structures and power relations might be explained in evolutionary terms as institutional and ideological constructions, which have survived from pre-colonial and colonial times because they have been reworked to be suitable for the regulation of capitalist production relations. Moreover, the Veblenian hypotheses about human agency might account for the influence of institutional and ideological constructions on individual aims and desires. Finally, the primacy given to class relations as a major distinguishing trait of capitalism allows the role of class inequalities to be emphasised even when they are intertwined to non-class inequalities rooted in culture and religion.

The interpretative potential of the Marxist/Institutionalist framework will be tested in the case of Provincial India in the remainder of the book. I will use the representation of the capitalist economy introduced in this chapter as a guideline for my analysis, with the aim of pointing out the distinguishing traits of India's provincial capitalism. I focus first on Provincial India as a whole and then on Arni town.

Consistent with the eclectic framework, I will explore, in turn, economic organisation, class structure, and the impact of ideologies and institutions on production relations. This will be done for Provincial India as a whole in Chapters 3, 4 and 5, and for Arni in Chapters 6, 7 and 8.

3 Introducing non-farm capitalism in Provincial India

1 Introduction

The analysis of the non-farm economy in Provincial India begins with this chapter. I explore first the organisation of economic activity, and then I turn to class structure in Chapter 4 and to the influence of ideologies and institutions on social production relations in Chapter 5. The Marxist/Institutionalist framework introduced in Chapter 2 provides the conceptual tools for my analysis.

I build on the assumption that the injection of capital associated with the high-yielding varieties (henceforth HYVs) deeply impacted on the spatial and intersectoral allocation of resources in Provincial India, imprinting a new direction to capitalist development. My argument is twofold. First, I argue that the economy of Provincial India is *diversified* and *informal*, i.e. activities from different sectors – agriculture, industry and services – co-exist in the same area, while transactions are informally regulated. I take diversification and informality as outcomes of historical specificity: long-term features of Provincial India that have become the pillars of social production relations in the aftermath of the Green Revolution (henceforth GR). Second, I argue that the growth of rural non-farm activities (henceforth RNFAs) in Provincial India and the 'quality' of employment they generate are the outcome of the interplay of society and economy within a naturally and historically bounded territory.

The chapter is organised as follows. Section 2 introduces the historical context in which capitalist development in Provincial India has been taking place since the GR; Section 3 explores the nature and significance of economic diversification; Section 4 deals with informality; Section 5 proposes a Marxist/Institutionalist conceptualisation that focuses on the interplay of economy and society within a bounded area; and Section 6 concludes.

2 The historical context

India has more than doubled her GDP annual growth rate since the mid-1960s, from an average 3.2 per cent in 1960–1965 (Third Five-Year Plan) to an average 8.4 per cent in the period 2009–2011, falling to 6.9 per cent in 2011–2012.[1] This spectacular growth is much debated. Its origin and causes are controversial, as are its consequences in terms of poverty and inequality.

From Green Revolution to economic liberalisation

Some analysts ascribe India's growth to post-1991 economic liberalisation (Joshi and Little, 1998; Ahluwalia, 1999; Bhagwati, 1999), while others stress the continuity of the reform process over the decades, pointing to the shift from the socialist planning of Jawaharlal Nehru to the pro-business strategy initiated by Indira Gandhi and Rajiv Gandhi that was consolidated and developed with the post-1991 reforms. This latter view is widely supported by the literature, which stresses the lack of evidence of a significant acceleration in the growth rate after 1991 (Byres, 1997: 5; Torri, 2000: 717; Rodrik and Subramanian, 2004a: 27; see also McCartney, 2009).

The State played a major role in enhancing economic growth (McCartney, 2009). The governments led by Indira Gandhi (1966–1977 and 1980–1984) laid the foundations for a pro-business strategy, creating a favourable environment for capital accumulation by means of three major policy interventions (Torri, 2000; Rodrik and Subramanian, 2004a; Basu and Maertens, 2007).

The first was the GR. After pilot programmes in 1960–1961 and again in 1964–1965, the GR was part of the 'new strategy of agricultural development' launched in the Fourth Five-Year Plan (1969–1974). Together with agricultural credit subsidies, it included a technical package based on HYVs and on the 'expansion' of the supply of fertilisers and pesticides and the improvement of irrigation (Planning Commission, 1970: Chapter 7). It was addressed to the 'better-endowed' regions with the aim of enhancing accumulation by promoting intensive agriculture and increasing yields and the marketed surplus (Patnaik, 1997: 181; Rao, 1997: 132; see also Gulati, 1999, and Bhalla, 2007). The second intervention was the nationalisation of the banks (1969). This had a significant impact on accumulation because it made savings 'easier and safe' for the rural population by forcing the banks to open branches in distant regions (Basu and Maertens, 2007: 159–160). Finally, the third intervention was the programme of 'expansionary adjustment', which Indira Gandhi's government negotiated for a loan of Special Drawing Rights (SDR) 530 million from the IMF and SDR 266 million from the Compensatory Financing Facility. The programme – adopted in 1980 after the second oil shock and the 1979 drought – included measures to enhance exports and to cut trade barriers – both tariff and non-tariff (Joshi and Little, 1998: 58–59; Torri, 2000: 700).

Rajiv Gandhi carried on and strengthened Indira Gandhi's pro-business strategy adopting a series of measures of economic liberalisation from 1985 to 1989. These measures, more wide-ranging than the previous ones, consisted of industrial and import deregulation, export incentives, depreciation of the exchange rate, reduction of direct taxation, and financial liberalisation (Joshi and Little, 1998: 62–62; Torri, 2000: 717–719; see also Rodrik and Subramanian, 2004b).

Yet, neither Indira Gandhi's nor Rajiv Gandhi's measures represented a radical break with Jawaharlal Nehru's planning. The fracture occurred in 1991 when, to face the macroeconomic crisis after the Iraqi invasion of Kuwait, Narasimha Rao's government negotiated a programme of economic stabilisation and structural adjustment for a loan from the IMF. By means of the new economic policy – implemented in several steps after 1991 – the Indian State deeply influenced the mobilisation and allocation of the economic surplus, combining economic and institutional reforms (McCartney, 2009: 179 et seq.).

The post-1991 reforms relied on three pillars: (i) the retreat of the State from the economy by cutting investment, industrial and import licences, and by privatising the public sector; (ii) the creation of a 'friendly' environment for private investment by reducing the fiscal burden and increasing investment in infrastructure; and (iii) the opening of India's economy to international competition by means of the reform of the trade regime, new regulation of foreign investment (direct and portfolio), and the reform of capital markets (Torri, 2000: 755–757; Rodrik and Subramanian, 2004a, 2004b; Basu and Maertens, 2007). These reforms marked the end of the import-substitution policy (and the related protection for infant industry) that India had maintained since Independence.

Growth and inequality

While its impact on poverty is controversial, few doubts remain that India's economic growth has been associated with increased inequality. Relying on the data supplied by the National Sample Survey Organisation (henceforth NSSO), Datt and Ravallion (2010) show that, after a steady increase of poverty since 1950, the pace of poverty reduction accelerated after the 1991 reforms. Yet they argue that, despite the growth impact of the 1991 reforms, inequality has increased in economic and human development terms. Also Sen and Himanshu (2004a, 2004b: 4370–4372) point to the sharp increase of inequality 'in all its dimensions', stressing that inequality itself has constrained poverty reduction, preventing the decline in the 'absolute number of poor'. Basu (2008: 54) reaches a similar conclusion, arguing that, while inequality ('no matter how one measures it') is growing, poverty is declining, but at a rate that is 'unacceptably low'.

Another widely analysed aspect is the unequal distribution of the gains from growth across states, sectors, classes and individuals. Ahmed and Varshney (2008) stress the increasing inequality in literacy rates and the gender gaps in education and income, while Bardhan (2009), Bhaskar and Gupta (2007), and Kar and Sakthivel (2007) document the increasing sectoral and regional inequality.

A heavily debated issue is the poor quality of India's economic growth as shown by the features of the employment generated by economic liberalisation. Assuming that the benefits of growth are transferred to the working poor through employment, it is widely argued that economic liberalisation has not produced *adequate* employment and that this failure is responsible for the increasing inequality and for the persistence of poverty (Dev, 2002; Chandrasekar and

Ghosh, 2006; Unni and Raveendran, 2007; S. Bhalla, 2007; Papola and Sahu, 2012).

The emphasis is on the *quantity* and *quality* of jobs in post-reform India. Focusing on manufacturing, Alessandrini (2009: 2–3) argues that a pattern of jobless growth has been emerging since 1991. This is a consequence of the international openness of the country, on the one hand, and of the shift from labour-intensive to capital-intensive activities, on the other. The exposure to international competition, and the subsequent restructuring, determines the loss of jobs in inefficient production units (Ghosh, 2006), while the shift to capital-intensive activities reduces the quantity of labour per unit of capital. Also the nature of the jobs created across sectors changed after liberalisation. Since 1991, the vast majority of the new employment is 'informal': a phenomenon largely depending on the growth of the tertiary sector following the international opening of India's economy (NCEUS, 2008: 3–4; see also Joshi, 2004; S. Bhalla, 2007; Bosworth *et al.*, 2007; Basile and Harriss-White, 2010; Srivastava, 2012).

Growth and inequality in Provincial India

Economic liberalisation has impacted on Provincial India in contradictory ways. The end of the import-substitution strategy and the signing of the Agreement on Agriculture were expected to benefit agricultural producers by increasing agricultural prices and improving the domestic terms of trade between agriculture and industry, enhancing the competitiveness of India's agricultural production on international markets (Bhalla, 1997: 31; Gulati, 1999: 123; Ghosh, 2006: 6; Bhalla, 2007: 223 et seq.).[2] By contrast, the growth of agricultural exports has been below expectations (mainly owing to price volatility), while the exposure to international competition revealed the inadequacy of India's agriculture, negatively impacting on food security and living standards (Bhalla, 2007: 265).

Bhalla shows that the deterioration of food security in the post-reform period is the joint effect of the decline in per capita availability of foodgrains, the large fluctuations in food production, and the mixed evidence in relation to access to food (2007: 281 et seq.). Patnaik (2004: 10, Table 4) denounces the sharp decline in per capita foodgrains absorption (from 177 kg to 155 kg). The decline – which Patnaik establishes on the basis of official data on production and trade – results from divergent trends in urban India (where food consumption is rapidly increasing) and rural India (where it is rapidly decreasing); and it is ascribed to the neoliberal reforms that have reduced agricultural incomes and public expenditure on rural development (Patnaik, 2004: 13).[3] Also, for Ghosh (2006: 16) a major cause for the deterioration of food security is the reduction of agricultural incomes, owing to the collapse of agricultural employment and the increasing incidence of poverty and indebtedness among farmers and agricultural labourers.

After the steady decline in the 1990s, the agricultural rate of growth recovered between 2000 and 2005, yet it remained well below the non-agricultural one (1.7 per cent against 8.7 per cent) (Chandrasekhar, 2007: 2). This had an impact on employment – which showed only a slight growth, largely determined by an increase of the number of self-employed women. It also affected rural poverty (Mishra, 2007). The incidence of rural poverty constantly remains above that of urban poverty.[4]

While the large proportion of the population below the poverty line shows the failure of India's pattern of growth at being 'inclusive', the urban/rural gaps show the progressive marginalisation of rural areas – a phenomenon with more serious implications than the decline of agriculture in development.

3 Economic diversification

Indeed the performance of agriculture goes far in explaining urban/rural gaps in terms of living standards and participation in growth. Yet, Provincial India extends beyond agriculture, also including RNFAs, which generate employment and income.

Economic diversification is a long-established trait of Provincial India. The literature widely documents the existence of RNFAs in colonial India, when, in the context of agricultural stagnation, they provided a transient and flexible source of livelihoods (Saith, 1992, 2001; Roy, 1999; Chadha, 2003). With a major injection of capital into India's provincial economy, the GR enhanced the process of economic diversification, leading to the expansion of RNFAs, which developed in close integration with agriculture and with the territory in which they were located.

This process is explored in this section. I first introduce the main conceptual issues about rural diversification, turning then to the evidence for India.

3.1 Issues in economic diversification

There is a widespread consensus in the literature that special attention should be paid to RNFAs for their contribution to employment and income generation in rural areas, where high and increasing labour surpluses exist. The growth of RNFAs is said to prevent urbanisation, limiting the pressure on urban infrastructure (Ellis, 1998; Scoones, 1998; Start and Johnson, 2004) and contributing to poverty reduction.[5]

The non-farm economy in rural areas (henceforth RNFE) is highly diversified and heterogeneous. It includes activities in manufacturing and services, which also differ in the quality and quantity of employment and the pattern of local/ global integration (Coppard, 2001; Davis, 2004; Davis and Bezemer, 2004; Haggblade *et al.*, 2007: 13). For these reasons, a positive definition – of what is included in the RNFE rather than of what is not – is difficult, as the spatial and socio-economic boundaries are uncertain.

To define the RNFE, two major approaches exist: in the *locational approach* the RNFE includes activities located within an area defined as 'rural', while in the *linkage approach* the RNFE includes activities demonstrating growth linkages with the rural population through input and output markets. An empirical compromise is to combine the two criteria and to include the RNFAs that generate growth and are located in the countryside and in small and intermediate urban centres (Islam, 1987: 3; J. Harriss, 1991: 434 and 456fn; Saith, 2001).

Urban centres concentrate economic activity and social intercourse serving rural areas. Following Renkow (2007: 195–196), three major types of functions are observed. (i) Marketing functions: rural towns collect and distribute agricultural and non-agricultural goods from the hinterland and supply consumption and investment goods for consumers and producers in the hinterland. (ii) Production functions: several productive activities are localised in rural towns, from agricultural processing to manufacturing and services. Hence, rural towns are also 'employment centres' for workers from the surrounding area. (iii) Service functions: rural towns supply services for individuals and firms, and public utility infrastructure (see also Davis, 2004: 12). It follows that the RNFE is also *spatially* diversified, because activities may be located both in towns and in villages.

Another major characteristic is the sectoral composition of the RNFE. Haggblade *et al.* (2007: 5) estimate that service activities account for between 50–75 per cent of rural non-farm employment worldwide, while rural industry accounts for 20–25 per cent. Yet they also point out that significant differences exist across countries, which are explained by country-specific factors – such as resource endowments, the agrarian structure, and social structure. These factors also account for the trajectories of rural diversification.

In its contemporary form, rural diversification is an outcome of the structural transformation of the economy, and in particular of agricultural decline, which, by freeing resources, creates the condition for the growth of RNFAs (Chenery and Syrquin, 1986). Two 'scenarios' are possible. In the first – which Hazell *et al.* (2007: 83 et seq.) call the 'pull scenario' – rural diversification is produced by agricultural growth. The introduction of technical change increases resource productivity, feeding the growth of RNFAs with the agricultural resources freed by technical change and with the demand emanating from increased income. In the 'push scenario' the decline of agriculture induces the growth of RNFAs, but here the decline is determined by agriculture's distress, and resources leave the sector for better returns and living standards. While the two 'scenarios' describe two opposite trajectories of diversification, situations of 'multiple causality' also exist (Coppard, 2001: 25).

That different trajectories of diversification are possible is important for empirical analysis, as it explains discrepancies in the sectoral composition of the RNFE across countries and regions, accounting also for the variety of organisational forms and production relations.

Focusing on the enterprise as the unit of analysis, a variety of organisational forms exists – from micro and small to large firms (Liedholm, 2007). Moreover, enterprises in the RNFE operate in 'vertical supply chains' (Haggblade, 2007b: 352 et seq.; see also Haggblade, 2007a) or in sectoral concentrations, such as 'districts' and 'clusters', through which the supply of inputs and the marketing of output are organised (Davis, 2004: 27 et seq.). By contrast, focusing on labour, and having the household as the unit of analysis, the RNFE is diversified in relation to the status of employment. The basic distinction is between self-employment and wage labour, to which other forms are accreted on the basis of personal and household features, while a minority are labour-employing households.

The social features of households and workers account for the choice to engage in RNFAs faced with alternative choices, such as urban migration versus farm work (Reardon *et al.*, 2007). While education, gender, caste and ethnicity explain why workers have access to RNFAs with different rates of return (Lanjouw, 2007), the features of the household, in terms of farm/non-farm linkages and participation in caste/ethnicity/business networks, provide incentives to diversification, accounting for the scale of RNFAs and their pattern of local/global integration (Haggblade, 2007a).

3.2 Provincial India as a diversified economy

While there is a widespread consensus that RNFAs contribute to economic growth in Provincial India by creating employment and ensuring high rates of return to resources (Planning Commission, 2008: 171), their actual relevance in socio-economic terms is widely debated. The debate is partly stimulated by their heterogeneity, which makes a comprehensive assessment difficult, but also by the lack of adequate information on their size and contribution to India's GDP.

The available macro evidence mainly consists of information on rural non-farm employment (henceforth RNFL), which is provided by the quinquennial rounds on employment and unemployment of the NSSO.[6] The official information is supplemented by micro studies on specific cases. In this section I explore this field, relying on both sources of information. I comment first on the main trends in economic diversification as they emerge from the NSSO data for 2009–2010, and then I explore the case literature to identify the main features of the RNFE.[7]

The long-term expansion of RNFL

The NSSO long-term data on employment and unemployment provides strong evidence that the high rate of growth of India's economy has been accompanied by a long-term decline in the rate of employment growth. As Papola and Sahu (2012: 5) show, the rate of employment growth has been constantly declining over the period, from 2.4 for the period 1972/1973–1977/1978 to 0.22 per cent for the period 2004/2005–2009/2010.[8] This overall outcome results from different performances of employment in rural and urban areas, with the growth of urban employment being systematically higher than the growth of rural employment over the period.

Focusing on rural employment, Papola and Sahu also show that RNFL has performed better than agricultural employment, growing at 4.6 per cent per year during 1972/1973–1977/1978 and at 2.83 per cent per year during 2004/2005–2009/2010 (against 1.6 and –1.65 for agricultural employment in the same years) (Papola and Sahu, 2012: Table 4). Accordingly, the share of RNFL over India's rural employment has increased from 15 per cent in 1973 to 27 per cent in 2004–2005 and again to 32 per cent in 2009–2010 (corresponding to slightly more than 100 million workers).[9]

The increasing trend of RNFL in relation to rural employment is shown in Table 3.1, which also includes a description of its sectoral composition. In 2009–2010, the industrial sector as a whole employed more than half of the RNF workers, while the tertiary sector reduces its share over the last decade. Construction is the main activity (employing about 30 per cent of RNFL), while manufacturing, which has progressively reduced its share, employs slightly more than 20 per cent of RNF workers. In the service sector, trade and social services represent the largest activities.

The NSSO data for 2009–2010 provides a thorough evidence of the increasing trend of RNFL, showing that, as far as employment is concerned, the performance of the rural non-farm sector deeply contrasts with the stagnation of overall employment and the decline of agricultural employment. This conclusion challenges the uncertain picture of rural diversification provided by the previous NSSO surveys, which, since mid-1970s, show subsequent phases of expansion and retrogression in RNFL (S. Bhalla, 1997: 167 et seq.; Chadha, 1997: 187 et seq.). The most recent data also confirms the constant reduction of agricultural employment, showing that India is stable on the track of her structural transformation, overcoming the major anomaly – for a high-growing capitalist country – of a large percentage of the population employed in agriculture.[10]

Table 3.1 Sectoral composition of rural employment

Sector	1993–94	1999–2000	2004–05	2009–10
Agriculture	78.43	76.23	72.58	67.93
Non-agriculture	21.57	23.77	27.42	32.07
Total	*100.00*	*100.00*	*100.00*	*100.00*
Distribution within non-agriculture				
Mining and quarrying	2.58	2.09	1.79	2.01
Manufacturing	32.46	31.15	29.47	22.32
Utilities	1.06	0.55	0.47	0.43
Construction	11.02	13.96	17.81	29.32
Total secondary sector	*47.12*	*47.74*	*49.53*	*54.08*
Trade, hotels etc.	19.86	21.59	22.62	20.33
Transport and communication etc.	6.71	8.66	9.11	9.00
Financing, insurance, real estate and business services	1.36	1.52	1.76	1.70
Community, social and personal services	24.96	20.49	16.98	14.89
Total tertiary sector	*52.88*	*52.26*	*50.47*	*45.92*
Total non-agriculture	*100.00*	*100.00*	*100.00*	*100.00*

Source: Papola and Sahu (2012: Table 7).

44   *Analysing non-farm capitalism in Provincial India*

The process in itself is physiological and, together with the increasing trend of RNFL, represents a turning point in India's pattern of growth.

Socio-economic and spatial unevenness

The pattern of rural diversification, as described by the NSSO data for 2009–2010, shows a notable variability among Indian states. First, while RNFL is widespread in the country, a remarkable percentage is found in Kerala and West Bengal, while a notable low percentage is found in Gujarat, and Maharashtra (Table 3.2).

Table 3.2 Non-farm workers as percentage of the rural workforce in 2009–2010

	Non-farm	Agriculture	Total
Andhra Pradesh	23.7	76.3	100.0
Arunachal Pradesh	13.6	86.4	100.0
Assam	13.9	86.1	100.0
Bihar	17.0	83.0	100.0
Chhattisgarh	8.6	91.4	100.0
Delhi	100.0	0.0	100.0
Goa	89.3	10.7	100.0
Gujarat	7.8	92.2	100.0
Haryana	18.4	81.6	100.0
Himachal Pradesh	13.0	87.0	100.0
Jammu and Kashmir	10.7	89.3	100.0
Jharkhand	27.2	72.8	100.0
Karnataka	19.4	80.6	100.0
Kerala	57.4	42.6	100.0
Madhya Pradesh	12.1	87.9	100.0
Maharashtra	7.8	92.2	100.0
Manipur	65.0	35.0	100.0
Megahlaya	26.7	73.3	100.0
Mizoram	16.5	83.5	100.0
Nagaland	15.2	84.8	100.0
Orissa	23.8	76.2	100.0
Punjab	17.6	82.4	100.0
Rajasthan	27.4	72.6	100.0
Sikkim	35.1	64.9	100.0
Tamil Nadu	27.6	72.4	100.0
Tripura	86.5	13.5	100.0
Uttarakand	7.1	92.9	100.0
Uttar Pradesh	14.4	85.6	100.0
West Bengal	57.7	42.3	100.0
A and N Islands	57.6	42.4	100.0
Chandigarh	100.0	0.0	100.0
Dadra and Nagar Haveli	31.7	68.3	100.0
Daman and Diu	11.9	88.1	100.0
Lakshadweep	41.5	58.5	100.0
Puducherry	30.7	69.3	100.0
All India	20.6	79.4	100.0

Source: NSSO, 2011: 140.

Second, the extreme variability among states is also confirmed in Table 3.3, in which the distribution of RNF workforce among sub-sectors is reported for each state. Broadly, manufacturing, and public administration and education are the RNFAs that absorb the large proportion of RNFL in the vast majority of the states. A notable exception is Rajasthan, in which construction dominates. Also the workforce employed in services to individuals and enterprises is very variable among states. While trade and hotel is a major RNFA in Karnataka and Maharashtra, transport and finance employ a significant proportion of RNF workforce in Bihar and Gujarat. Third, the variability among Indian states is high also in relation to the sex of the employees and to employment status (see Table 3.4, which refers to rural employment as a whole).

While the percentage of women among regular workers is lower than that of men in the majority of Indian states (with the interesting exception of Kerala), the percentage of women among casual labourers is often higher than that of men and very variable, reaching its peak in Karnataka, Tamil Nadu and Andhra Pradesh.

Factors and processes of diversification

The variability of the structure and size of RNFL among Indian states reflects the existence of several trajectories of rural diversification, which in turn depend on several factors of diversification. The literature distinguishes *internal* from *external* factors. In the first case, rural diversification is seen as the outcome of processes that originate from within agriculture; and in the second case, the 'prime movers' are to be found outside agriculture, in the pattern of economic development (Unni, 1998: A-39).

We explore the internal factors, comparing the 'pull' scenario to the 'push' scenario and paying particular attention to the introduction of the GR and to its impact on rural diversification.

The analysis of the linkages between agriculture and rural differentiation has largely been carried out within the theoretical framework proposed by Mellor (1976) in his analysis of the GR. According to Mellor, technical change in agriculture may enhance the growth of the RNFE activating agricultural *production linkages* – which include both forward linkages of agriculture to the processing and marketing of agricultural goods and backward linkages with input suppliers – and *consumption linkages* – which develop from the impact of farmers' consumption on the local production of goods and services. The new technology accelerates the pace of structural transformation with a twofold impact: it increases resource productivity, freeing resources (mainly labour) that supply the emerging RNFAs; and it increases farmers' incomes, enhancing demand for consumption and investment goods. Through agricultural linkages, the impact of technical change in agriculture crosses sectoral boundaries, increasing the competitiveness of local industries.

Mellor's framework has been very influential in the analysis of rural diversification in India. Part of the literature confirms its main propositions in several

Table 3.3 RNF workers (u.s.) by state and broad industry division (NIC 2004) (% of total RNFL)[a]

	Mining and quarrying	Manufacturing	Electricity and water	Construction	Trade and hotel	Transport	Finance	Public admin. and education	All
Andhra Pradesh	2.95	42.19	0.00	16.88	18.57	1.27	0.84	17.30	100.0
Arunachal Pradesh	0.74	5.15	0.00	27.21	14.71	0.00	0.00	52.21	100.0
Assam	0.00	20.14	0.00	6.47	20.14	0.00	1.44	51.80	100.0
Bihar	0.00	48.24	0.00	2.94	12.35	5.88	0.00	30.59	100.0
Chhattisgarh	3.49	15.12	0.00	38.37	16.28	8.14	0.00	18.60	100.0
Delhi	0.00	0.00	0.00	87.01	0.00	0.00	0.00	12.99	100.0
Goa	3.92	6.83	0.00	0.00	4.26	2.02	0.45	82.53	100.0
Gujarat	0.00	21.79	0.00	30.77	12.82	6.41	0.00	28.21	100.0
Haryana	0.00	29.35	0.00	13.59	14.13	0.54	0.00	42.39	100.0
Himachal Pradesh	0.00	10.00	1.54	33.08	7.69	0.77	0.77	46.15	100.0
Jammu and Kashmir	0.00	51.40	0.00	5.61	1.87	1.87	0.00	39.25	100.0
Jharkhand	2.21	40.07	0.00	33.82	3.31	2.21	0.00	18.38	100.0
Karnataka	1.55	35.05	0.00	11.86	27.32	0.52	0.52	23.20	100.0
Kerala	0.87	32.40	0.87	11.67	11.85	1.22	5.05	36.06	100.0
Madhya Pradesh	2.48	38.84	0.00	38.84	6.61	0.00	0.00	13.22	100.0
Maharashtra	1.28	26.92	0.00	15.38	26.92	0.00	0.00	29.49	100.0
Manipur	0.00	28.31	0.00	37.38	28.46	0.00	0.00	5.85	100.0
Megahlaya	3.37	11.99	0.00	23.60	37.08	0.37	0.00	23.60	100.0
Mizoram	0.00	1.21	0.00	51.52	30.91	1.21	0.00	15.15	100.0
Nagaland	0.00	13.16	1.32	34.21	20.39	0.00	0.00	30.92	100.0
Orissa	0.84	44.96	0.00	25.63	10.50	0.00	0.42	17.65	100.0

									Total
Punjab	0.00	22.73	0.57	5.68	7.95	0.00	1.14	61.93	100.0
Rajasthan	0.36	6.93	0.00	81.75	3.28	0.73	0.00	6.93	100.0
Sikkim	0.00	0.28	0.00	33.05	13.68	0.00	0.28	52.71	100.0
Tamil Nadu	0.36	42.39	0.36	27.90	14.49	0.00	0.36	14.13	100.0
Tripura	0.23	13.99	0.00	73.53	1.85	0.00	0.12	10.29	100.0
Uttarakand	0.00	9.86	0.00	35.21	2.82	0.00	4.23	47.89	100.0
Uttar Pradesh	0.00	43.75	0.00	13.89	18.06	0.69	0.00	23.61	100.0
West Bengal	2.43	64.64	0.00	1.73	7.97	0.69	0.87	21.66	100.0
A and N Islands	0.87	22.40	0.00	17.36	14.93	0.52	0.35	43.58	100.0
Chandigarh	0.00	0.00	0.00	5.40	0.00	0.00	0.00	94.60	100.0
Dadra and Nagar Haveli	0.00	53.00	0.00	12.93	19.56	0.00	0.00	14.51	100.0
Daman and Diu	0.00	68.91	0.00	0.00	12.61	0.00	0.00	18.49	100.0
Lakshadweep	0.00	0.00	0.00	19.04	4.34	19.76	0.00	56.87	100.0
Puducherry	0.00	27.69	0.00	33.55	30.62	0.00	1.95	6.19	100.0
All India	1.46	36.41	0.00	25.24	13.59	0.97	0.97	21.36	100.0

Source: NSSO (2011: 140).

Note
a u.s. = usual status.

Table 3.4 Rural workers (u.s.) by employment status, sex and state in rural India (% of total RNFL)[a]

	Rural male			Rural female			All
	Self-employed	Regular employees	Casual labour	Self-employed	Regular employees	Casual labour	
Andhra Pradesh	41.9	9.3	48.8	39.5	3.7	56.9	100.0
Arunachal Pradesh	76.8	19.0	4.2	89.1	8.2	2.8	100.0
Assam	71.8	9.1	19.1	65.3	10.8	23.9	100.0
Bihar	52.0	3.3	44.7	47.9	2.6	49.5	100.0
Chhattisgarh	37.9	7.1	55.0	40.2	1.1	58.7	100.0
Delhi	8.1	62.0	29.9	0.0	13.1	87.9	100.0
Goa	32.5	58.5	9.0	1.8	83.9	14.4	100.0
Gujarat	53.1	8.8	38.2	59.8	2.5	37.7	100.0
Haryana	54.9	20.0	25.1	75.4	7.1	17.5	100.0
Himachal Pradesh	54.8	21.2	24.0	89.4	6.1	4.4	100.0
Jammu and Kashmir	63.0	19.7	17.3	94.7	4.3	1.1	100.0
Jharkhand	60.1	5.7	34.3	77.5	3.3	19.2	100.0
Karnataka	48.4	6.9	44.7	42.8	5.6	51.6	100.0
Kerala	38.8	17.6	43.5	42.1	23.8	34.2	100.0
Madhya Pradesh	55.2	6.0	38.7	49.6	1.7	48.7	100.0
Maharashtra	47.9	10.2	41.9	49.9	1.8	48.3	100.0
Manipur	77.6	14.6	7.9	70.7	3.8	25.5	100.0
Meghalaya	54.1	11.6	34.4	67.4	5.5	27.1	100.0
Mizoram	83.4	12.5	4.0	88.0	2.5	9.6	100.0
Nagaland	79.9	19.2	0.9	88.8	5.5	5.6	100.0
Orissa	55.9	7.1	36.9	55.4	4.3	40.4	100.0

Punjab	48.4	13.6	38.0	81.1	7.7	11.2	100.0
Rajasthan	67.7	8.4	23.9	71.3	1.9	26.8	100.0
Sikkim	58.5	28.7	12.8	64.7	22.3	12.9	100.0
Tamil Nadu	33.2	12.2	54.5	33.3	6.6	60.1	100.0
Tripura	50.2	10.4	39.4	22.0	8.1	70.0	100.0
Uttarakand	63.1	13.3	23.6	89.8	2.1	8.1	100.0
Uttar Pradesh	66.8	5.3	27.9	78.2	2.6	19.2	100.0
West Bengal	45.2	8.3	46.4	50.9	8.9	40.3	100.0
A and N Islands	48.1	37.4	14.7	53.7	34.6	11.7	100.0
Chhandigarh	12.6	65.2	22.2	5.7	94.3	0.0	100.0
Dadra and Nagar Haveli	51.3	13.8	34.9	10.8	5.4	86.5	100.0
Daman and Diu	19.1	41.9	39.0	22.1	10.5	67.4	100.0
Lakshadweep	41.5	28.0	29.3	55.2	31.0	13.8	100.0
Puducherry	22.0	22.1	55.9	28.9	5.3	65.8	100.0
All India	53.5	8.5	38.0	55.7	4.4	39.9	100.0

Source: Source: NSSO (2011: 127–128).

Note
a u.s. = usual status.

empirical exercises, showing that a positive relation exists between agricultural growth and the RNFE.[11] Moreover, it has been argued that the growth of RNFAs also has a positive impact on the primary sector – the so-called *reverse linkages* (Haggblade *et al.*, 2007: 144) – increasing the demand for food, improving the provision of industrial goods and service to farm workers, and increasing agricultural wages through the tightening of rural labour markets (Murthy, 2005).

However, another part of the literature challenges the positive relation between the introduction of technical change in agriculture and the RNFE (and, with it, also, the rosy picture of the balanced intersectoral growth produced by rural diversification). In a seminal study on NSSO and Census data on 16 states, Vaidyanathan (1986) shows that a positive relation exists between RNFL and the unemployment rate, and on the basis of this empirical result he advances the well-known 'residual sector hypothesis', according to which the growth of RNFL is not necessarily the outcome of technical change in agriculture, being instead a possible consequence of agricultural distress. In this case, the RNFE is a 'residual sector', to which rural workers turn for last-resort jobs. Like Mellor's framework, the residual sector hypothesis has been very influential and widely debated.[12]

Mellor's framework has been also criticised on theoretical grounds. A major critique refers to the concept of *locality* on which the whole edifice of growth linkages relies. Initially raising this critique, Barbara Harriss (1987a) argues that it is not possible to assess a priori whether farm demand does or does not become an incentive for *local* enterprises. The actual impact depends on the life and consumption styles of the agricultural population which might choose to increase their consumption of *non*-local and *non*-national products, instead of the local/national ones, with the consequence that agricultural investment does not induce rural *local* development. Moreover, she also points out the difficulty in conceptualising locality in the case of traded goods, which is a classification derived from international trade and might not be necessarily accurate or appropriate to a local economy.

The critiques of the theoretical construction of growth linkages lead the way to the conceptualisation of the role of external factors on rural diversification. Broadly, the literature suggests that rural diversification cannot be analysed in relation only to the rural sector, but needs to be contextualised in the structural transformation of India's economy. Proceeding from a structuralist view of economic change, several empirical analyses show that processes such as urbanisation, changes in consumption patterns, improvements in education, and the growth of transport infrastructure, exert a positive impact on rural diversification in many Indian states (Hazell and Haggblade, 1991; Alagh, 2005; S. Bhalla, 2005). The positive impact of government expenditures has also been discovered (Vaidyanathan, 1986; B. Harriss, 1987b; S. Bhalla, 1997; Sen, 1997).

Developing her argument that the performance of agriculture plays a marginal role in rural diversification, Sheila Bhalla argues that other regional trajectories exist that explain the growth of RNFAs. Relying on district and state level data, Bhalla points to diversified rural areas – which she calls 'corridor districts'

(1997: 167 et seq.; 2005: 84 et seq.) – along road and rail lines linking urban industrial centres. Focusing on the case of the north-west corridor that links the Delhi–Faridabad–Gurgaon industrial complexes – also known as Golden Corridor (Breman, 2004: 250) – she shows that rural diversification is a by-product of a global pattern of multisectoral growth which involves the rural population thanks to the development of transport and communications.

Among the external factors of rural diversification, the literature also stresses the growth of small-sized rural towns. Proximity to rural towns is widely seen as an incentive to rural diversification: it promotes urban/rural migration and commuting (Unni, 1998; S. Bhalla, 1997; Jayaraj, 2004); it increases RNFL and workers' productivity (and wages) (Papola, 1992); and it provides marketing structures and services to support the growth of RNFAs (B. Harriss, 1991; Coppard, 2001).

The empirical and theoretical debate on the factors leading to rural diversification in contemporary India does not reach an unequivocal conclusion. Clearly, a variety of trajectories of diversification are developing – from success stories, in which the growth of RNFAs is a consequence of agricultural prosperity, to agricultural distress scenarios and cases in which agricultural performance has no influence at all. A major implication can be drawn that rural diversification in India is the outcome of a multiplicity of factors and takes a multiplicity of forms. This variety is mirrored in the internal composition of the RNFE.

Dimensions of diversification

India's RNFE is composed of activities showing a high degree of diversification in relation to three main dimensions: the sectoral composition, the spatial distribution, and the scale of operation/structure of firms.

Sectoral diversification is the key trait of the RNFE. Manufacturing and services co-exist in rural space, employing local resources (to a variable degree and in variable forms). The proportion of manufacturing and services also varies. Moreover, several sub-sectors are usually included in each sector. As Fisher *et al.* (1997: 79) show, manufacturing includes a large variety of activities, from food processing, to textile garment and carpet production, to construction, to diamonds and gem cutting, to ceramics and other homeware products; while services include services to enterprises and to individuals (including tourism), repair and maintenance, retail and wholesale trade, and transport.

Services are the most important non-farm activity in terms of employment and the number of enterprises. Yet, rural industry has long been seen as the leading sector in the RNFE.

As Chadha's careful review shows (2003: 22 et seq.), the importance of rural industry for India's economy was established since the first debates on the country's development strategy. While industrialisation was a widely shared aim, two major views confronted each other: the long-term strategy proposed by J. Nehru and P.C. Mahalanobis, aimed at building an industrial structure starting from the investment goods sector, and M.K. Gandhi's strategy of rural industrialisation.

The latter had the explicit aim of supporting the 'village economy', rooted in rural industry – and in particular in *khadi* production (Fisher *et al.*, 1997: 8–10; Chadha, 2003: 13) – with the conviction that rural labour-intensive activities could enhance employment and promote social objectives, while at the same time satisfying the basic needs of an increasing population.

The strategy for heavy industrialisation prevailed. Yet, the role of rural industrialisation was explicitly acknowledged, and, since 1948, India's industrial policy walked on 'two legs' (Chadha, 2003: 30). With different weighting, the Five-Year Plans paid attention to rural industry, which was described as an artisan-based sector, inhabited by tiny and small enterprises involved in *khadi* and other 'traditional' activities, strictly interlinked with local agriculture through input and output markets (see also Alagh, 2005: 115).

Indeed, in addition to Mahatma Gandhi's legacy, the key role of rural industry among the RNFAs is supported by the evidence for its dynamism, extending to the development of scale economies (derived from the introduction of new technology), while the service sector is stagnant, being often composed of 'traditional', low-income and backward activities.

The evidence from contemporary rural India challenges this view. Exploring the growth potential of RNFAs, Fisher *et al.* (1997: 55 et seq.) argue that services and manufacturing are found both in 'modern' and 'traditional' RNFAs. They classify subsectors in the RNFE into three groups – high-share, high-growth, and emergent – on the basis of physical conditions of production (including the size and structure of the enterprises), demand, and intersectoral linkages (Fisher *et al.*, 1997: 58), showing that each group comprises firms operating in both services and in manufacturing.[13] Papola and Sharma (2005: 509) also note that 'non-manufacturing segments' of the RNFE can grow faster than manufacturing when they are located in rural towns. Finally, the earlier evidence of a rural town in South India (Arni) shows that i) in certain circumstances, service activities might be as dynamic as manufacturing, and ii) there is a strong interdependence between the two groups of activities (B. Harriss, 1991; Harriss-White, 2003a, 2003b).

The second important dimension in rural diversification is the location of activity in rural space. The literature shows that in India RNFAs are located in rural towns as well as in villages, and that location influences their performance. Contrary hypotheses have been generated to account for this: (i) that rural towns enhance rural diversification and improve the performance of RNFAs; and (ii) that rural towns depress RNFAs in villages.

Empirical analyses at state/region level support the first argument, stressing that the growth of rural towns has a positive impact on the RNFE by improving the access to urban infrastructure (marketing, the provision of intermediate goods, credit, education, and transport); they also stress that this positive impact is directly correlated with improvements in local transport for commuting (Unni, 1991; Papola, 1992; Visaria and Basant, 1994; Jayaraj, 2004). Papola (1992) also shows that the spread of urban centres better activates urban/rural linkages, enhancing rural diversification and rural development. The argument that rural towns have a positive influence on rural diversification in villages is also found in Fisher *et al.* (1997: 12), who stress that towns are better equipped as input and output markets (while villages never reach an adequate size in the demand for these commodities).

For Papola and Sharma (2005: 509), the relation between towns and villages runs in the opposite direction. Diversification in villages enhances the emergence of RNFAs in rural towns. This occurs as the investible surplus (generated in villages) is utilised in towns – owing to the latter's competitive advantages. Yet, they believe this to be a 'healthy development towards rural–urban linkages and integration', as it leads to an improvement in access to urban infrastructure. Insisting on the positive role of rural towns for activating urban/rural linkages, they also stress the priority of the development of small rural towns in rural development policy (512). A similar conclusion is reached by Mitra and Mitra (2005: 135), who argue that growth in the RNFE should be imputed to the development of small urban centres, and in particular to the growth of services. A contrasting opinion comes from Kundu *et al.* (2005), who, in their exercise on Census data (1981 and 1991), do not find evidence of the positive influence of rural town on rural diversification.

Finally, Harriss and Harriss (1984), in research on North Arcot, show that the local rural town (Arni) plays a dual 'parasitic' and 'generative' role towards the villages in the hinterland, with the balance varying over time. Building on the observation that the growth of the town in the 1980s was largely due to the silk manufacturing sector, and that there were no growth linkages between the silk sector and local agriculture, they argue that urban (local) growth did not affect rural diversification, while the growing urban economy induced increasing inequality between the town and the villages.

The third dimension of diversification in rural India refers to the scale of operation and the structure of firms. With important exceptions of large firms, the non-farm sector in rural India, both in manufacturing and services, is dominated by small and micro enterprises based on individual and family labour forces, which largely employ 'artisanal' technologies (Unni, 1998, 2000; Nayyar and Sharma, 2005). As capital requirements to enter the sector are low, there are no (or few) barriers to entry and competition is high (Fisher *et al.*, 1997; Aswasthi, 2007).

Rural petty producers have a contradictory class location.[14] They are simultaneously workers and entrepreneurs, and the borders between these roles are blurred (Das, 2003). While in possession of some – 'specific and restricted' (Harriss-White, 2010b: 10) – means of production, they have an incomplete control over production, being expropriated of the bulk of their entrepreneurial functions by middlemen and subcontractors who mediate between them and the markets. They are 'pseudo-entrepreneurs' (Aswasthi, 2007: 475), who employ a low-skilled labour force – mainly unpaid family labour – and use primitive technology.

While internal differentiation exists in relation to the scale of production and to the amount of the means of production they control, rural petty producers are usually disguised wage-workers (Harriss-White, 2010b; Lerche, 2010). They are exploited – as they are excluded from access to certain productive resources, while their exclusion generates advantages to middlemen and subcontractors – and self-exploited – investing a greater working time in production for a return that is less than the prevailing wage (Harriss-White, 2010b: 10).[15]

Moreover, the 'quality' of labour arrangements in India's RNFE is very variable – from low-paid casual work to regular well-paid work – depending on the scale of operation but also on the degree of local/global integration of the firms (Lerche, 2010: 67–69). The quality of RNFL improves when firms operate in a 'healthy' economic environment, such as the one provided by networks of firms in the same sector or in interlinked sectors, as in the case of value chains and clusters. Relying on their comparison of competitive advantages of RNFE subsectors in India, Fisher *et al.* (1997: 217) argue that value chains and clusters improve the competitiveness of rural firms, reducing the constraints on economic activity, ensuring the provision of services, marketing and market research, raw material and equipment.[16] Coppard (2001: 35) takes a similar view, seeing the clustering of firms as a major factor in the dynamism of the RNFE. Finally, the quality of RNFL is also enhanced by the proximity to towns, owing to the availability of transport and marketing infrastructure (Nayyar and Sharma, 2005: 12).

The variable quality of RNFL corresponds to variable rates of return to agents, which, in turn, depend on aspects of personal and family identities and other social features influencing their access to RNFAs. While Wandschneider (2003: 7) emphasises the 'key role' of caste in 'enabling and constraining' the access to high income RNFAs, Unni and Rani (2005) show that gender is the 'key factor' in explaining women's segregation in casual jobs in low-income, marginal segments of the RNFE, a phenomenon that is also explained by gender differentials in education and in the domestic workload (Fisher *et al.*, 1997: 35–37). The low level of education accounts for the marginalisation of women in RNFL and thus their constant low participation across different phases in the development of the RNFE (Chadha, 1997: 207; see also Unni and Raveendran, 2007: 197 et seq.).

4 Informal development

A major feature of India's RNFE is the *informal* socio-economic organisation, which is observed in particular in employment arrangements (Das, 2003; Aswasthi, 2007). Complementing the analysis of rural diversification, this aspect is analysed in this section. First I review the main conceptualisations of informality and, then, I turn to India.

4.1 Old and new concepts of informality

Since the 1970s, when it was first identified in Africa, the informal economy has been the object of increasing attention both in academic and political circles. Introduced by the British anthropologist Keith Hart in his study of economic organisation in Accra, the concept of the 'informal sector' provided the analytical framework for the employment missions of the International Labour Organization (henceforth ILO) in Africa in the 1970s, starting with the mission in Kenya in 1972.

According to the ILO the informal sector is distinct from the formal sector in the nature of job opportunities – self-employment as opposed to formal wage earning – and it is characterised by: (a) ease of entry; (b) reliance on indigenous resources; (c) family ownership of enterprises; (d) small scale of operation; (e) labour-intensive and adapted technology; (f) skills acquired outside the formal school system; (g) unregulated and competitive markets (ILO, 1972: 6).

The ILO's pioneering analysis proposed a dualistic approach to informality. The informal sector is a residual sector, with no link to the formal sector, and the inferior segment of a dual labour economy emerging in the transitional phase in which the formal sector is not (yet) able to absorb the labour that is leaking from the 'traditional' (low-productivity) sector. Informalisation is then a transitory and positive phenomenon, which reduces the social cost of the capitalist transition, while its ultimate fate is to be absorbed by the formal sector once the structural transformation is over (Perry *et al.*, 2007).

Two alternative approaches emerged in the 1980s and 1990s proposing more complex views of informality: the structuralist approach and the legalist approach. Both use the idea that the informal sector is composed of small and unregistered firms, but they make different interpretations of the processes generating informality and of the link between formal and informal sectors.

The structuralist analysis builds on the evidence of a continuum between the informal and the formal sector and explores the working of the economy as a whole, focusing on the relations between its parts (Moser, 1978; Castells and Portes, 1989). Supplying cheap labour and inputs, the informal sector is functional to capitalist development in the formal sector, while informal workers are subaltern to the large registered firms. This situation emerges particularly in crises and socio-spatial restructuring, when, to cut their costs, firms in the formal sector engage in decentralised and flexible production. Providing 'flexibility' to the capitalist system (ILO/WTO, 2009), informality ceased to be a transitory feature of a segment of the economy, to become instead a phenomenon that crosses sectoral borders and a necessity for the capitalist system as a whole. By contrast, the legalist school sees the informal sector as composed of micro entrepreneurs who chose to operate informally to avoid the costs associated with formal economic activity. Accordingly, informality is the outcome of the voluntary choices of small and micro firms, when the costs of the laws and procedures associated with formal economic organisations exceed the benefits.

Despite the predictions of its eventual demise by the dualist view, the informal economy has continued to prosper. There is abundant evidence in capitalist development that economic activity is increasingly informalised. With the expansion of the informal economy, the academic and political debate has become more lively and widespread, leading to the development of a new and comprehensive conceptual framework that establishes a new definition of informality and lays out new guidelines for the theoretical and empirical analysis.

With the joint effort of the ILO and the global research policy network Women in Informal Employment: Globalizing and Organizing (henceforth WIEGO), the definition of the informal sector has been broadened to include informality in all its manifestations. The focus has shifted from unregistered firms to the employment relationship, introducing the concept of 'informal employment' to refer to all conditions of unprotected and unregulated employment relationships.

This shift prefigures a major theoretical change in the analysis of informality, allowing the inclusion of all employment arrangements in which workers live and work in conditions of unregistered subordination, even when the employment relationships are ambiguous, disguised or not clearly defined (Chen, 2007: 8; see also Chen, 2005). This is the case for self-employed and own-account workers in all forms of sub-contracting: being deprived of entrepreneurial autonomy in production, their role as 'entrepreneurs' is uncertain, while, as subaltern workers, they are employed without social and labour protection (ILO/WTO, 2009).

The shift from the firm to the employment relationship brings a new complexity into the analysis of the informal economy. For, as the evidence suggests, the informal economy is composed of different segments, and the position of workers within them depends on their individual and social attributes of class and identity, and on their bargaining power. Moreover, the demand for workers in each segment is determined by the features of the firms, while the relationship between the different segments creates the conditions for the growth of output and employment (ILO/WTO, 2009: 47).

Chen (2005, 2007) summarises this new view of the informal economy, focusing on the significance and permanence of the informal economy, its segmented structure, its links with the formal economy, and its legality/illegality. The informal economy is seen as a basic (non-marginal) component of modern capitalist economies: a permanent, long-term, phenomenon. A continuum exists between the formal and the informal economy, while production units and workers move along this continuum and/or operate simultaneously in both components of the economy. The informal and the formal components are 'dynamically' linked in their operations, while the links among firms depend on the nature of the production system of which the firms are components: individual firms in the formal component may transact with individual firms in the informal component; alternatively links may be 'structured' in networks, such as sub-sectors or value-chains (ILO, 2002: 38; see also Chen, 2005).

The extent and variety of the informal economy raise the issue of the 'quality' of informal employment. Building on the distinction between self-employment in informal firms and wage-employment in informal jobs, Chen distinguishes between employers, own-account operators and unpaid family workers, in the first case; and between wage-workers and casual and temporary workers, in the second. Then, she identifies a hierarchy of segments of informal employment showing differences in earnings, which depend on individual features of workers and their status as suppliers, purchasers and employers (2007: 3).

Unregistered firms and unregulated employment arrangements cannot be considered fully illegal. The goods and services produced in the informal economy are largely legal; moreover, the criminal economy – which is the part of the informal economy that explicitly operates outside the law – is only a limited part (Chen, 2005). The non-criminal part of the informal economy remains unregistered, in part to escape the regulatory framework and in part also because firms are exempt from registration (because of their small scale of operation). While employers escape registration in order to reduce costs and to increase flexibility, to operate outside the regulatory framework often represents a cost for unregistered workers who would greatly benefit from the social and labour protection that would be guaranteed by registration. The lack of social and labour protection for subaltern workers is the cause of the increasing deficit of 'decent work' in the informal economy (ILO, 2002).

A major issue in the debate on the informal economy is its relation to the State. This is also linked to the more general issue of the regulation of informal activities.

Castells and Portes (1989: 27) argue that 'the informal sector as a whole tends to develop under the auspices of government tolerance'. In this sense, the encouragement of informal activities is a way to manage – and to resolve – social conflicts and 'to promote political patronage', while informality is 'useful' as it leads to the expansion of the productive base of society. Then, despite the lack of formal (state) control over informal activities, informalisation is often legitimated by the State.

Considering the three 'offices' in which the State manifests itself – 'the regulator, the policeman, and the tax collector' – Centeno and Portes (2003: 30) argue that there is a 'definitional antithesis between the State power and informality' and that the aim of informal activities is to 'avoid' the contact with the State in each of these offices, or to neutralise state action by means of 'bribes'. Moreover, assuming that state regulation depends both on the State's 'regulatory intent' and on its 'regulatory capacity', they identify a typology of state forms corresponding to different forms and trade-offs of regulation, which ranges from the 'liberal state' – high state regulatory capacity and low state regulatory intent – to the 'frustrated state' – high regulatory intent and low regulatory capacity – passing through the 'welfare' state, the 'totalitarian' state, the 'absent' state, and the 'enclave' state. Finally, they draw attention to the role of the 'social structure and culture of the population' in influencing the forms taken by state regulation (2003: 8; see also Kus, 2006: 12). They focus in particular on the regulative capacity of civil society, arguing that a large majority of Third World countries in which the informal economy is extensive should be considered as 'self-regulated rather than informal' (Centeno and Portes, 2003: 9).

4.2 Provincial India as an informal economy

Despite the relevance of the phenomenon in the country, the analysis of informality in India is not an easy task.[17] As the Committee on Unorganised Sector Statistics (2012) points out, the available information is inadequate to support a thorough assessment of the size of the informal sector, of its linkages with the formal sector, and of its internal dynamics.[18]

The basic information is provided by the NSSO, which has collected information on informality within the survey of employment and unemployment since the 55th round (1999–2000). In the 55th round no information was collected on the features of the workers and the coverage was limited to non-agricultural activities. However, wider and more consistent information on informal workers and on their conditions of employment have been collected in the 61st round (2004–2005) and again in the 66th round (2009–2010). In these rounds, the surveys cover both non-agricultural activities and the activities in the agricultural sector, with the exclusion of growing crops, market gardening, horticulture and growing of crops combined with farming of animals (henceforth AGEGC activities) (NSSO, 2012: 1).

The NSSO adopts the conceptualisation of informality established by the 15th and the 17th International Conferences of Labour Statisticians (1993, 2003). Accordingly, it distinguishes between employment in the *informal sector* – an 'enterprise-based concept' which covers persons working in units with 'informal' characteristics – and *informal employment* – a 'job-based concept' which includes the workers, such as own-account workers, employees, family workers, who are employed in jobs without the legal protection and employment benefits of the jobs in the formal sector (NSSO, 2012: 20–21; ILO, 2012: 2).

Operationally, the information is collected on 'usual status' (u.s.) workers employed in the 'unincorporated enterprises' identified by the type of ownership as proprietary and partnership (henceforth p&p).[19] Then, p&p enterprises are considered as the *informal sector* (NSSO, 2012: 14 et seq.).

The NSSO data for 2004–2005 and 2009–2010 are employed in this section to describe the features of India's informal employment. The information coming from NSSO is also integrated with the analysis coming from the literature and from the elaboration/interpretation of the NSSO data for 2004–2005 produced by National Commission on Employment in the Unorganised Sector (henceforth NCEUS).[20]

Employment in India's informal economy

According to the NSSO estimates for 2009–2010, about 71 per cent of the workers in AGEGC and in non-agricultural activities are engaged in India's informal sector. The proportion is higher in rural areas (74 per cent) than in urban areas (67 per cent); in urban India the proportion is higher for women than for men.[21] It is worth noting the significant reduction of employment in the informal sector since 2004–2005, from about 77 per cent to 71 per cent (Table 3.5).

Table 3.5 Workers in the *informal sector*: proportion of workers (u.s.) employed in p&p enterprises, 2004–2005 and 2009–2010 (% of total workers in AGEGC and non-agricultural activities)[a]

	Rural		Urban		Rural + urban	
	2004–2005	2009–2010	2004–2005	2009–2010	2004–2005	2009–2010
Male	79.2	74.2	73.9	68.5	76.7	71.5
Female	86.4	74.4	65.4	61.6	79.7	69.8
Person	81.6	74.2	72.2	67.3	77.5	71.1

Source: NSSO (2012: 39).

Notes

a u.s. = usual status; p&p = proprietary and partnership.

Broadly, 93 per cent of workers in rural and in urban areas engaged in AGECG activities work in p&p enterprises. The proportion is significantly lower for non-agricultural activities, both in urban and in rural areas (71 per cent and 67 per cent respectively). Both in urban and in rural areas, the highest proportion is found among self-employed workers – with more than 90 per cent of them engaged in the informal sector for each type of activity – and among casual workers in other than public work – with a proportion of workers engaged in the informal sector always higher than 70 per cent (Table 3.6). The situation is largely unchanged since 2004–2005 (Table 3.7). The gender bias in the case of regular wage labour should be stressed. Also in relation to gender participation in the informal sector, no significant changes are observed since 2004–2005 (Table 3.8).

Table 3.9 summarises the available information on workers in the informal sector according to industry group. While over 90 per cent of employment in AGEGC is in p&p enterprises, p&p enterprises in non-agricultural activities employ slightly more than 70 per cent of the total workers. In rural areas, the most informalised sectors are manufacturing, wholesale and retail trade, and hotel and restaurants (with a similar proportion of men and women). The situation is largely confirmed for urban areas; yet, the proportion of informalised activities is lower than in rural areas (in particular for women). Significant exceptions are manufacturing, and wholesale and retail trade, in which women appear to be largely informalised as in rural areas. A significant gender bias is to be observed in the case of manufacturing, in which 87 per of women are employed in the informal sector against 75 per cent of men (Table 3.9). Yet, a significant contraction is found in the proportion of women working in non-agricultural informal activities since 2004–2005, both in rural and in urban areas (respectively from 86.4 to 74.4 and from 65.4 to 61.6) (Table 3.10)

The vast majority of rural workers in the informal sector have their workplace located in rural areas (88 per cent). It is interesting to note that the proportion is significantly higher for women than for men (95.4 per cent and 85.9 per cent respectively). The situation is largely unchanged since 2004–2005. Yet, it is

Table 3.6 Workers in the *informal sector*: proportion of workers (u.s.) in p&p enterprises for different employment statuses in employment, 2009–2010 (% of total workers in AGEGC and non-agricultural activities)[a]

	Rural			Urban		
	AGEGC	Non-agriculture	AGEGC and non-agriculture	AGEGC	Non-agriculture	AGEGC and non-agriculture
Male						
Self-employment	95.6	91.8	92.2	96.8	94.9	94.9
Of which:						
• Own-account workers	95.5	91.7	92.1	97.1	94.4	94.5
• Employers	100.0	94.8	94.9	100.0	97.0	97.0
• Helper in household enterprise	95.8	92.2	92.8	94.9	96.3	96.3
Regular wage/salaried employees	58.7	41.4	41.7	47.9	42.7	42.7
Casual labour in other than public work	85.3	74.4	74.8	88.9	75.7	76.0
Total	90.6	73.0	74.2	88.3	68.3	68.5
Female						
Self-employment	97.3	94.6	96.0	99.1	96.5	96.7
Of which:						
• Own-account workers	97.2	92.6	94.9	98.8	96.0	96.3
• Employers	100.0	91.2	92.1	100.0	99.5	99.5
• Helper in household enterprise	97.4	97.3	97.4	99.7	97.3	97.5
Regular wage/salaried employees	87.1	26.8	27.4	61.0	28.8	28.8
Casual labour in other than public work	86.2	68.2	69.7	82.5	62.1	62.3
Total	95.0	64.1	74.4	97.7	60.1	61.6

Person					
Self-employment	96.8	92.4	93.5	98.0	95.2	95.3
Of which:					
• *Own-account workers*	96.6	91.9	92.8	97.9	94.7	94.8
• *Employers*	100.0	94.6	94.8	100.0	97.1	97.1
• *Helper in household enterprise*	97.1	94.5	95.5	98.3	96.6	96.7
Regular wage/salaried employees	62.2	38.6	39.0	49.2	40.2	40.2
Casual labour in other than public work	85.6	73.4	74.0	88.1	73.4	73.7
Total	93.4	71.3	74.2	92.5	66.9	67.3

Source: NSSO (2012: 42).

Notes

a u.s. = usual status; p&p = proprietary and partnership.

Table 3.7 Workers in the *informal sector*: proportion of workers (u.s.) in p&p enterprises for different employment statuses in employment, 2004–2005 (% of total workers in AGEGC and non-agricultural activities)[a]

	Rural			Urban		
	AGEGC	*Non-agriculture*	*AGEGC and non-agriculture*	*AGEGC*	*Non-agriculture*	*AGEGC and non-agriculture*
Male						
Self-employment	93.7	95.0	94.8	92.1	97.3	97.2
Of which:						
• *Own-account workers*	95.5	93.7	94.6	94.5	91.4	97.1
• *Employers*	100.0	98.5	98.6	100.0	98.4	98.4
• *Helper in household enterprise*	95.8	93.6	96.7	96.0	94.2	97.8
Regular wage/salaried employees	58.7	65.4	44.0	44.5	60.9	46.5
Casual labour in other than public work	85.3	74.4	86.3	80.5	80.8	88.2
Total	90.4	78.1	79.2	86.8	73.7	73.9
Female						
Self-employment	97.6	96.6	97.2	95.2	96.8	96.6
Of which:						
• *Own-account workers*	97.3	96.4	96.9	96.0	96.1	96.1
• *Employers*	100.0	96.3	97.5	100.0	98.5	98.5
• *Helper in household enterprise*	97.7	96.7	97.4	94.6	97.7	97.3
Regular wage/salaried employees	72.7	25.8	26.3	41.7	27.8	27.8
Casual labour in other than public work	90.1	73.8	76.0	90.9	68.9	69.3
Total	97.2	77.1	86.4	94.9	63.5	65.4

Person						
Self-employment	96.6	95.4	95.8	94.1	97.2	97.1
Of which:						
• Own-account workers	96.1	94.9	95.2	93.6	96.9	96.8
• Employers	100.0	98.4	98.5	100.0	98.4	98.4
• Helper in household enterprise	97.1	96.7	96.9	94.6	97.8	97.5
Regular wage/salaried employees	66.0	40.5	41.1	60.5	42.9	42.9
Casual labour in other than public work	87.5	79.4	80.0	88.7	82.3	82.4
Total	95.2	77.9	81.6	91.2	71.7	72.2

Source: NSSO (2012: 42).

Notes

a u.s. = usual status; p&p = proprietary and partnership.

Table 3.8 Workers in the *informal sector*: proportion of workers (u.s.) employed in p&p enterprises by status of employment and by sex (% of total workers in AGEGC and non-agricultural activities)[a]

	2004–2005			2009–2010		
	Male	Female	Person	Male	Female	Person
Rural						
Self-employment	94.8	97.2	95.8	92.2	96.0	93.5
of which:						
• *Own-account workers*	*94.5*	*96.9*	*95.2*	*92.1*	*94.9*	*92.8*
• *Employers*	*98.6*	*97.5*	*98.5*	*94.9*	*92.1*	*94.8*
• *Helper in household enterprise*	*96.0*	*97.4*	*96.9*	*92.8*	*97.4*	*95.5*
Regular wage/salaried employees	44.5	26.3	41.1	41.7	27.4	39.0
Casual labour in other than public work	80.8	76.0	80.0	74.8	69.7	74.0
Total	79.2	86.4	81.6	74.2	74.4	74.2
Urban						
Self-employment	97.2	96.6	97.1	94.9	96.7	95.3
of which:						
• *Own-account workers*	*97.0*	*96.1*	*96.8*	*94.5*	*96.3*	*94.8*
• *Employers*	*98.4*	*98.5*	*98.4*	*97.0*	*99.5*	*97.1*
• *Helper in household enterprise*	*97.7*	*97.3*	*97.5*	*96.3*	*97.5*	*96.7*
Regular wage/salaried employees	46.6	27.8	42.9	42.7	28.8	40.2
Casual labour in other than public work	85.3	69.3	82.4	76.0	62.3	73.7
Total	73.9	65.4	72.2	68.5	61.6	67.3

Source: NSSO (2012: 44).

Notes
a u.s.=usual status; p&p=proprietary and partnership.

worth noting that in 2009–2010 the workplace was located in the dwelling unit for about 40 per cent of the women (NSSO, 2012: 51); the proportion was much higher in 2004–2005 (65.8 per cent) (NSSO, 2006: 49).

The NSSO data also provides information on the features of enterprises and the condition of employment. This information, which broadly confirms the conceptualisation of informality reviewed in Section 4.1, is summarised below (NSSO, 2012: 53 et seq.).

First, in rural areas only 12 per cent of the workers employed in p&p in AGEGC and non-agricultural activities use electricity for production purposes (it was 9.4 per cent in 2004–2005). By contrast, the proportion is 26 per cent in urban areas (it was 20 per cent). The proportion is much higher for the manufacturing activities (26.6 per cent and 52.2 per cent, respectively, in rural areas and in urban areas) and is increasing in relation to 2004–2005. Second, the vast majority of workers are employed in enterprises with fewer than six workers. In the case of p&p enterprises, the proportion is 77 per cent in rural areas and 70 per in urban areas. The proportion is higher for women than for men and shows

Table 3.9 Workers in the *informal sector*: proportion of workers (u.s.) in p&p enterprises by industry group, 2009–2010 (% of total workers)[a]

	Rural			Urban		
	Male	*Female*	*Person*	*Male*	*Female*	*Person*
AGEGC	90.6	95.0	93.4	88.3	97.7	92.5
Mining and quarrying	63.8	62.9	63.7	24.3	34.9	25.1
Manufacturing	82.9	92.6	86.1	75.0	87.3	77.8
Electricity	9.8	0.0	9.1	14.9	0.0	13.4
Construction	69.2	36.7	63.6	72.6	65.9	72.0
Wholesale and retail trade	90.8	95.6	91.4	91.4	93.0	91.6
Hotels and restaurants	91.8	90.5	91.6	87.8	90.0	88.1
Transport	82.2	80.6	82.2	69.1	44.5	68.4
Financial intermediation	24.9	80.4	31.0	23.2	24.3	23.3
Real estate	79.8	76.7	79.6	61.6	40.6	59.1
Education	24.3	24.1	24.2	30.1	34.8	32.3
Health and social work	60.3	21.6	43.3	48.9	44.4	47.1
Other service activities	82.5	75.5	81.0	75.3	68.2	73.0
Non-agriculture	73.0	64.1	71.3	68.3	60.1	66.9
AGEGC and non-agriculture	74.2	74.4	74.2	68.5	61.6	67.3

Source: NSSO (2012: 49).

Notes

a u.s.=usual status; p&p=proprietary and partnership.

Table 3.10 Workers in the *informal sector*: proportion of workers (u.s.) in p&p enterprises in AGEGC and non-agriculture activities (% of total workers)[a]

	2004–2005				2009–2010			
	Rural		Urban		Rural		Urban	
	Male	*Female*	*Male*	*Female*	*Male*	*Female*	*Male*	*Female*
AGEGC	90.4	97.2	86.8	94.9	90.6	95.0	88.3	97.7
Non-agriculture	78.1	77.1	73.7	63.5	73.0	64.1	68.3	60.1
AGEGC and non-agriculture	79.2	86.4	73.9	65.4	74.2	74.4	68.5	61.6

Source: NSSO (2012: 50).

Notes

a u.s.=usual status; p&p=proprietary and partnership.

a decrease since 2004–2005 (81 per cent and 74 per cent respectively for rural areas and urban areas). Third, the earnings of workers in informal employment show significant differences for regular wage/salaried employees and for casual labourers. With Rs.177 per day, the regular wage/salaried workers engaged in p&p enterprises earn more than workers engaged in the employer's household (Rs.100), but much less than the average pay per for all type of enterprises for all India (Rs.321). Moreover, a systematic bias is observed in the case of rural areas and of women. By contrast, for casual labourers, no significant difference is found in comparison to the workers in all types of enterprises. Yet, a significant bias for women and rural areas is confirmed. Forth, 82 per cent of workers in rural areas and about 74 per cent in urban areas do not have written contracts. The proportion is significantly higher in 2009–2010 than in 2004–2005, while no significant gender bias is observed. Construction and manufacturing are the industry groups in which the phenomenon is stronger. Fifth, slightly more than half of the regular wage/salaried employees in rural areas are engaged in temporary employment (about 40 per cent in urban areas) and the situation is largely unchanged since 2004–2005. Sixth, 70 per cent of the employees (u.s.) in non-agricultural activities are not eligible for paid leave (60 per cent in urban areas and 80 per cent in rural areas), the highest proportion being among casual labourers. A significant increase is to be seen from 2004–2005. Finally, 74 per cent of all employees (u.s.) in non-agricultural activities are not eligible for any social benefit (65 per in urban areas and 82 per cent in rural areas) and the proportion is higher for casual labourers in rural areas (97 per cent). A minor increase is observed since 2004–2005.

The analysis conducted by the NCEUS on the NSSO data for 2004–2005 points out important features of India's informal economy that complement the information coming from the NSSO for 2009–2010.

First, the NCEUS stresses the systematic gender bias in India's informal sector: women are fewer (in numbers) than men, both in rural and urban India; however, the proportion of female workers in total employment in the informal sector is higher than the proportion of male workers. Moreover, women are employed relatively more in agriculture than in industry and services (NCEUS, 2008: 32). Second, the NCEUS points out that, while the level of education in the informal sector is systematically below that of the formal sector, the difference is higher for rural India and for women, and increases for higher levels of education. Third, urban India and rural India differ in their labour arrangements. Own-account workers, unpaid family workers and casual workers are the main categories in rural India while in urban India own-account workers and regular wage employees prevail. Significant discrepancies also exist between men and women: in rural India, over 50 per cent of the female workforce in the informal sector is employed as unpaid family labour and over 30 per cent as casual workers, while in urban India the gender bias is less strong (NCEUS, 2008: 34 et seq.). Finally, the distribution of informal sector workers by social groups varies between rural and urban India: more than one-third of informal workers in the informal sector belong to Scheduled Castes (SCs) and Scheduled Tribes (STs) in rural areas (more women than men), while in urban India the percentage is around 20 per cent (once again, more women than men) (NCEUS, 2008: 87).[22]

The degree of employment informalisation is higher in rural India than in urban India (NCEUS, 2008: 139). However, significant differences exist among states. Focusing on rural areas, the vast majority of Indian states show a proportion of informal employment well above 90 per cent of total employment, with the significant exception of Kerala (slightly above 80 per cent). By contrast, in urban areas, with the exception of Uttar Pradesh (nearly 90 per cent), the degree of informalisation of employment in India is below 85 per cent, with a large number of states – Gujarat, Maharashtra, Kerala, Karnataka, Tamil Nadu and Orissa – below 80 per cent.

Important information on the economic potential of the informal economy is drawn from exploring its contribution to GDP. Using an original methodology, the NCEUS estimates that in 2004–2005 the informal sector contributes nearly 50 per cent to India's GDP (it was over 55 per cent in 1999–2000).[23] While 'informal' agriculture is confirmed the main sector (with 35.5 per cent of informal sector GDP (43.5 per cent in 1999–2000) and 95 per cent of total agricultural GDP), manufacturing contributes nearly 9 per cent (8 per cent in 1999–2000) and trade is 22 per cent (18 per cent in 1999–2000) (Table 3.11). Over the period, the GDP growth rate of the informal sector as a whole was below the growth rate of the overall GDP (4 per cent against nearly 6 per cent (computed at 1999–2000 constant prices)). Mining had a negative growth rate (–5.5 per cent), as did electricity, gas and water (–1.7 per cent) and public administration (–33.4 per cent), which contrasts with growing sub-sectors, such as construction, retail trade, and financial services (Table 3.12).

Table 3.11 Informal sector contribution to gross value added (GVA) by industry group (%)

	Informal sector to sectoral GVA		Informal sector to total informal GVA	
	(1999–2000)	*(2004–2005)*	*(1999–2000)*	*(2004–2005)*
Agriculture	96.55	94.48	43.55	35.55
Mining	30.00	18.00	1.26	1.07
Manufacturing	28.85	26.84	7.84	8.68
Electricity, gas and water	4.00	3.00	0.18	0.13
Construction	44.66	46.33	4.60	6.03
Trade	77.35	75.08	18.12	22.35
Hotels and restaurants	56.19	50.80	1.26	1.42
Transport and storage	57.27	44.45	7.71	7.80
Banking, finance and insurance	7.43	9.29	0.79	1.09
Real estate, renting and business services	77.24	63.44	9.98	10.91
Public administration and defence	3.65	0.40	0.45	0.05
Education	13.81	12.33	0.97	0.92
Health and social work	21.80	23.19	0.61	0.86
Other community, social and personal services	61.04	69.44	2.38	2.72
Private household and extra territorial organisation	80.11	95.29	0.30	0.41
Total	55.42	49.94	100.00	100.00

Source: NCEUS (2008: 56).

Table 3.12 Growth rate (GDP at 1999–2000 constant prices) for the informal sector and for the economy by industry group (1999–2000/2004–2005; %)

	Informal sector	Total economy
Agriculture	1.15	1.59
Mining	−5.50	4.67
Manufacturing	4.91	6.44
Electricity, gas and water	−1.69	4.14
Construction	9.59	8.79
Trade	7.46	8.10
Hotels and restaurants	5.39	7.53
Transport and storage	7.06	12.63
Banking, finance and insurance	10.61	5.78
Real estate, renting and business services	3.31	7.46
Public administration and defence	−33.43	3.60
Education	3.35	5.71
Health and social work	12.00	10.62
Other community, social and personal services	7.31	4.58
Private household and extra territorial organisation	11.00	7.22
Total	4.08	5.99

Source: NCEUS (2008: 57).

The poor quality of informal employment

A major issue in the analysis of informal economy refers to the *quality* of informal employment, a concept which includes pay and income, terms and conditions, entitlement to social security, security in terms of employment and work conditions (NCEUS, 2009: 130). The main source of information about the quality of informal employment is again the NCEUS.

The NCEUS (2007) builds on a basic distinction between wage-workers and self-employed workers. Despite the differences, both categories share common features in terms of limited access to resources and to education, which are explained by workers' personal features and social status. The majority of wage-workers and self-employed workers in the informal sector are landless or holders of less than 0.4 hectares (over 70 per cent) and a large proportion of them belong to low-status and marginalised social groups (SCs, STs and Muslims). Moreover, they differ from workers in the formal sector in terms of years of schooling (5.6 years against 9), and then have lower opportunities in terms of labour market entry (NCEUS, 2007: 15 et seq.).[24]

Despite these common features, and despite the fact that they share 'deplorable' working and living standards (NCEUS, 2007: 27), wage-workers and self-employed workers have different socio-economic profiles in relation to conditions at the workplace, employment contracts, and earnings. Moreover, 'internal' differences also exist. Among wage-workers, the profile of casual workers differs from regular wage-workers and self-employed workers. Further, these all change according to the nature of the enterprises in which they are employed. We will discuss wage-work and self-employment in turn.

The precarious working conditions of wage-workers in India's informal economy largely result from the lack of decent conditions at work in terms of: space and illumination requirements, health hazards (determined by temperature and humidity, and the use of dangerous inputs and tools) and the lack of safety measures. A major consequence is a high rate of occupational diseases and accidents (NCEUS, 2007: 33–34). Precarious living standards are often associated with precarious conditions at work. These might occur when informal workers are employed in clusters in which the expansion of productive activities reduces the space for housing, with a subsequent deterioration of water, drainage and sanitation facilities (Vijayabaskar, 2005, 2010). Working and living standards may deteriorate further owing to long working hours and the lack of weekly holidays, which, as the NCEUS says, 'seem to be a normal feature of unorganised sector in India' (NCEUS, 2007: 36) despite the existing legal norms (see also Harriss-White, 2003a).

While informal workers might be recruited when 'standing at the factory gate', recruitment mainly occurs through caste, family and community networks and through labour contractors (De Neve, 2010; Lerche, 2010). The nature of the employment contract varies according to the sector, the features of the workers and their relations with the contractors. However, it is observed that contract workers enjoy lower security of employment and receive lower wages than other categories. Moreover, they often pay part of their wages to contractors as 'informal commissions'.[25]

Overall, informal wage-workers appear a weak transacting part in the labour market, a weakness that is also mirrored by the fact that the vast majority of them do not have written contracts, remaining outside the protection of India's labour legislation.

Indeed, the bulk of India's informal workforce takes the form of self-employed workers, a heterogeneous category that includes: (i) own-account workers, (ii) unpaid family workers, and (iii) employers with fewer than ten workers. The internal heterogeneity of self-employed workers is a major determinant of the complexity of India's informal economy.

Self-employed workers have a twofold characterisation. They are workers, but they are also involved – to a variable degree and in variable forms – in the management of the enterprise in which they operate. So, while they use their labour power as workers, as entrepreneurs, they might also use other individuals' labour power and be involved in several entrepreneurial decisions in relation to production and marketing (Harriss-White, 2010b). Several attributes therefore need to be considered when analysing the performance of self-employed workers, from the degree of exploitation and self-exploitation, to the nature, size and forms of entrepreneurial activities. In other words, it is necessary to take into account, together with the features of work, the nature of the enterprise.

According to the NCEUS, about 87 per cent of informal enterprises in India are own-account enterprises (henceforth OAEs). In rural India the proportion is even higher, with 94.2 per cent of enterprises employing more than 87 per cent of informal workers; moreover, nearly 62 per cent of informal workers are employed in OAEs operated by the owner. By contrast, in urban India the con-centration of OAEs is lower (78.4 per cent), as it is the percentage of informal workers employed in them (58.7 per cent) (NCEUS, 2007: 51).

Major differences in terms of economic performance exist between OAEs with or without hired workers. Relying on NSSO data for 1999–2000, the NCEUS provides estimates of the value of the assets and of the contribution to GDP for the two types of OAE. OAEs without hired workers are small-scale firms, operating with an average level of fixed assets of Rs.39,000 per enterprise. This generates an average gross value added (henceforth GVA) per worker per year of Rs.19,000. In the case of rural OAEs, the values decrease to Rs.20,000 and Rs.14,000. These OAEs are unregistered (90.4 per cent in rural areas) and nearly half are run from within household premises (46 per cent in rural areas). The performance of OAEs with hired workers is markedly different. The average value of fixed asset is nearly Rs.300,000 (Rs.130,000 in rural areas), while the average GVA per worker per year is Rs.39,000 (26,000 in rural areas). More-over, 75 per cent of these OAEs operate from fixed premises with a permanent structure, and 90 per cent of them are registered (NCEUS, 2007: 52 et seq.).

An intermediate category in between self-employed and wage-workers is con-stituted by home-workers. According to the NSSO data for 1999–2000, home-workers are about 12 per cent of non-farm informal workers (8.2 million), 4.8 million of which are women. The main difference between self-employed workers and home-workers is that, while the former are in charge of several entrepreneurial decisions in production and marketing, the latter usually work under the putting-out system. While bearing some of the costs of production and not being directly supervised, they are deprived of a large part of entrepreneurial choices.

Regulation exerts a major impact on the quality of informal employment. The issue of regulation clearly emerges at two points in the NCEUS analysis: (i) when the regulative role played by civil society institutions – as an alternative to state institutions – in the recruitment of informal workers is described; and (ii) when the reliance of the vast majority of OAEs on non-market relations (as in the case of unpaid family workforce) is stressed. The regulative role of social institutions, such as gender and patriarchy, also emerges from the strong gender bias in India's informal economy.

Indeed, the issue is widely addressed in other literature, which provides a detailed analysis of the main regulative institutions shaping the process of infor-malisation. This literature complements the quantitative picture supplied by the NCEUS, providing a 'qualitative' picture of India's informal economy.

While this literature will not be reviewed here, it is useful to point out three main indications that emerge from it. First, social regulation in India's informal economy takes a variety of forms on the basis of the regulative institutions that, in each context, appear to stabilise and support capital accumulation. Regulative institutions – such as caste, ethnicity, family, gender, and patriarchy – are rooted in India's culture and history, and social regulation is path dependent. In this sense, the informal economy is 'embedded' in civil society (Basile and

Harriss-White, 2000; Harriss-White, 2003a; Harriss-White, 2010a; Kapadia, 2010). Second, state regulation and social regulation should not necessarily be considered opposing forces. On the contrary, according to the needs of capital accumulation, they complement each other in a comprehensive and multifaceted regulative framework (Mezzadri, 2010; Ruthven, 2010). Third, the regulative framework changes according to the change in the institutions on which it relies. As institutional change is a terrain of conflicts involving parts of civil society and the State, the regulative framework of the informal economy is also the outcome of social dialectics and change in different contexts (Basile and Harriss-White, 2010).

5 The distinguishing traits of India's provincial economy

In this chapter I have introduced the diversified and informal economy of Provincial India, showing that activities from different sectors co-exist in the same area and production is mostly organised in own-account enterprises.

Employment diversification is a widespread phenomenon, which in 2009–2010 involves more than 30 per cent of the rural workforce. Moreover, the trend of diversification is clearly increasing, being largely explained by the reduction of the proportion of agricultural workforce in the total workforce. Also informality is a pervasive phenomenon. Together with agriculture, in which more than 90 per cent of employment is informal, also the RNFAs are informalised, with a proportion of informal employment around 80 per cent, in particular in trade, construction, services and manufacturing.

Variety

India's provincial economy shows a high degree of internal variation. RNFAs differ in relation to sector, localisation, scale and organisation of production, intersectoral relations, and local/global integration. Trajectories of diversification also differ. The performance of agriculture influences diversification, but the endowment of non-agricultural resources and the institutional framework matter too: diversification trajectories are path-dependent and history-specific, and RNFAs take a locality-specific form, involving multiple agents – individuals, firms and institutions – that operate in the same (rural) locality. Thus, India's RNFE is a mosaic of different economic systems, each one composed by a different mix of RNFAs, each one emerging from a specific trajectory of diversification.

Another aspect of variability is constituted by the way in which the RNFE is locally organised and regulated. As the evidence on informality reveals, self-employment, casual labour, and unpaid family labour are the main employment arrangements, while social institutions, such as gender, caste, and family, regulate workers' recruitment and employment relations.

Poor-quality employment

Workers are the weakest transacting part and are systematically marginalised. Poor working conditions and poor living standards are the outcome of the subordination to entrepreneurs and contractors in the informal economy, which is shown by the lack of written contracts for casual workers and self-employed alike and by the deficit of autonomy for self-employed workers. Moreover, a twofold gender bias exists: women are discriminated against, being segregated in low-wage and low-quality jobs; and they are over-represented (together with SCs and STs) among casual labour and unpaid family workforce, being deprived of their rights as workers. Their marginalisation is increased by social regulation.

Poor economic performance

According to the NCEUS' estimates, the informal sector contribution to India's GDP has been decreasing since 1999–2000. No official estimates are available for the informal activities in rural areas. However, an indirect confirmation of the poorer performance of the rural economy in comparison to the urban one is provided by NCEUS' estimates of the GVA per worker and the value of fixed assets in rural OAEs without hired workers, which are lower than those in all other types of OAEs, both in urban and in rural India. Current explanations for this poor performance refer to the low level of investment per worker, which, in turn, is ascribed to a 'poor business environment', in which petty production, employing unpaid family workforce, prevails.

The influence of capitalist (local/global) change

Diversification and informality are an outcome of the structural transformation of India's economy. While the local availability of resources for diversification largely depends on agrarian structure and agriculture's performance, and while diversification is endemic in rural India as a 'distress resort' in agrarian crises, the emergence of new RNFAs is largely determined by the delocalisation of industrial and service activities to rural areas. In turn, this is influenced by the local availability of infrastructure and by the cost differential. Capitalist development also supports informal organisation. Supplying cheap labour and inputs, the informal sector contributes to the growth of the formal sector. This occurs especially when firms in the formal sector engage in decentralised production to cut their costs: informality provides 'flexibility' to the capitalist system. Being deeply informalised, the RNFE increases the flexibility of India's capitalism as a whole by facilitating the access to cheap rural resources.

A Marxist/Institutionalist conceptualisation

The growth and change of India's RNFE in the post-GR period can be usefully interpreted by means of the conceptual categories introduced in Chapter 2.

While the quantity of the available physical and human resources defines the context in which the RNFE can grow, the institutional framework within which economic activity takes place shapes the *actual* pattern of RNF development. Institutions influence the quantity and quantity of the available resources, regulating the access to them and their use. Moreover, they can be used to manipulate power relations between individuals and groups, with a determining impact on capital/labour relations. Finally, they regulate the access to external resources and the participation in business networks, shaping the relations with the external environment (surrounding villages and towns and/or distant regions) according to the interests of individuals and groups. These multiple and intertwined modes of influence prefigure a situation of *institutional embeddedness* of change in the RNFE.

Indeed, our analysis also shows another dimension of embeddedness, which is revealed by the linkages between economic activities and the area in which they are located. We may call it *spatial embeddedness*.

Institutional embeddedness and spatial embeddedness are intimately connected. Spatial embeddedness descends from (and is perpetuated by) the use of resources drawn from agriculture. By employing former agricultural resources, the RNFAs also absorb culture and habits that are embodied in the institutions that regulate social intercourse in the primary sector. The outcome is a form of integration of economic activity and locality that takes, at the same time, a geographical dimension and a cultural/institutional dimension. This explains why a large proportion of the relations that support production and marketing in the RNFE occurs within a delimited locality.

Together with informality and diversification, institutional embeddedness and spatial embeddedness enlighten the complexity of India's provincial economy. They show that each socio-economic system is an institutional and spatial entity that follows a trajectory of capitalist development consistently with its history-specific socio-economic and cultural features. Accordingly, they account for the variety of socio-economic systems composing Provincial India, showing that each one of them is embedded in a geographical and cultural environment, in which institutional and spatial linkages exist between economic activities and human and physical resources.

Indeed, informality and diversification, and institutional and spatial embeddedness account also for the flexibility of India's provincial economy. While informal organisation enhances the flexibility of production relations, economic diversification in a delimited locality supports the flexibility in the use of resources, enhancing the re-allocation of resources among sectors. The whole process is further supported by social regulation. Jointly, they account for the economic performance of Provincial India and for the poor living and working conditions.

While the analysis conducted in this chapter is a major step in the conceptualisation of capitalism in Provincial India, institutional embeddedness and spatial embeddedness reveal that the analysis of economic organisation is not enough to understand the working of the economy and to assess the quality of the development. Through institutions, other aspects exert a major impact on production relations and need to be taken into account. So, the processes of exploitation and marginalisation of the workforce – a structural feature of the informal economy – require a specific focus on the nature of social classes and on the intertwining of class and non-class stratification. Similarly, the weakness of the working class in capital/labour conflict cannot be accounted for without specific attention to the institutional and ideological infrastructures that influence the perception of individual and group interests, ultimately determining aims and choices.

4 Exploring class structure in Provincial India

1 Introduction

Moving to the second step of my assessment of India's provincial economy, in this chapter I focus on class structure. My aim is to find out who owns and who employs the means of production.

Relying on the available literature, read through Marxist/Institutionalist lenses, I show that Provincial India's class structure is history-specific, being the outcome of the intertwining of capitalist production relations with power relations rooted in institutions and culture. I also show that class dialectics occur between the antagonist classes of capitalists and subaltern workers, which represent capital and labour. My conclusion is that understanding capitalism in Provincial India requires a 'redefinition' of capital and labour to keep account of the historical specificity of production relations.

The chapter is organised as follows. Section 2 deals with class structure reviewing the major debates since Independence. Section 3 proposes a Marxist/Institutionalist reading of evidence and argument coming from the literature on class structure and class dialectics in India's provincial economy. Section 4 concludes, pointing out the specific features of the antagonist classes in India's provincial economy.

2 The debate on class structure

The analysis of class structure in Provincial India after Independence is part of a broader debate on the transition to capitalism. Involving a large number of Marxist and non-Marxist scholars who confront themselves over the terms and extent of capitalist transformation and the reasons for the backwardness of rural areas, the debate revolves around two major issues: the nature of classes and the trajectory of class formation. Before reviewing this debate, I briefly point out its theoretical background.

2.1 The theoretical background

From a theoretical point of view, the pre-requisites of the transition to capitalism are the capitalist transformation of agriculture and the formation of the antagonist classes of the capitalist economy: while the first ensures the availability of resources (capital and labour) for the emerging capitalist economy, the second generates the social structure which supports capitalist production relations. Both influence the pattern and the timing of the transition.

The analysis of the transition to capitalism begins with Marx and Engels who elaborate on both processes. While Marx (1894, Part 3: 194 et seq.) describes the English path to capitalism, Engels (1894) explores the capitalist transition in Europe, showing that only Great Britain and Prussia have been able to solve their agrarian questions. He also points out the major differences in terms of class formation between the English path – in which a class of improving landlords succeeds in generating a capitalist agriculture – and the Prussian path – in which the feudal landlord class transforms into a capitalist class. In relation to class formation, Marx identifies two major alternative paths: the artisan (worker) path, i.e. when the producer starts to accumulate to hire in labour and to organise production on a capitalist basis; and the merchant path, i.e. when the merchant enters the production process – by providing raw materials to producers and by selling their products – and starts to organise capitalist production (Marx, 1894, Part 1: 400). In both cases, the capitalist transition requires the formation of an entrepreneurial class that 'learns' how to accumulate.

Lenin (1899) and Kautsky (1899) also analyse capitalist transition. They focus on agrarian change: Kautsky explains the different pace of capitalist change in agriculture and industry; and Lenin compares different paths of agrarian transition. Building on Engels, Lenin compares the English path and the Prussian path to the American path, in which peasants transform into agrarian capitalists, stressing that two opposite patterns of capitalist transition emerge, which he calls 'capitalism from above' and 'capitalism from below' (Lenin, 1899, 1907; see also Byres, 1996).

The twentieth century debates on capitalist transition build on the contributions of these Marxist scholars. The first debate originates from Dobb's research on the transition from feudalism to capitalism in Europe.[1] Dobb (1962) shows the complexity of class formation, arguing that the formation of two distinct classes – a class of 'free' workers who sell their labour power on the market and a class of individuals who accumulate 'wealth' – is not enough to ensure the capitalist transition. The transformation of 'wealth' into the means of production is also necessary, which, in turn, requires new behaviour and lifestyles of the accumulating class. Brenner (1976) further enlarges the scope of the debate, moving to 'macro' processes.[2] Challenging the conventional interpretations of the emergence of capitalism – i.e. the demographic and the commercialisation models – Brenner explains capitalist transition in terms of a change in class relations, which obliges producers to specialise, submitting to market imperatives.

2.2 Two debates

The broad issue of the transition to capitalism dominates the literature on economic change in rural India after Independence, giving birth to two main debates:

the debate on the Indian modes of production (henceforth IMP) – which involved a large number of scholars on the pages of *Economic and Political Weekly* and a few other journals for more than a decade since the end of the 1960s – and the debate on intermediate classes (henceforth IC) – which builds on Kalecki's concept of 'intermediate regimes' first applied to India by Raj in 1973.

Begun with an empirical exercise in which it was shown that no capitalist farmers existed in Punjab (Rudra *et al.*, 1969), the IMP debate analysed capitalist transition in agriculture in theoretical and empirical terms.[3] Challenging the definition of capitalist farmer employed by Rudra *et al.* and with the support of an extensive fieldwork, Patnaik (1971a, 1971b, 1972) argued that the process of capitalist accumulation in India was not in its 'pure' form as it retained pre-capitalist features. According to Patnaik, colonial rule influenced capitalist transformation, owing to the large share of surplus transferred outside agriculture, with the consequence of undermining primitive accumulation and inhibiting productive investments. Moreover, this process of 'blocked' capitalist transition created a labour force that only appears to be free, but is in reality bonded.

Developing the idea of a 'distorted or blocked' capitalism, Bhaduri (1973) argued that Indian agriculture had more in common with feudalism than with industrial capitalism and advanced the idea of a 'semi-feudal' mode of production, in which the spreading of sharecropping and the indebtedness of tenants and land-less farmers went together with the concentration of usury and land-ownership in the hands of the same class. Alavi (1975) dismissed the idea of the semi-feudal mode of production and, elaborating on the British influence, advanced the idea of a 'colonial mode of production': a form of subaltern capitalism in countries with a colonial past holding the position of a colony in world economy. The search for alternative typologies of capitalism to fit with the Indian situation was criticised by Chattopadhyay (1972a, 1972b), who argued that the use of different definitions of capitalism was wrong, while the evidence of labour commoditisation was enough to consider Indian agriculture as capitalist.

The controversy over the nature of mode of production also extended to rural class structure. There were those who, like Rudra (1978: 999), talked about 'hybrid' classes that were 'in part capitalist, in part feudal' and those who, like Bhaduri (1973), stressed the concentration in the same class of land and money, and the related overlapping of two forms of exploitation; and there were also those who, like Patnaik (1972), pointed to the practice of unproductive investment and to the lack of a proper class of wage-workers. Broadly, the consensus on the existence of the two antagonist classes – the capitalist farmers and the wage-workers – was rather limited, and the IMP debate reached the paradoxical result of describing Indian agriculture as a capitalist system in which the conventional capitalist classes were limited in their occurrence.

The distinctiveness of Indian class structure is also central to the IC debate, which builds on Kalecki's idea of 'intermediate regimes'.

Kalecki used the term 'intermediate regimes' in his analysis of the class nature of the State in countries – such as India, Indonesia, and Egypt – which shared three basic features: (i) an unfinished capitalist transition; (ii) a strong involvement of the State in the management of the economy; (iii) the inability of the native upper-middle-classes 'to perform the role of "dynamic entrepreneurs" on a large scale' (Kalecki, 1972: 163). In a similar context, while the State played the role of a 'dynamic entrepreneur', a composite class force acted as ruling class, generating state forms that Kalecki called 'intermediate regimes'. The class coalitions supporting intermediate regimes were highly heterogeneous, including self-employed, middle and rich peasantry, white-collars, and the most prosperous members of the working classes; they dominated in numerical terms and were stable, their cement being the participation of the State in the management of the economy (Kalecki, 1972: 164). The regimes emerging in those contexts were 'intermediate' in a twofold sense: they were located in the middle between feudalism and capitalism and they represented the interests of the lower-middle classes and of the rich peasantry. For these features, intermediate regimes differed from 'classical' capitalist economies (Kalecki, 1972: 167).

Applying Kalecki's idea to India, Raj (1973) employed the term 'intermediate classes' for indicating the social strata that 'stand between the proletariat and the bourgeoisie' and that support intermediate regimes (Raj, 1973: 1189). Like the intermediate regimes, classes are 'intermediate' in a twofold sense: they are the class structure of a phase in between the two ends of the capitalist transition – neither feudalism nor capitalism; and they are in between the bourgeoisie and the proletariat – neither capital nor labour.

Stressing the heterogeneous composition and the numerical dominance of intermediate classes in post-Independence India, Raj included in them individuals who were, at the same time, owners and users of the means of production: 'small proprietors in agriculture, industry and commerce (dependent to some degree on hired labour) … the self-employed … [individuals] engaged in professions … clerical and administrative work and teaching' (Raj, 1973: 1191).

In spite of criticism from the Marxist side for neglecting the role of big bourgeoisie (Byres, 1997), the concepts of intermediate regimes and intermediate classes has been since utilised for the analysis of Indian social stratification. In his influential book on economic stagnation, Jha (1980) pointed out the importance of the intermediate classes in explaining Indian economic policy. Acknowledging his debts toward Kalecki and Raj, he argued that the intermediate class is not 'a transitional class' but, rather, the 'nascent bourgeoisie of early capitalism' (Jha, 1980: viii).

Jha explained economic stagnation in India between 1965 and 1980 as the outcome of the privatisation of public goods and services by intermediate classes. He showed that their economic prosperity increases in times of market shortage, in which rich peasants and farmers may control the timing of their supplies to obtain higher prices, and small businesses and traders may increase their prices and engage in black-marketing, avoiding state controls. The prosperity of the intermediate classes enlarges the room for manoeuvre of corrupt bureaucrats and civil servants who seek to increase their income by selling their services for bribes. The outcome of the diversion of public investments in favour of the intermediate classes and of the increased corruption is economic stagnation.

Jha's interpretation of economic stagnation in India has been criticised for having neglected the conflicts within the coalition of intermediate classes, the contradictions between small capital and big capital, and the differences in their economic and political behaviour (McCartney and Harriss-White, 2000: 10–15). However, its contribution to the analysis of contemporary India has been acknowledged. McCartney and Harriss-White (2000) argue that, because of its emphasis on the role of interest groups and on the embeddedness of state and markets, Jha's model offers 'a powerful political economy of development' that generates strong predictions (McCartney and Harriss-White, 2000: 29). Harriss-White (2003a), employing it for the analysis of peripheral capitalism in post-liberalisation India, sees Jha's approach as 'historical and dialectical' (Harriss-White, 2003a: 57). Her argument is that intermediate classes are resilient and that continue to be a dominant class coalition in contemporary India despite economic liberalisation and the 'direct attacks' to their hegemony. Economic liberalisation has undermined their dominance in three ways: (i) through the crisis of state capitalism and planning induced by the financial crisis and the inflow of international capital; (ii) by undermining their interests through the 'marketisation' of the Indian economy induced by the 'delicencing' and 'the removal of investments limits'; and (iii) owing to the consolidation of a new 'middle class' – identified by modern professions and westernised lifestyles – that engage in new links with the big bourgeoisie through shared ownership, insurance, etc. (Harriss-White, 2003a: 60–61). The impact of economic liberalisation adds to the 'direct attacks' by means of state reforms. Particularly relevant are the fiscal reforms – that tend to increase the fiscal pressure on small and medium-size firms – and the cuts in public transfers and investments in agriculture. However, despite the dissolution of the pre-conditions for intermediate regimes and the 'attacks' to their political dominance, the intermediate classes continue to be a locally hegemonic class coalition that resists the end of its political power and the emergence of a new dominating class force by increasing the forms and intensity of tax evasion and corruption, by refining the 'mafianisation' of the economy, and by 'informalising' socio-economic organisation (Harriss-White, 2003a: 64). This analysis is widely shared by McCartney (2010) who emphasises the role of intermediate classes in capital accumulation after economic liberalisation. According to McCartney, the power of intermediate classes is particularly strong at local level, where their aim has been to capture 'regional politics' with the aim of controlling local states (McCartney, 2010: 158–159)

2.3 A critique

The IMP and IC debates point out key traits of class structure in Provincial India: the former stresses the persistence of pre-capitalist production relations, while the latter points to the resilience of a class force that is a 'combination' of capital and labour, in which rent-seeking and corruption are widespread. They show that India differs from mature capitalist countries in the existence of classes that appear to be inconsistent with capitalism. Enlightening this trait, they reveal the historical specificity of India's class structure, in which institutional features intertwine with capitalist production relations.

However, a major problem with the IMP and IC debates is that participants fail to understand the implication of historical specificity in terms of class relations and conflicts. In my opinion, this failure is due to the use of a conceptual framework built on the idea of a 'purely capitalist economy', which is inhabited by 'pure classes'. Accordingly, the difference between India's class structure and the class structure of mature capitalist countries is taken to be the consequence of the incomplete capitalist transition, while the existing classes are seen as 'spurious', being neither capital nor labour. A corollary of this view is that a successful capitalist transition will cancel out these 'anomalies'.

This critique is particularly cogent for the IMP debate, which is carried on within a classical Marxist approach. As Chakrabarti and Cullenberg (2003: 55–56) point out, this debate does not add much to the classical Marxist view of capitalist development and appears more an academic dispute within the same interpretative paradigm than a real contribution to the understanding of Indian economy and society. Participants confront over two contrasting epistemological standpoints within historical materialism: empiricism and rationalism. While for the first the primacy is with reality, for the second the 'essence' of the reality cannot be observed, being only 'captured by the correct theory', which 'determines and validates' the facts. Both positions show serious drawbacks: empiricism leads to economic reductionism and rationalism focuses on class as the sole determinant of socio-economic processes. This explains why the IMP debate does not consider the influence on production relations of non-economic and non-class factors, such as caste and religion.[4]

Conversely, the inadequacy of the concept of the intermediate classes relies on its being largely descriptive and empirical. While having the major advantage of drawing attention to a key social force largely neglected by conventional Marxism, it only provides a description of the coalition without analysing its role in class dialectics.

In between the distinctive classes of the capitalist economy, the intermediate classes are the outcome of the complexity of capitalist social structure and are made of individuals with contradictory 'class locations' who might be at the same time employees and employers or, alternatively, neither employers nor employees. However, their contradictory class locations do not imply their 'neutrality' in capital/labour relations. It follows that, while the empirical analysis of capitalist production relations requires acknowledging the existence of intermediate classes as distinct from the capitalist class and the working class, it also requires explaining their interests and their position in capital/labour conflicts.

Indeed, the concept of intermediate classes stresses the composite nature of class structure. However, it assumes that the class interests of the intermediate classes are different from the interests of the dominating classes in the capitalist economy, so overlooking their class position in relation to capital and labour. Being built on Marxist categories, and then relying on a concept of class based on the relations with the means of production, it does not consider the self-perception of class interests and status and whether, in part or as a whole, intermediate classes gravitate toward pro working class consciousness or toward pro capitalist consciousness.[5]

In empirical terms, the description of intermediate classes as a coalition containing both owners and users of the means of production is only the first step of analysis. A second – major – step should be the assessment of intermediate classes' position from three different standpoints: in relation to economic and political power in social relations and structures; in relation to the interest in exploiting their power as a class; and in relation to the 'ideological' attitude towards capital/labour conflicts. If this assessment is missing, nothing can be said about how intermediate classes' interests and actions influence social production relations and the level of exploitation in the economy. We would then be left with a description of the intermediate classes as a pressure group operating with rent-seeking behaviour.[6]

3 A Marxist/Institutionalist class analysis

Focusing on the non-farm economy of Provincial India as a diversified and informal socio-economic system with a low performance and poor working and living conditions, my aim in this section is to show that its class structure is polarised around two antagonist classes – capitalists and subaltern workers – which represent capital and labour.

3.1 Paths of class formation

Analysing the emergence of a class of capitalists in Provincial India, the literature stresses two major 'paths' of formation that are linked to different agrarian structures.

The first path is influenced by the changes in the agricultural sector after the GR. Baru (2000) analyses the role of 'regional capitalists' with 'rural roots or agrarian links going back not more than one generation' (Baru, 2000: 214) in the industrialisation of different Indian states. Reviewing the literature on Andhra Pradesh, Gujarat, Tamil Nadu and Maharashtra, he shows that during the 1970s and 1980s an increasing number of capitalist farmers and landlords have moved into manufacturing, creating a 'rural-urban' entrepreneurial class and giving birth to a diversified economy – strongly rooted in agrarian capitalism – covering several industries, such as textiles, cement, sugar, chemicals, fertilisers, pharmaceuticals, electronics, steel and engineering goods (Baru, 2000: 215). His conclusion is that agrarian change plays a crucial role in the capitalist class's formation and that the capitalists with agrarian roots differ from other types of capitalists rooted in trade and money lending for the regional scope of their activities and for their political linkages with regional parties (Baru, 2000: 226).

The agrarian roots of the capitalist class in Provincial India are also emphasised by Rutten (1995) in a research on two villages in Gujarat. He shows that the accumulation of capital in agriculture is the basis for rural industrialisation, and that capitalists are the outcome of the class transformation of capitalist farmers. While the GR increases their wealth, capitalist farmers cannot increase their land due to land ceilings. The only possibility left for productive investments is economic diversification of activities in manufacturing, services and trade. Economic diversification occurs thanks to 'the institution of the joint family and the business partnerships' that make it possible for large farmers 'to mobilise the financial and managerial resources needed for their different types of business operation in agriculture, trade and industry' (Rutten, 1995: 349). Ruttern adds that a similar process is observed for small-scale industrialists who employ their increase in wealth – indirectly due to the GR *via* consumption – to diversify their economic activity in agriculture and services. Again, economic diversification is possible due to the joint family and to the business partnerships.

The outcome of these processes is the formation of an entrepreneurial class that operates in all sectors of the diversified economy. Both the capitalist farmers and the small-scale industrialists that give birth to the provincial capitalist class move from an entrepreneurial background, and their class formation only requires the learning of the practice of economic diversification.

The formation of the capitalist class in Provincial India is analysed in empirical terms also by Upadhya (1997) who deals with coastal Andhra Pradesh. She argues that – in addition to the practice of economic diversification in manufacturing, services and trade – the making of the capitalist class also requires ideological and cultural changes that contribute to define the homogeneity of the class itself. Upadhya stresses the need of 'cultural re-orientation and social re-structuring': two processes that 'take place simultaneously and reinforce one another' (Upadhya, 1997: 73). Then, the formation of the capitalist class also implies the convergence on similar lifestyles and values, and the adoption of similar political attitude and practices: class formation entails not only capital accumulation, but also the transformation of social and cultural identity.

The second agrarian path to capitalist class formation has been recently theorised by Chari (2000, 2004) who talks about a 'worker's path' to accumulation. Chari explores capitalist class formation in the industrial cluster of Tiruppur, pointing to the local textiles and knitwear capitalists as a class of self-made men which he describes as an evolution of a class of agricultural workers of the Gounder caste (Chari, 2004: 28–29).

Chari points out two keys to class formation. The first key is individual behaviour in the production process. Chari's capitalists are self-made men who become capitalists by means of their 'toil': the 'institutional memory' of their agrarian work conditions (2000: 589) that represents their starting 'capital' (581). Then, the agricultural contribution to capitalist development is not confined to physical resources, including also a 'cultural' resource that is summarised in the word 'toil'. Toil is then the 'key resource' that transforms agrarian workers into members of a class of small-scale industrialists (589). The second key is the 'fraternal' link within the caste that ensures class-like solidarity in capital accumulation among workers showing similar features and being moved by similar cultural and economic forces.[7]

While Chari presents a type of agricultural worker's path to industrialization, other types of worker's paths are discovered in the literature on economic diversification in Provincial India. Saith (2001) stresses the artisan origins of small-scale industrialists arguing that there are 'inadequate grounds' to link the growth of rural industrialisation to successful agricultural performance.[8] Cadène (1998a) takes a similar position, arguing that the development of clusters in India in small urban centres is a direct result 'of artisanal traditions which sometimes go back several centuries' (142). An artisan origin has also been found for a large part of the production units in Agra's footwear district (Knorringa, 1998).

The role of artisans in Indian industrialisation remains controversial (Bagchi, 2002: 78–79). As Rutten (2002) points out, many analysts – building on Weber's 'cultural' view of entrepreneurship – have stressed that Indian artisans 'did not form an important source of entrepreneurial talent in modern industrial development' for their lack of 'entrepreneurial values and motives' resulting from the Indian religion and caste system that work as an obstacle to social mobility and change (Rutten, 2002: 5).

The 'cultural' view of entrepreneurship is also used to explain why the merchant path to capitalist class formation is scarcely relevant in Provincial India. While there are scholars who believe that traders played a major role in the growth of industrial districts (for instance Kattuman, 1998: 236 and Cadène, 1998b), others have argued that Indian merchants (and money-lenders) never showed a marked entrepreneurial behaviour.[9] The reason is that, while entrepreneurial behaviour is confined to few mercantile castes (Bagchi, 2002: 80), Indian merchants are often committed towards 'rapid and not necessarily honest profits' and employ profits for conspicuous consumption (Rutten, 2002: 5).

The nexus caste/entrepreneurship is central in the literature on the emergence of the new capitalists in high-growing India. While Nath (2000) stresses the role of caste communities in explaining the capitalist development of regions and sectors, Shinoda (2000) explores entrepreneurship in small-scale industry in Gujarat focusing on the social background of entrepreneurs and paying a special attention to backward classes. With a specific focus on caste, the analysis shows that the distribution among activities is determined by the social mobility of communities, which is, in turn, influenced by the level of education, the existence of networks, and the pattern of capital accumulation. Also Damodaran (2008a, 2008b) establishes the key role of caste networks in his analysis of big business. Reviewing the history of the main merchant communities in independent India, Damodaran points out three paths to capitalist class formation according to caste groups: shop to factory for mercantile castes; office to factory for Brahmins and other scribal castes; and field to factory for castes rooted in agriculture and related activities. His conclusion is that the role of caste culture for the growth of entrepreneurship might be enhanced by politics and globalisation.

Apart from the trajectories of class formation, as a class, provincial capitalists present a number of features that distinguish them from other capitalist classes.

These refer to: (i) organising/regulative principles; (ii) economic behaviour; (iii) lifestyles; and (iv) political behaviour.

i   The class of provincial capitalists is socially regulated. Internally generated and/or controlled institutions regulate intra-class relations and the relations between the class faction and the external world (i.e. other classes, and local and central state). The regulative role of caste is widely recognised (Upadhya, 1997; Rutten, 2002; Bagchi, 2002) but the joint family and caste groups play a major role too (Rutten, 1995).[10] While the joint family provides the necessary resources for economic diversification, caste appears to be the major means to articulate class identity and to consolidate class positions (Upadhya, 1997: 49; Damodaran, 2008a, 2008b; Prakash, 2010). Caste plays a twofold role. First, caste-based networks are the basis for business activities. Second, caste-consciousness – reinforced by caste-based networks – enhances class-consciousness of the dominating classes, while preventing class-consciousness of the exploited classes. Jointly, caste and family influence accumulation trajectories, creating a network of social relations that tend to exclude (or reduce) social and economic intercourse outside caste and family circles.

ii These regulating institutions differentiate the class of provincial capitalists from the conventional entrepreneurs described by economic theory. The existence of caste and family networks and of joint family firms transforms entrepreneurship in a sort of 'collective function'. This explains the practice of economic diversification of the family investment portfolio – i.e. when the members of the same family mobilise their financial resources for different types of activities in agriculture, industry and trade – which contrasts with the specialisation of the entrepreneur/innovator described by Schumpeter (1934). While caste and family networks provide the basic support for economic diversification, as they make available the necessary resources, they also make economic diversification necessary to meet the needs of caste and family institutions in terms of occupation and social status. In this sense, the diversified provincial economy appears to be the outcome of investment decisions of a 'plural' economic agent that challenges the stereotype of the individual capitalist.

iii The focus on the plural dimension of entrepreneurship in the diversified provincial economy also furthers our understanding of the conspicuous consumption of provincial capitalists (who employ their income in luxury goods, such as expensive homes, gold ornaments, consumer durables and extravagant foods). The expensive lifestyles of provincial elites do not appear to be interfering with investment (i.e. the mobilisation of resources with a potential productive use), but play a twofold function: they mark the social status of caste and family institutions; and they increase the consumption of goods and services produced within and for the class itself. The distinction between 'productive' and 'unproductive' ways to dispose of profits loses part of its validity (Rutten, 1995: 352).

iv   Finally, the caste dimension of economic life explains the political behaviour of the provincial capitalist class. This class is 'characterised by the
successful promotion of common interests in the political arena' (Rutten,
1995: 352). While this is a phenomenon with a major local dimension, it has
also produced significant policy incentives to small-scale industries and to
clusters at central and regional level. This has required the systematic and
widespread use of corruption and fraud and has reinforced the practice of
rent seeking (Harriss-White, 2003a). Again, this behaviour has a plural
dimension that relies heavily on caste identity and interests.

3.2 Forms of labour commoditisation

As we have seen in Chapter 3, poor working and living conditions are widespread in Provincial India. The literature shows that this situation is a consequence of workers' structural and enduring subordination to capital, which
takes a plurality of forms.

Subaltern workers are forced into informal labour relations by a 'powerful
stratum of small-scale capitalists' whose aim is to keep low the level of managerial costs and to increase flexibility (Harriss-White, 2003a: 17–18), employing a
mosaic of capital/labour contracts that give birth to several forms of labour commoditisation. Wage labour is neither the only nor the most important form of
labour commoditisation while other categories of informal workers exist. A large
part of these categories do not fit under the conventional Marxist category of
'working class' as they do not exchange their labour power for a wage and, thus,
are not commoditised in the form described by Marx. Nevertheless, informal
workers in Provincial India are commoditised, and their commoditisation takes a
multiplicity of forms that are the outcome of the institutional and cultural framework regulating social intercourse (Lerche, 2010: 69 et seq.).

The literature provides important insights on the multiple forms of labour
commoditisation. There exist cases of autonomous commoditisation (when the
carrier of labour power is also its possessor), as well as cases of heteronomous
commoditisation (when the carrier of labour power is not its possessor). Moreover, there are situations in which carriers sell directly their labour power, as
well as situations in which someone else – who 'owns' their labour (i.e. who
controls their bodies) – does it.

Self-employment and wage labour are the major forms of autonomous commoditisation. Both generate multifaceted – and in many senses ambiguous – categories of workers.

Self-employment is a label that hides different types of agreements, in many
cases forcing workers 'into extreme self-exploitation' (Breman, 1996: 159;
NCEUS, 2007). As Breman argues (1999b: 412), the term 'self-employment' –
which should only be used for 'own-account work' – often includes forms of
'sub-contracted work and job-work' that are 'indirect' and 'mediated' forms of
wage-work agreements. While having the appearance of self-employed workers
in micro enterprises, a large number of labourers in India's provincial economy

lack the necessary autonomy (Harriss-White, 2010b). For a large proportion of these micro enterprises the production process is organised by 'middlemen' who mediate between capital and labour. This mainly occurs by means of contracting and sub-contracting. The basic form of these contracts is when the capitalist 'bears all production costs other than labour', while labour is supplied by the contractor (Breman, 1996: 157). The contractor sells to the capitalist the services of labour that he buys directly from workers. Workers are 'self-employed' in a twofold sense: because they do not enter any wage contract with capital; and because they are their 'own capitalists', in the sense that they exploit themselves in the attempt to increase their return. Another important form of employment is when capitalists contract out phases of the production process to self-organised groups of workers. In both cases, the aim of capitalists is to avoid the employer's responsibility toward the workers as employees (Breman, 1996: 158). In contracting and sub-contracting, the relations between capital and labour do not assume the form of wage contracts. While they appear to be cases of autonomous labour commoditisation, they differ from the one theorised by Marx, as the seller of labour to capital is the contractor rather than the worker.

Wage labour is the other important form of autonomous labour commoditisation in Provincial India. Wage labour is widely casualised and is unprotected and unorganised, as are other categories of informal work. Harriss-White (2003a: 24) points out that labour casualisation is the main instrument by which capital achieves flexibility. Workers only have 'verbal work contracts' that do not guarantee their rights, while legal regulations to protect labour exist but are not enforced (Breman, 1999b: 411).

Another important category of worker in India's provincial economy is represented by home-workers. Home-workers are the least visible and most vulnerable group of informal labourers. They are mainly women and children who work at home and are employed by means of the 'putting-out' system. Usually, it is a part-time activity that is 'easily' combined with housekeeping. The form of commoditisation of home-workers depends on their personal attributes and on the quality of family relations. In the case of child labour, we have a form of heteronomous commoditisation, as children's wages are usually given to the parents who have the control over their children's labour. A similar situation also occurs in the case of women's work, depending on the power relations within the joint family that constrains women's autonomy (Breman, 1996; NCEUS, 2007, 2009). Finally, the basic traits of heteronomous commoditisation are found in the case in which contractors are involved in the employment relation, mediating between subaltern workers and entrepreneurs (Breman and Guérin, 2009; De Neve, 2010).

For all categories of subaltern workers in Provincial India, life and working conditions are particularly difficult (NCEUS, 2007). The workplace is usually small and unsafe and the premises are often used for domestic purposes. No retirement age exists for informal workers, both wage labourers and self-employed. Caste and class regulate the access to better jobs, while low castes and classes are relegated to the bottom of the economy (Lerche, 2010). Yet, what makes life and working conditions of subaltern workers particularly hard is the widespread practice of debt bondage (Breman, 1996: 169). Bondage changes the terms of labour commoditisation.

Bondage is not a new phenomenon in India (Srivastava, 2005). The use of bonded labour in agriculture has been widely analysed by participants in the IMP debate, who have seen it as a significant example of pre-capitalist production relations. Yet, in contemporary India bondage assumes a different significance and does not appear to be a pre-capitalist form or a residual (Lerche, 1995, 2007; Breman, 1999a, 1999b; Breman and Guérin, 2009), but rather an instrument of contemporary capitalism.

As Breman points out (1996: 162–163), bondage in the pre-capitalist agrarian economy is a form of interpersonal, permanent link – involving economic and extra-economic obligations that could be extended into the next generation – that neither the farm servant nor the master has an interest in ending. By contrast, the form of bondage that we observe in contemporary Provincial India has a different nature. Breman (1996: 163–169; see also Breman and Guérin, 2009) introduces the concept of 'neo-bondage' to refer to a form of 'less personalised, more contractual and monetised' bondage (Breman, 1996: 69), which involves workers and employers/contractors, and which does not provide, as in the past, 'protection' and 'a subsistence guarantee' to bonded workers.

Labour is tied by means of debts, advance payments, the provision of accommodation, and by linking 'in a single-agreement the terms and the conditions for labour with those on land, money and product markets', including also 'the non-contractual obligations of patronage that may also require the work of the women and children' (Harriss-White, 2003a: 24). In this sense, neo-bondage is not a feudal residual, but rather a device used by capitalist employers and contractors to keep labour costs low.

Neo-bondage is a phenomenon rooted in the asymmetry of power relations between capital and labour embodied in institutions and culture and, when it prevails, it influences the form of labour commoditisation, bringing about a form that is intermediate between the autonomous commoditisation of wage labour and the heteronomous commoditisation of slavery (van der Linden, 2008: 23). In this form, the carriers of labour do not have full control over their labour power.

Subaltern workers are the weakest part of Indian society and lack the power over the process of production and over the terms and conditions of their own work. While there are some who, like family workforce and bonded labourers, do not have control over their own labour power, others, like home-workers and sub-contracted workers, do not have control over their means of production and over the product of their work. All categories are commoditised in forms that depend on the pattern of interpersonal relations within the family and within society, and that differ from wage labour commoditisation. For all categories the degree of exploitation and/or of self-exploitation is very high.

4 Capital and labour redefined

Capitalists and subaltern workers are the two antagonistic classes of non-farm capitalism in Provincial India.

Provincial capitalists are small-scale entrepreneurs who diversify their economic activity in agriculture, manufacturing and services by employing a surplus generated, directly and indirectly (*via* consumption), by the introduction of the GR. Coming from different sections of the economy, they differ in the trajectories of class formation and in their patterns of capital accumulation, but they are 'segments' of the same dominant class: they share the control over the means of production and commoditise labour.[11] Moreover, they have a basic social and cultural homogeneity and are linked by the common interest of perpetuating their social and political hegemony.

Subaltern workers are also a class made of different segments with distinct nature and origin, while sharing lifestyles and working conditions.[12] Despite their distinct positions in production, they are commoditised and do not have control over the means of productions, and often over their own labour power and their bodies too.

In Provincial India, classes need to be redefined (Bagchi, 2002). Capitalists seem more similar to *rentiers* than to capitalists. Their conspicuous consumption and expensive lifestyles, the family-based dimension of their economic, political and social life, the importance of caste in economic strategies, the rent-seeking behaviour and the use of corruption and fraud, all are elements showing how far provincial capitalists are from the sober capitalists described by Smith, who maximise their profits and practise the 'abstinence' that, according to Marx, makes accumulation possible.[13] Similarly, workers live in a condition of subordination that is far from the situation of the 'free' workers selling their labour force for a wage. To mark their distance from the 'free' workers of the capitalist economy, the subordination of workers often originates outside the production process (and outside the market), as in the case of family workforce. Yet, despite their 'anomalies', both capitalists and subaltern workers are subordinate to the 'imperatives of competition, accumulation, profit-maximisation, and increasing labour-productivity' dictated by the spreading of the capitalist market (Meiksins Wood, 2002: 6–7).

Capitalists represent the interests of capital. Their behaviour is consistent with their class. They have a wide and deep control over India's provincial economy and society. Their investments are aimed at the re-enforcement of their control over all components of the diversified economy. Their social and economic behaviour is consistent with the same aim and intends to promote their cultural and political hegemony as individuals *and* as a class. Indian institutions and culture are their tools, as much as are the wages they pay. Similarly, subaltern workers represent labour and are a class that is antagonist to provincial capitalists. Despite the multiplicity of contractual arrangements between labour and capital, labour commoditisation is widespread, while the degree of exploitation and self-exploitation is high. In their essence, the relations between capital and labour in Provincial India are typical of capitalism. Capitalist transition is no longer an issue.[14]

The classes dominating the process of economic diversification in Provincial India do not correspond to abstract theoretical categories, yet they are the forms that capital and labour assume in the present phase of capitalist development. Their distinctiveness – their 'backwardness' – is an outcome of the interplay between capitalist production relations and the institutional framework, which relies, among other institutions, on caste, gender, patriarchy and ethnicity. This interplay gives birth to structures and relations that might appear inconsistent with capitalism – such as unpaid family labour, bonded labour and child labour – but do not mask the capitalist character of production relations.

Pointing out the distinctiveness of class structure as a major trait of the variety of capitalism prevailing in Provincial India – and *not* as an indicator of an incomplete capitalist transition – this chapter widely contributes to the conceptualisation of the nature and working of India's provincial economy and society. Indeed, key questions are still unanswered and more analysis is required. In particular, we need to explore the mechanisms through which cultural and social institutions influence economic choices and we need also to unveil their interplay with market institutions in the capitalist economy. I will deal with these issues in the next chapter. My focus will be on caste – still a major organising principle of India's society – and my aim will be the assessment of its impact on social production relations.

5 Caste-based interest representation and the hegemony of capital in India's civil society

1 Introduction

In this chapter I explore the influence of caste on production relations in contemporary India. While other institutions – such as gender, patriarchy, ethnicity and religion – also exert a significant impact, I take caste as a privileged key. Despite the formal abolition of caste discrimination in the Indian Constitution, caste still impinges on individual and social behaviour, being legitimated by Hindu religion. Moreover, despite its secularisation, caste has acquired new roles in the economy, society and polity following the Mandal Report and the implementation of the Reservation Policy for backward classes.

I analyse the influence of caste by observing the organisation of civil society. I take civil society – defined as the association of non-state associations – as the sphere in which particularistic interests are expressed and represented, and I assume that the organisation of India's civil society reveals the intertwining of the interests of capital and labour with other typologies of (non-class) interests deriving from power relations rooted in India's colonial and post-colonial past.

Taking caste as an influential social institution in contemporary India, I analyse it by means of Marxist/Institutionalist categories. I argue that caste impacts on individual and social behaviour for its twofold role as *institution* and as *ideology*, and I advance the hypothesis – which relies on Gramsci's theory of hegemony (introduced in Chapter 2, Section 2.1) – that it generates a corporatist civil society in which particularistic interests are represented through non-voluntary caste-based associations and the hegemony of capital over labour is negotiated and enhanced.

The chapter is organised as follows. Section 2 focuses on interest representation in civil society. Section 3 deals with caste in independent India. Section 4 presents the Gramscian hypothesis on the role of caste in contemporary India. Section 5 concludes.

2 Interest representation in civil society

I introduce below the concept of civil society as the non-state sphere for the representation of particularistic interests. While several theoretical approaches to civil society exist, I explore the Marxist one, reviewing in particular Gramsci's theory. Then, building on Gramsci's, I show that in the case of the corporatist civil society the participation in association is non-voluntary. I conclude by distinguishing between state corporatism and societal corporatism.

2.1 Introducing Gramsci's civil society

A key concept in Western social theory, civil society is firmly rooted in the Enlightenment. The Enlightenment philosopher Adam Ferguson (1723–1816) was the first to introduce the modern concept of civil society, linking it to the increase of commerce and to the needs of the emerging capitalism. However, it was Hegel who proposed the first comprehensive theory, establishing a clear-cut separation between the public sphere of the State and the private sphere of civil society and pointing out the contrast between them. For Hegel, civil society is included in the sphere of ethical life, being 'intermediate between the family and the state' (Hegel, 1821 [2001]: 154). It is not the product of 'natural life', but the result of a historical process that transforms nature in order to meet human needs (138), defining the material conditions of life and covering the sphere of economic relations and class formation.

While harmony is a feature of the family, which is the first 'ethical root of the state' (Hegel, 1821 [2001]: 193), 'private interests' pursued by 'private persons' dominate civil society (157).[1] The 'constituent element' (191) of civil society is the 'corporation' (association), whose aim is the administration of private interests in 'societies, trades and professions' (234). However, the pursuit of private interests in corporations is subordinated to the higher interest of the State. The State is the synthesis and warrant of the universal interest against the particularistic interests expressed by civil society, and ensures the unity of civil and political societies. Hence the contrast between the State as the sphere of political institutions, and civil society as the sphere of economic institutions.

Marx's concept of civil society markedly differs from Hegel's (Femia, 2001). Marx has a Hobbesian view of civil society as an ensemble of hostile individuals who fight over economic interests: the spirit of civil society is then the spirit of 'egoism, of *bellum omnium contra omnes*' (Marx, 1844: 58). While the character of the 'old society' – i.e. the feudal society – was 'directly political', with the bourgeois revolution the 'essence' of community breaks and individuals are separated from the State. So, civil society is 'an expression of man's *separation* from his *community*, from himself and from other men' (Marx, 1844: 58). This separation is the origin of conflicts over particularistic interests, among which economic interests have the primacy. It follows that the purpose of civil society – and with it also of citizenship, i.e. the status of individuals participating in the bourgeois society – is to preserve and enhance the rights and the interests of the members of the capitalist economy.

Gramsci builds on Hegel – and not on Marx – presenting a deeply innovative concept of civil society. For Gramsci, civil society does not contain only economic relations (as for Hegel) but also ideas and institutions that enhance particularistic interests. It combines together two spheres of human life: economic interests and ideological factors. The associations that create civil society are seen as the outcome of individual and group interests, on the one hand, and of ideologies by which consent is gained and interests imposed, on the other. So, ideology is a major building block of civil society, while civil society is a form of organisation that supports the hegemony of the dominant classes.

For Gramsci civil society is distinct from the State and it located within the superstructure:

> We can for the moment fix two major superstructural layers: the one that can be called 'civil society', that is the ensemble of organisms commonly called 'private', and that of 'political society' or 'the state'. The two layers correspond on the one hand to the function of 'hegemony' that the dominant group exercises throughout society, and on the other hand to that of 'direct dominance' or rule exercised through the state and the juridical government.
> (Gramsci, 1975: 1518–1519, my translation)

The participation in the associations of civil society appears as 'voluntary'. By means of ideology, the dominant classes gain the 'spontaneous' consensus of the subaltern classes who enter the groups in which the alliances with hegemonic classes take their shape. Hence comes the distinction between the State – the realm of coercion – and civil society – the realm of hegemony.

Gramsci's theory provides important insights on the nature and working of civil society, which is described, at the same time, as an association of 'voluntary' associations and as ideological construction. The associations that compose it are the outcome of particularistic interests that are imposed by means of ideology: their life is univocally determined by the nature of the underlying interests, and they are historical constructions. There is an essential complementarity between the State and civil society: both are the outcome of specific production relations and represent the interests of the dominant classes; and both are the outcome of a process of negotiation over conflicting interests.

2.2 Interest intermediation in corporatist civil society

A form of civil society's organisation in which the role of ideology is crucial and the interplay between interest representation/organisation and production relations is particularly visible, is corporatism. Corporatism has been widely studied for its impact on economic growth and its significance in terms of democracy.

Schmitter (1974) conceives corporatism as the *institutional structure* – and *not* as a form of *policy-making* – that exists when the relationships between individuals and the State are mediated by interest groups.[2] This situation strongly differs from 'pluralism', i.e. the alternative institutional system in which the relationship between individual and State is direct and unmediated. Comparing corporatism with pluralism, Schmitter gives birth to a rich debate that explores the forms taken by corporatism in contemporary economies.[3]

The legitimacy of the comparison between corporatism and pluralism is controversial, as it is the definition of corporatism. Williamson (1989) argues that the very concept of pluralism is too abstract to be useful in the analysis of the real world.[4] He compares it with neoclassical economics, suggesting that pluralism is based on methodological individualism: society is explained in terms of individual preferences and values; the activity of interest groups is open and competitive; the State is a 'persona non grata', and state institutions are neutral (Williamson, 1989: 52). This situation can hardly exist and real political systems show a variable degree of interest organisation.

Indeed, as an abstract category, pluralism helps us understand the nature of corporatism. In corporatism, interest representation is state-licensed or state-recognised or even delegated by the State, and interest associations are hierarchically organised in their internal structure as they need to have specialised leaders and staff in order to carry out their work. By contrast, in pluralism, interest associations, when they exist, do not depend on the State – i.e. are not state-licensed or state-recognised – and are not hierarchically organised – and then they do not require any formal organisation.

The debate on corporatism has focused on the significance of a corporatist system and its impact on economy and society. A key issue is the nature of the function performed by interest associations. While in his 1974 definition Schmitter emphasises 'representation', in a later definition he shifts the emphasis to 'intermediation' (Schmitter and Lehmbruch, 1979). The shift to a broader concept is necessary to the cases in which associations 'distort' the representation of members' interests or 'teach' them what their interests should be, playing not only a representative role, but also a 'regulatory' role, contributing in determining members' interests. This regulatory role is enhanced in their intermediation with the State: associations not only negotiate agreements on members' behalf, they also apply the contents of such agreements to their members. They act as intermediaries, assuming public powers and taking part in policy-making. Interest intermediation extends public regulatory functions into the domain of private associations: associations assume a 'quasi-public nature' (Williamson, 1989: 99).

The regulatory function performed by interest associations takes us to the issue of democracy. Here the question is whether the corporatist organisation of interests enhances democracy or whether it restricts it. If one takes the organisation of interests as a way to limit the power of the State, to enlarge participation and to ensure 'voice' for different opinions, then a corporatist system should be considered as a substantial enhancement of democracy. However, if one observes that competition is not open, being restricted by a monopolistic representation for each category, that there is no alternative form of representation open to individuals, and that – as Schmitter's definition stresses – membership is compulsory, then corporatism should be seen as a restriction of democracy as, due to barriers to individual participation, inequalities are re-enforced by the politics of organised interests. Another aspect of corporatism that qualifies its contribution to democracy is internal organisation: associations are widely seen as bureaucratic and anti-democratic top-down-led bodies.

2.3 State corporatism and societal corporatism

The contribution of the organisation of interests to the enhancement of demo-cratic politics is crucial in assessing the viability of corporatism in liberal states. According to Schmitter two basic types of corporatism should be distinguished: *state corporatism*, in which the institutional structure of organised interests is imposed by the State; and *societal corporatism*, in which the institutional struc-ture of organised interests emerges from below under the pressure of social groups. In the first case, the corporatist institutional structure is found in author-itarian regimes, such as the ones experienced by Fascist Italy, and by Spain and Portugal in the central decades of the twentieth century. In the second case, the corporatist institutional structure is found in contemporary liberal democracies and goes under the name of *neo-corporatism*.

Cawson (1985: 8) provides a useful definition of neo-corporatism:

> a specific socio-political process in which organisations representing mono-polistic functional interests ... engage in political exchange with state agen-cies over public policy outputs which involves those organisations in a role that combines interest representation and policy implementation through delegated self-enforcement.

In neo-corporatism the relationships between state and corporatist associations are based on political exchange, usually involving state, capital and labour. The use of coercion is not necessary because the State may 'bargain' with the part-ners, the associations being aware that, in principle, enforcement is possible: neo-corporatism appears then as a 'benign' system of social integration. More-over, coercion is often substituted by the use of ideological mechanisms that deny the relevance of class and particularistic interests in favour of 'general' cross-class interests.

Neo-corporatism combines together the intermediation of functional interests – performed by the associations and by the State – with joint decision-making – i.e. 'policy concertation'. It is a closed system based on political exchange rather than competition: participation in policy concertation is open only to the groups recognised as institutional counterparts (and not to individuals). While the tripar-tite bargaining – state, capital and labour – ensures stability, the State is not simply a neutral arbiter, but organises its action according to the asymmetrical distribution of power between capital and labour.

The reasons for the choice of a neo-corporatist institutional structure are found in its economic and social impacts. The literature emphasises that cor-poratism ensures social stability and, then, economic growth. The representation and intermediation of interests is a way to organise and to control conflicting interests; moreover, the leaders of associations may adapt members' demands while representing members' interests. This twofold action ensures stability and allows for the implementation of public policies.

Recent research shows that corporatism has a significant macro-economic impact on employment and inflation. This is largely due to policy concertation and to the practice of coordination of wage setting. Streeck and Kenworthy (2005: 456–458) point out three 'causal mechanisms'. First, by 'engendering wages restraint', interest organisation keeps inflation and unemployment low, as coordinated wage negotiations reduce the risks associated with bargaining at firm level. In the face of an aggressive request for a wage increase, a firm can react in five basic ways: raising productivity, raising prices, reducing profits, reducing investment, reducing employment. In the case of individual bargaining, these actions do not necessarily have an adverse impact on the economy, being in principle limited to a single firm. So unions, being unconcerned about the macro-economic consequences of wage bargaining, may be led to a 'strategy of wage militancy'. By contrast, in the case of coordinated wage setting, unions are aware of the likely macro-economic consequences of firms' reactions in terms of employment and inflation, and then they may have 'an incentive for wage moderation', reducing the negative impact of aggressive bargaining on the economy.

Second, the practice of coordinated wage setting may have a significant impact on economic growth, and then – in the medium run – also on employment, as an agreement between employers and workers on the wage level may often include a greater level of investment. In turn, a greater investment may induce an increase in production and, then, in employment.

Third, governments in countries where the wage level is set within a corporatist institutional structure are able to adopt expansive economic policies, as policy-makers are more confident about a moderate increase of labour costs, and then are less worried about 'wage-push' inflation. By contrast, policy-makers in countries with 'fragmented bargaining' are led to adopt restrictive policies in order to reduce the risk of inflation, with the consequence that the level of unemployment is kept higher.

Due to the interplay in corporatist regimes between civil society's organisation and policy concertation, civil society, political society and economy overlap. This 'confusion' between society and polity – which, according to Gramsci, is typical of the corporatist framework (1975: 763) – is the joint outcome of tripartite bargaining and of the non-neutrality of the State, which transfers to the political sphere the constraints coming from the economic structure, and vice versa. In this context, participation – both of interest groups in political exchange and of individuals in associations – is compulsory, because non-participation de facto implies the exclusion from the political process and, then, condemns individuals to a second-class citizenship.

3 Caste as an institution and an ideology

In this section I review how caste influences the organisation of India's society. After an introduction to the nature of caste, I point out the main changes in the post-Mandal period and I explore the caste/class nexus. Finally, I present a Marxist/Institutionalist interpretation of caste as an ideology and an institution that produces a corporatist civil society.

3.1 Caste in independent India

Caste is a system of beliefs and rituals that has long been among the major organising principles of Indian society (Béteille, 1983, 2002; Dirks, 2002). Moreover, it is a form of social stratification based on a concept of inequality that finds its legitimacy in Hindu religion and culture (Sharma, 1994).

Caste is governed by the concepts of purity and impurity, which define a hierarchical order, and the relationships among individuals of different caste groups are regulated in terms of blood, food and occupation (Shah, 2002; Béteille, 2012). Caste defines a *closed* and *segmented* system of stratification in which individual mobility is denied and in which all castes recognise the hierarchy and accept their position in it by force of religious legitimacy. In this sense, it is a 'consensual system [of stratification] based on complementarity' (Deshpande, 2003: 103).

Because of its twofold nature – a system of beliefs and rituals and a form of social stratification – caste has been frequently analysed in dual terms.

The emphasis on the values and beliefs is found in the literature that analyses caste by means of religious texts, rituals and customs about marriage and commensality. This is the approach of the 'book view' of caste mainly supported by Dumont's controversial *Homo Hierarchicus* (1980). Here, caste is a system of ideas: an ideological construction that defines a social order. By contrast, the emphasis on caste stratification and on the interests that caste stratification creates is found when caste is analysed in terms of power relations (Deshpande, 2003: 103). A major contribution to this approach is M.N. Srinivas' 'field view' of caste, in which the social order of caste is seen as the origin of power structures and relations influencing economy and polity (M.N. Srinivas, 1996).

A dual explanation of caste is also found in Marxism. Broadly, Marxists explain caste in terms of class. However, two views exist, caste being seen to belong alternatively to *superstructure* – as ideology – or to *structure* – as a form of social stratification. According to the classical Marxist view (Shah, 2002), caste is a 'false consciousness', which manipulates the perception that workers have of their position in production relations, and a pre-capitalist residual that capitalism will dissolve.[5] According to the alternative Marxist view, caste is the form taken by class in India and then, as class structure, it belongs to structure (Chakrabarti and Cullenberg, 2003: 114–115).

In early post-Independence India, caste was considered incompatible with democracy. Nehru believed caste to be 'an aristocratic ideal' in contrast with the 'democratic conceptions' of the Indian State (1954, quoted by Shah, 2002: 4), and the common aspiration of the post-Independence political elites was to 'annihilate' it.[6] After the formal abolition of caste discrimination in the Indian Constitution, caste soon became a non-issue to most economic and political commentators, who shared the conviction that 'modernisation' would lead to its dissolution. The Mandal Commission and the subsequent Mandal Report imprinted a different direction to Indian history and since the early 1980s caste was re-invented as a 'modern institution' (Deshpande, 2003: 124).[7]

3.2 Caste hierarchy, caste identity, caste politics

The Mandal Report – and in particular the implementation of the measures for the backward and most backward castes included in the Reservation Policy – induces a process of institutional change that leads, on the one hand, to the secularisation of caste and, on the other, to the emergence of new economic and political roles for it.

As the authoritative words of the late M.N. Srinivas (2003: 459) suggest, there is a major 'paradox' in the change of caste in the post-Mandal period: 'while caste *as a system* is dead or dying, individual castes are thriving'. This paradox involves all India, but is particularly manifest in rural areas, in which capitalist change undermines village economy and the caste-based division of labour on which it relies (Shah, 2007). The paradox is revealed by the change in caste hierarchy and caste identity.

The territorial dispersal of caste members following urban/rural and international migrations – in a sort of 'globalisation of caste' (Shah, 2007: 111) – leads to the breaking of the boundaries of sub-castes, giving birth to larger castes. This process is reinforced by *caste mobility* and *in-caste class differentiation* (Sharma, 1994: 7–8).[8] A major by-product is the increasing separation between caste and occupations (Béteille, 2007: 951).

Identity is the tool through which castes face the problem of preserving their unity and their boundaries. Caste identities are socially constructed, and their construction undermines caste hierarchy. Often without the support of textual tradition, caste histories are invented, and qualities and skills of each caste – as well as their religious descents – are celebrated (Narayan, 2004a). This process relies on caste 'rhetoric', which is elaborated and locally disseminated through caste associations (Michelutti, 2004).[9] While the construction of a 'suitable' past for castes is not a new phenomenon, neglected and undervalued practices are rediscovered and enhanced in the post-Mandal period (Gupta, 2004: xix; Michelutti, 2004: 49). So, if the Mandal Report accelerates the death of caste as a system, it also gives new life to its elements, enhancing the assertion of caste identity (Shah, 2007).

Indeed the post-Mandal change has not much to do with the religious legitimacy of caste. Instead, it brings about economic and political roles for it, leading to the emergence of caste politics (GDP, 2008).

The politicisation of caste identity and the use of caste as a vehicle to represent and to organise interests in the party political arena is confirmed as a major trait of the post-Mandal era. Following the emergence of new caste interests generated by the Reservation Policy, castes behave as pressure groups, organising interests by means of caste associations and political associations, and even caste-based parties (Sharma, 1994: 6–7; Bayly, 1999; Sheth, 1999; Shah, 2002: 18; Harriss-White, 2003a: 194–196; Bhanu Mehta, 2004; Michelutti, 2004; Narayan, 2004a, 2004b).

The role of caste politics as an instrument of democratic politics, in particular for the representation of lower castes, is highly controversial (Corbridge and

Harriss, 2000; Narayan, 2004b; Béteille, 2007; Wankhede, 2008; Desai and Dubey, 2011). In very broad terms, the controversy refers to the nature of caste/ class relations and to the influence on them of Reservation Policy: does caste inequality determine class inequality? Has caste discrimination a negative impact on class mobility – determining a significant under-representation of lower caste groups in Indian society and economy? To what extent does class upward mobility (induced by positive caste discrimination) reduce caste-based inequality or does Reservation Policy work only to the benefit of powerful caste-based constituencies?

There are few doubts that, after the Mandal Report and as a consequence of the Reservation Policy, caste and caste politics have become highly sensitive issues in contemporary India. Major evidence is the decision of the Indian Government – taken in August 2010 – to conduct a caste census in 2012.[10]

3.3 Caste and class

Caste and class are different forms of social stratification. While both define a hierarchical order, the former is based on culture and religion and the latter on the relations to the means of production. However, as caste classifications also rely on the occupational status, caste inequalities have often been analysed in terms of class. As Shah (2002: 11–12) argues, socio-anthropological research has shown that the origin of caste is associated with the production of an economic surplus, since caste is a tool 'to accommodate' the inequalities generated by the surplus itself. Relying on field research by Srinivas (1952), Béteille (1996a) and Klass (1980), he also argues that hierarchies of landownership and hierarchies of caste often overlap. A similar situation was observed in British India, in which 'the landlords, big landowners, wholesale traders, moneylenders' belonged essentially to the high castes and low-class individuals to the lowest castes and tribes (Mukherjee, 2000: 334–335; see also Sheth, 1999). Also Deshpande (2003: 109–120) shows – on the basis of NSSO data – that caste-divide continues to be manifested in terms of income and wealth, while Vaid (2007) shows that high castes dominate professional, business and large farming classes.

Moreover, while the conceptual difference between caste and class stratifications cannot be denied, caste and class intertwine, influencing socio-economic organisation and production relations. For Thorat and Newman (2007: 4122), caste discrimination is a form of 'forced' social exclusion that restricts the access to capital, labour, land, education, and other inputs to low-caste individuals, denying rights and preventing the mobility on the class ladder. The outcome is twofold: the structural inefficiency in resource allocation and the perpetuating of the class subordination of the lower castes. This situation is particular manifest in the labour market, in which, as Madheswaran and Attewell (2007) show (by means of NSSO data), caste discrimination results in the segregation of lower castes to the low quality/low paid jobs. Lerche (2010) shows how the joint action of class and caste increases the segmentation of rural subaltern workers, segregating them to the bottom of Indian labour hierarchy. Exploring India's non-corporate capitalism, Harriss-White (2003a) stresses the role of caste in the regulation of the informal production organisation, worsening working and living conditions for subaltern workers. While the issue is increasingly addressed in literature, we may conclude with Heyer (2010) that, in post-Mandal India, caste appears to be a tool in the hands of the hegemonic classes, and as such it concurs in creating a favourable environment for the marginalisation and exploitation of the lower castes/classes.

3.4 A Marxist/Institutionalist analysis of caste

The intertwining of caste and class takes two major forms: the ideological use of caste to control the level of class conflicts and to pursue the interests of the hegemonic classes (Bardhan, 1994: 415–416; Bandyopadhyaya, 2002); and the creation of caste-based institutional constructions to support specific classes – or segments of classes – in becoming hegemonic (Sheth, 1999).

In Marxist terms (Bardhan, 1994; Sharma, 1994; Ranadive, 2002; Shah, 2002), caste prevents the formation of class-consciousness. As a 'false consciousness', it substitutes caste-consciousness for class-consciousness, leading the exploited classes to absorb – and become committed to – values and interests of the dominating classes. Caste values and interests contrast with class values and interests: if the latter are tools to mobilise the exploited classes against the exploiting classes, enhancing class conflicts, the former prevent class conflicts. Moreover, caste creates non-class institutions – caste associations and caste-based associations – that represent and organise particularistic interests vested in caste identity, so breaking the unity of the exploited classes by dividing them according to their caste (Bhambhri, 2005). This action assists in constraining class-consciousness, slowing down class unity.[11]

Caste impacts on class also through the formation of new classes across the caste hierarchy, creating 'new alliances and antagonisms' (Mukherjee, 2000: 338). This process, that Sheth (1999: 2508) calls the 'classisation of caste', is shown in particular by the emergence of the new 'middle class' that is the outcome of inter-caste mobility and in-caste class differentiation (Béteille, 2007). The new middle class is a composite stratum that includes members of several castes who share lifestyles and the self-consciousness of belonging to the same class (Varma, 1998; Sheth, 1999: 2508–2509).

While including several castes, the new middle class is rapidly acquiring a specific self-identity: members share interests and lifestyles with other members of the class rather than with individuals of the same caste, becoming progressively more distant from the rituals specific to their caste (Sheth, 1999). It is then a class in the making, its cement being economic and political interests and lifestyles (Harriss-White, 2003a: 61).

The new class formation does not require the dissolution of individual caste identities. Caste still provides the cultural background of social and political life: 'identity politics [i.e. caste politics] has come to prevail over class politics'

(Béteille, 2007: 951), while caste-based associations and parties represent the main instrument to organise and represent interests. Then, vested interests are expressed in terms of caste identity and, at the same time, caste provides the organisational structure to participate in the political arena and to seek favour from the central and local state.

Through Marxist/Institutionalist lenses, caste appears at the same time an *ideology* and an *institution*. As a system of values and beliefs, caste is part of the mental processes that shape human agency, influencing social intercourse. As an institution – when it transforms from ideas into social norms – caste defines widely accepted patterns of civil society organisation, constructing and legiti- mising social differences. Relying on these roles, it is a major organising prin- ciple of Indian civil society.

Both as an ideology and as an institution, caste is part of the superstructure and is involved in a double interplay with structure: it influences production rela- tions and production forces, and is influenced by them. As such, it is a historical construction, which evolves according to the change in social production relations.

As an institution, caste has shown to be 'fit' to pass on from colonial India to independent India, undergoing a 'cumulative process of change' in which its nature and its role have adapted. While the changes in India's economy and society have induced its change, caste has impacted on the organisation of India's economy and society and on production relations. The outcome is a form of civil society's organisation in which caste provides a major vehicle for the representation and organisation of particularistic (class and non-class) interests emerging in the economy and polity. Also as an ideology, caste has undergone a deep change since Independence, progressively weakening its religious character to gain instead a political connotation.

Emphasising the role of caste as institution and as ideology, the Marxist/Insti- tutional interpretation shows the limits of the classical Marxist analysis which, assuming a one-way relation between structure and superstructure, stresses the role of caste as 'false consciousness', neglecting caste-based organisation and representation of interests. The Marxist/Institutionalist interpretation explains how caste institutions and caste ideologies shape human agency, accounting for their impact on the organisation of civil society and, then, on the organisation of production.

4 A Gramscian hypothesis on the role of caste in Provincial India

Then, caste is much more than a 'false consciousness' that undermines the unity of the working classes. It is a major force in civil society's organisation in which ideology 'materialises'. Reading it through Gramsci's theory of hegemony, this twofold nature corresponds to a twofold role: as ideology, caste ensures that the intellectual and moral leadership of the elites is 'spontaneously' accepted through shared values and ideas, supporting the hegemony of the dominant classes over the subaltern ones with the use of caste idioms and symbols; as civil society, caste produces a network of associations in which subaltern and dominant classes enter 'voluntarily', and in which the necessary consensus over hegemony is negotiated. Both the ideology and the civil society that the ideology produces are the outcome of social production relations. While ideology ensures that dominant classes also have moral and intellectual leadership over subaltern classes, this dominance is rooted in the structure of the economy: jointly, caste and production relations constitute the historical bloc that creates the conditions for economic growth in any specific phase of capitalist development.

The Gramscian hypothesis on the twofold role of caste will be explored for Arni in Part II of this book by means of qualitative and quantitative data from field research. However, it might be useful to set the scene for such an exercise, reviewing the main conclusions of Chapters 3 and 4, with the aim of describing in broad terms the social production relations prevailing in non-farm capitalism in Provincial India and of specifying the forces that participate in the historical bloc. This exercise helps us to outline the empirical analysis.

In Chapter 3 I have described India's provincial economy as a diversified and informal system consisting of micro and small firms based on casual labour, self-employment and an unpaid family workforce, which shows a poor economic performance and low-quality employment. I have shown in Chapter 4 that two antagonist classes – which represent capital and labour – inhabit this socio-economic system. These classes are segmented: the first is made of individuals who control the means of production and who commoditise workers in wage and non-wage forms; the second is made of commoditised workers who do not have the control over the means of productions, over their own labour power and often also over their bodies.

Assuming that the same ideological and institutional processes are at work in Provincial India as well as in urban and Metropolitan India, a Gramscian interpretation on the working of caste can be expressed in the following terms.

The capitalist class is hegemonic over the class of subaltern workers and dominates with the support of the shared values and beliefs that find a major expression in caste. Caste largely provides the ideological tools that make capital's hegemony possible, deconstructing class identities and substituting caste-consciousness for class-consciousness. Moreover, caste produces the network of civil society organisations in which subaltern workers enter 'voluntarily' and in which the hegemony of the rural non-farm capitalist class is negotiated.

The ideological use of caste values and beliefs to support capital's hegemony is a key factor for the growth of Provincial India as it prevents subaltern workers' perception of the conflicting interests of capital and labour.

Capitalists negotiate the consensus of subaltern workers for their hegemony in the associations of civil society, which include all classes of India's provincial NFE and in which subaltern workers agree to enter on the basis of shared values and beliefs. Caste is an instrument by which subaltern workers are led to accept the moral and intellectual leadership of capitalists, overlooking their class interests and in spite of their poor living and working conditions and their high levels of exploitation and self-exploitation; and it is also the cement to keep together the segments of the capitalist class and of the subaltern class. Ensured by caste, the 'alliance' between the capitalist class and the subaltern class enhances capital's interests against labour's interests. The participation of subaltern classes to the organisations of civil society is compulsory.

5 Caste, civil society, political society

In this chapter I have proposed an analysis of the influence of caste on production relations in contemporary India by means of the concept of civil society. However, the legitimacy of such an exercise is debated. Kaviraj (2001) argues that civil society is a concept of Western social theory, built on categories rooted in Western intellectual tradition and social history – such as individuality, self-interest, universality and society – which might not be suitable for countries with different social history and intellectual tradition (Kaviraj, 2001: 306 et seq.). The case of India is emblematic: owing to Hindu religious tradition, India has developed an alternative 'intellectual argument', which, consistently with caste and strongly contrasting with the Christian view of individual and society, relies on a different concept of 'the self' and on the idea of community.

On a similar position is Partha Chatterjee (2001), who challenges the adoption of the concept of civil society based on 'Western Christianity' in post-colonial democracies, and in particular in India, proposing an alternative conceptualisation of the relation between citizens and the State (170).

Revisiting Hegel's *Philosophy of Right*, Chatterjee argues that the emphasis on family as the 'elementary unit of social organisation' does not suit a non-Christian context, suggesting that 'family' should be substituted with 'population'. Then, focusing on post-colonial India, he distinguishes between *civil society* and *political society*, using the former to refer to the institutions of modern associational life based on 'equality, autonomy, freedom of entry and exit, deliberative procedures of decision-making, recognised rights and duties of members', and the latter to refer to the associational life of the vast mass of population that remains outside the domain of modern civil society. Civil society and political society strongly differ: the former is inhabited by urban elites and middle classes, which produce it in an attempt to replicate 'the forms' and 'the substance' of Western modernity; the latter is inhabited by urban poor and rural population and is built by governmental and non-governmental organisations 'to channel and order popular demands on the developmental state', with the aim of preventing the destabilisation of the democratic life (Chatterjee, 2001: 175–177).

Building on this argument, Chatterjee argues that the trait that distinguishes India from other capitalist countries is the co-existence of political society and civil society (2008a: 57). He also explains that, reproducing the model of Western bourgeoisie, civil society 'represents the domain of capitalist hegemony', which includes corporate capital and state structure; while political society is the domain of non-corporate capital, comprising the peasantry, artisans, and the petty producers in the informal sector (Chatterjee, 2008a: 57).

The divide between civil society and political society then overlaps with the divide between corporate and non-corporate capital, on the one side, and formal and informal sector, on the other.

Chatterjee relies on this distinction to explore the implications of economic growth on India's democracy. His argument, which has stimulated an interesting debate on EPW, is the following.[12] Owing to economic growth and to the hegemony of capital in the corporate sector, primitive accumulation is going to continue; as a consequence, the number of workers dispossessed of their means of production is due to increase; facing the unlikely possibility of being absorbed in the formal sector – a consequence of the high growth/low employment pattern of development in the current phase of capitalism – the dispossessed workers increase the size of the informal sector, being employed in low-income/low-quality jobs; the function of political society is then to compensate these workers in order to avoid the risk of transforming them into 'dangerous classes' for the democracy. For his argument, Chatterjee builds on the innovative conceptual analysis of capitalist accumulation in a high-growing country proposed by Sanyal (2007), sharing with the latter the conclusion that the '*narrative of transition is no longer valid*' in India (Chatterjee, 2008a: 55).

It seems to me that Chatterjee's distinction between civil society and political society cannot be employed as an analytical key to explore capitalism in Provincial India for the major reason that he does not provides a comprehensive analysis of the working and quality of the diversified economy. I see two major problems: i) the failure of understanding the crucial role of caste; and ii) the failure to grasp the implications of the interplay between the formal and informal sectors.

The lack of attention to caste in Chatterjee's analysis has been already pointed out by Shah (2008; see also Chatterjee's reply: 2008b: 90). However, my point here is not just that caste is another 'axis of power', but that caste and class are intertwined, the former being an instrument in the hands of the latter. The major implication is that an analysis neglecting caste is simply not possible. Moreover, caste/class intertwining is manifest in caste associations, which work as a major support for capital hegemony; yet, caste associations, through which caste/class interests are expressed and represented, cannot be accommodated in Chatterjee's dual framework, because they differ both from the elite structures that reproduce Western bourgeois civil society and from the mass associations created in political society to manage the demands coming from the dispossessed population. Since caste and caste-based interests are key components of social dialectics in contemporary India, this drawback undermines the interpretative power of the approach.

In relation to the second issue, the literature has recently challenged the distinction between formal economy and informal economy (see Chapter 3, 4.1), showing that: (i) informalisation is a process that involves both corporate and non-corporate capitalism; (ii) the existing differences in the organisation are an outcome of the needs of accumulation in the global economy and of local historical specificity; and (iii) a continuing interplay exists between informal sector and informal sector. Accordingly, the non-corporate informal sector cannot be taken simply as the residual sphere that absorbs the surplus of labour, while informal organisation is generated by inner class (and non-class) dialectics in the interplay with the corporate sector and, through it, with the global economy. As part of the capitalist economy, the non-corporate sector also produces a super-structural form of civil society in which particularistic interests are organised and represented, influencing production relations. Still a catalyst of conflicting interests in contemporary India, caste participates in the construction of civil society, both in corporate and in the non-corporate economy, and cannot be neglected.

It seems to me that the Gramscian reading of civil society that I have presented in this chapter – i.e. civil society as the association of associations for the representation/intermediation of interests in which the participation shows a variable degree of voluntariness (owing to the working of ideology) – is suitable to explain the nature and working of both the corporate and non-corporate sectors. The differences that exist in the forms taken by civil society in different corporate and non-corporate, formal and informal socio-economic contexts – in the variety of civil societies – are an outcome of the historical specificity of socio-economic organisation. They are then an aspect of the variety that is major trait of contemporary capitalism.

This chapter concludes the first part of the book, in which, after an introduction to the Marxist/Institutionalist framework (Chapter 2), I have presented the eclectic analysis of non-farm capitalism in Provincial India (Chapters 3, 4, and 5). My aim has been the identification of the distinguishing traits of India's provincial economy. In the second part of the book I will conduct a Marxist/Institutionalist analysis of Arni town. My aim is twofold: to understand how the macro processes pointed out for Provincial India as a whole are working at micro level; and to assess the quality of Arni's capitalist development in terms of working and living standards. I start with Arni's long-term change (Chapter 6), then I turn to class structure (Chapter 7), and finally I deal with ideological and institutional superstructure (Chapter 8).

Part II

A Marxist/Institutionalist analysis of capitalism in Arni

6 Long-term change in Arni's economy

1 Introduction

With this chapter I start the Marxist/Institutionalist analysis of Arni, a small-sized market town located in the rural district of Tiruvannamalai in Northern Tamil Nadu (henceforth TN), in which the GR was introduced at the end of the 1960s. Arni provides a unique opportunity to study empirically the features of capitalism in provincial India. Following the change in agricultural techniques, the town has experienced a major socio-economic transformation, which has been documented over the years through field research. A huge amount of quantitative and qualitative information on the town – and on its district – is available, allowing the recent historical perspective that is necessary to grasp the overall trends of capitalist change.

In this chapter, I introduce Arni and explore its long-term change; I focus on the socio-economic organisation of Arni's silk economy in Chapter 7; and I assess the impact of Arni's civil society on social production relations in Chapter 8.

This chapter is organised as follows. Section 2 introduces Arni and describes the theoretical background of the research on the town and the empirical context in which it was carried out. Section 3 summarises the analysis presented in published papers and books. Section 4 presents a Marxist/Institutionalist assessment of Arni's transformation after the GR, which relies on an original elaboration of long-term data. Section 5 concludes the chapter commenting on the variety of Arni's capitalism.

2 The empirical research on Arni

When the GR was introduced at the end of the 1960s, Arni was a small-sized market town located in a rural district on the Coromandel coastal plain of peninsular India, which was chosen for research on the introduction of the HYVs for its agro-climatic conditions.

Owing to the low – and variable – rainfall, the area is prone to periodic droughts that have produced famines and widespread poverty in the course of the nineteenth and twentieth centuries. Climatic conditions also determine agricultural seasons and the cropping pattern, which mainly consists of paddy on the wetland and groundnuts and pulses on the dryland.[1] Before the GR, it was an area of smallholder agriculture, and the vast majority of the population were dependent on agricultural production with an average land holding of 1.43 ha (Harriss-White *et al.*, 2004: 6). The introduction of the HYVs brought about a deeper penetration of capital into agricultural production, developing the process of commoditisation enhanced by colonialism (J. Harriss, 1982a: 209). Starting from agriculture and from the villages, capitalist change extended across sectors and to the town, deeply impacting on production relations and economic organisation.

2.1 The North Arcot surveys and the Arni surveys

Arni has been researched since the early 1970s (Harriss-White and Harriss, 2007). At that time, the town was a minor administrative centre – a *taluk* head-quarters – and an important market centre for the surrounding area in North Arcot district (in the northern part of TN).[2] The North Arcot district was chosen by an Indo-British team led by Ben Farmer (Cambridge University) for research on the progress and problems of the GR in a rice-growing semi-arid area in South India and eleven villages were randomly selected and surveyed (Farmer, 1977). Being one of the high-order service centres in the area for more than 100 villages, including the selected ones, the town was chosen for a study of urban–rural economic relations in the context of agrarian change.

The same area has been systematically researched two more times since: in 1982–1984 for research on the direct and indirect consequences of the GR (carried out by a team from the International Food Policy Research Institute (IFPRI) and the TN Agricultural University) (Hazell and Ramasamy, 1991a); and in 1993–1994 for research on the changes induced by economic liberalisation (carried out by a team from Oxford University and the Madras Institute of Development Studies (MIDS)) (Harriss-White and Janakarajan, 2004). While the primary focus of research was the villages, Arni provided again an important perspective on urban/rural relations and was re-surveyed by Barbara Harriss-White.[3]

Indeed, the research on Arni has also continued beyond the three rounds. In 1993–1994, as part of the major survey of the villages and town, a team from the MIDS led by K. Nagaraj, explored the development of silk handloom weaving in Arni and in the surrounding area, with the aim of explaining the increasing importance of the sector (Nagaraj *et al.*, 1996). In the following years, as a consequence of the detailed information available, Arni has become a sort of 'workshop' for the testing of socio-economic theories on development and change. As an outcome, other data and information have been produced.[4]

Arni never was a 'typical' town (Harriss-White, 2003b: 6). In 1973 it had a population of 38,664 (60,815 in 2001) and was a major trade centre for paddy, with an expanding sector of hand-woven silk saris.[5] In these features, it was basically similar to many small-sized market towns of which TN was rich.[6] Yet, while not being 'typical', Arni showed important features that contribute to explain its future role as a 'workshop'.

Arni was – still is – a 'rural' town – i.e. a small-sized town located in an economic environment in which agriculture was the dominant activity in terms of employment, while not necessarily in terms of income generation. Moreover, the town was – still is – a sort of accumulation point for economic activity and social intercourse in the district. As a 'market town', Arni was a trade centre for (local) socio-economic life. Yet, trade was only a part of an economy that also included a growing manufacturing sector, in which the production of hand-woven silk saris dominated but also other kinds of production were included (while neither the supply of raw materials nor the demand for the finished product were local). Again, the presence of a specialised and growing manufacturing activity was not exceptional for a market town in TN (Harriss-White, 2003b: 6). Yet, the specific combination of trade and production made of Arni a privileged place for the analysis of urban–rural relations in the course of economic change.

For its twofold role – as a market place and as a production centre – Arni was sensitive to agrarian change. This explains why the GR had a major impact on the town, as well as on the villages. After the introduction of the HYVs in agriculture the economic relations of the town with the villages increased, and Arni became a pole of attraction for the resources freed from agriculture, providing a paradigmatic case to test the most important theories of rural development and of rural/urban relations, as was done systematically in the studies on the town since the 1970s (Harriss and Harriss, 1984).

2.2 On the integration of the North Arcot surveys and the Arni surveys

Across the three rounds, the overall aim of the North Arcot project was to explore the process of change that, after the GR, was involving at one and the same time the countryside and the town, agricultural and non-agricultural activities, production and trade. Yet, despite this overall aim, a major theoretical divide is observed between the first and the second round, on the one side, and the third round, on the other. This divide is an outcome of the change in the intellectual and historical context brought about by India's economic and political liberalisation.

In the first two rounds, the aim was to assess how North Arcot's agriculture was reacting to the new technology. Firmly rooted in the debate on the GR, the first round intended to test whether the introduction of the HYVs was a means to solve the problems of poverty and hunger in the region or, on the contrary, was making them worse, as many observers of the period were arguing.[7] The assessment was carried out by means of Marxist analytical categories and was inspired by the IMP debate (Harriss-White and Harriss, 2007: 7). The introduction of the new seeds was seen as a factor leading to the capitalist transformation of Indian agriculture, while processes such as the differentiation of the peasantry and the growing importance of merchant and usurer's capital were at the core of the analysis (B. Harriss, 1981a, 1981b; J. Harriss, 1982a). In the second round, the intellectual context changed and the aim was to test the growth linkage effects of the

GR. Mellor's growth linkages theory provided the theoretical background. Accordingly, the introduction of scale-neutral agricultural techniques was seen as a factor increasing farm incomes and consumption, leading to the development of labour-intensive non-farm activities in the local economy, while the aim was the measurement of the direct and indirect effects of agricultural growth on the local economy.

Despite the difference in their theoretical backgrounds, both rounds focused on the transition process that would have been taking North Arcot's economy to a new and more 'advanced' situation in terms of production relations. In this context, the research on Arni explored the impact of the agrarian transition on the town and the subsequent change of urban/rural relations. In the first round, the relevant debate on urban/rural relations focused on the spatial dimension and the research question was whether or not the growth of Arni could have a positive impact on the growth of the local economy. In the second round, relying on Mellor's theory in which rural towns were given a special attention, the research on Arni complemented the project on the villages, exploring the resource flows between the town and the villages, and between the town and the global economy. The research on Arni was then functional to the North Arcot project as a whole.

In the third round, the North Arcot project had two distinct aims: (i) to discover what had become of the area after more than two decades since the introduction of the HYVs; and (ii) to explore, and also to forecast, the ongoing spatial and economic restructuring induced by local and global competition in the context of the retreat of the State (Harriss-White and Janakarajan, 2004). While the debate on the GR has lost its previous importance, what matters now is to draw some firm conclusion on the experience and the changes brought about by the new technology. The research provides evidence of an overall process of diversification going on in the area – from the diversification of crop varieties and patterns to the diversification of rural employment and the composition of incomes of peasant classes – and describes a grim picture of the retreat of the State as a factor increasing income inequality and food insecurity.

The research on Arni reflects this intellectual and political change. The last round focuses on the complexity of the socio-economic organisation in the town and on its suitability – in particular in relation to markets and to civic services – in a context of growth. For the town, as for the villages, the focus is on the retreat of the State and the aim is to speculate on its consequences in terms of economic efficiency and living standards. As for the villages, diversity is the key word. The town is observed to have 'a plethora of market forms' (Harriss-White, 2003b: 17–18) and an increasing number of new and old business activities: all are explored in order to assess contractual arrangements and power relations, and local/global patterns of market integration.

2.3 *What we know about Arni*

The research on Arni (and North Arcot) has given birth to a large number of publications from which it is possible to draw an extensive analysis of socio-economic change in the town and in the area. The publications on the town are based on the first two surveys and mainly refer to the period 1973–1983. I review below the contribution of these publications to the knowledge of Arni's economy and of the relations of the town with its hinterland. My aim is to set the scene for the assessment of Arni's long-term change in Section 4, in which the data from the three surveys will be jointly taken into account.

Arni's economic change

By 1983 Arni already showed a growing and differentiating economy. With an increase of 27 per cent in the urban population (from about 39,000 in 1971 to 49,000 in 1981), the town experienced a surprisingly high increase (about 400 per cent in constant prices) in the commodities flowing through it, with the remarkable growth of 61 per cent in the number of businesses. As in 1973, rice milling and paddy trading and the production of silk saris were the main activities. Other major activities were the production of basic consumption goods for the local markets (such as tailoring, pottery and tile making, and furniture). In comparison to 1973, there was a notable increase in the number of provision shops and general merchants, and new items were traded, from food to 'fancy' goods (such as cosmetics, plastics and steel furniture). Among service activities, transport, repair and financial services were particularly important, with a significant growth in the number of pawnbrokers and cooperative and commercial banks. Also the public sector showed a large, increase contributing to the increase in consumer demand (B. Harriss, 1991).

Yet, despite the increasing diversification (following the emergence of new activities in production and trading), Arni also specialised (Harriss-White, 2003b: 12). By 1983 the production of silk saris became Arni's major activity (increasing by a factor of 15), and the town progressively acquired a competitive trade advantage over other silk producing centres in TN and in other Indian states. At the same time, the town continued to be a trading centre for agricultural products.

A joint consequence of growth, diversification and specialisation was the increase in employment. With the only exception of a few large firms in rice and transport services, petty production dominated and family labour still represented a high percentage of total employment. Yet, over the decade it is wage labour that showed the largest increase. The case of silk weavers (whose number trebled in the period) is emblematic, leading to a large expansion of employment in the town and in the surrounding villages (with an increase of 175 per cent for male weavers in Arni and of over 300 per cent for male weavers in the villages (see J. Harriss, 1991: 448)). Despite the increase in employment, urban wages remained stationary, while rural wages increased.

The increase in the volume of trade was accompanied by a change in trade patterns. While only 10 per cent of the commodity flows passing through Arni had the town as final destination – i.e. the town has become a wholesale centre – a large quantity of the traded goods, especially for final consumption, were composed of imported products (B. Harriss, 1991). Then, Arni's economy showed a strong trade 'openness' that overcame the limits of the local economy.

On urban/rural relations in North Arcot

The first two rounds provide important insights on urban/rural relations. Building on Harvey's distinction between 'parasitic' cities – which do not contribute to the growth of their region – and 'generative' cities – which contribute to the growth of their region – Harriss-White (2003b: 8) argues that the very idea of 'generative urbanism' was untenable in the case of Arni for three major reasons.[8] First, the market services supplied by Arni did not reach the poorest people because they lacked 'effective demand for higher order urban products'. Second, Arni was not generating employment for the underemployed agricultural labour force and for the unskilled workers moving out of agriculture. Third, only a small percentage of the commodity flows passing through Arni had the town as final destination.

By testing Mellor's growth linkages theory, the second North Arcot survey also throws light on the relations between Arni and its rural district. The estimates of production and consumption linkages showed that the GR was having a fairly strong (and positive) impact on the non-farm economy, stimulating a 0.87 extra value added to the increase in the agricultural valued added (Hazell and Ramasamy, 1991b: 244–245). Also, the research on Arni confirmed a marked increase of the rural effective demand and strong consumption linkages. However, it also showed that the multiplier effect of farm incomes alone was not sufficient to explain the high increase in non-farm employment and incomes in the town as, together with agriculture, the main mover of the process was the silk industry, which largely contributed to the expansion in the demand for market and financial services. As the Arni studies pointed out, the estimates of consumption and production linkages were systematically biased for the inclusion of an activity such as silk sari production, which ought not to have been classified as a 'local' activity neither for the 'tradition' of the area nor for the source of inputs and destination of outputs.

This powerful conclusion undermines the theoretical approach of the overall project, demonstrating the ambiguities and fallacies in the use of the term 'local' in Mellor's theory[9] and revealing the theoretical and empirical weaknesses of agricultural demand-led models for economic analysis and policy purposes. Yet, while clearly showing that Arni's change in the 1970s and in 1980s was not led (only) by agricultural demand, this conclusion also shows that the empirical research did not provide a sound answer to the question of what was the role of the silk industry, of which mechanisms were at the origin of its growth, and of which factors were eventually responsible for Arni's long-term change.

The beginning of a process of growth and structural transformation

The comparison between the first two surveys clearly supports the conclusion that Arni was a growing economy and that its growth went together with a deep structural transformation. The town had undergone a process of diversification and specialisation that resulted from the emergence of new goods produced and traded and from the acquisition of new comparative advantages in manufacturing. Besides, the town was adopting urban life styles revealed by the spreading of new consumption goods for the local market.

In 1983 Arni appeared to be an 'open' town that was progressively losing its local dimension. It was still a market town with an increasing variety of traded goods, but the traded goods were progressively disposed on distant markets for distant consumers. It was also losing its rural dimension. Due to the spreading of urban lifestyles and consumption patterns, the town was progressively, if not perceptibly, weakening its cultural rural roots; the urban/rural growth linkages via consumption were also weakening. While there are few doubts that the GR had been the midwife of the process of economic growth-cum-structural transformation, the determinants of the process itself were not the ones that the mainstream theory of the period suggested.

Mellor's growth linkages were hardly at work in Arni. The impact of the introduction of technical change in its rural hinterland had not been inducing growth and change in Arni via consumption linkages. Classical economic theory that sees agriculture as a source of surpluses for urban and industrial growth seems to be a better explanation of the situation: the villages were providing the town with workforce and capital – through the increasing number of informal financial institutions – while the town was using the agricultural workforce and capital to specialise in manufacturing products for other urban markets.

In ten years, Arni underwent a deep process of change. Input and output markets changed, so did the origin of raw materials and the destination of the goods, as well as consumers' preferences. The pattern of capital accumulation also changed due to the emergence of new types of economic activity. Arni was still a market town, but it was both a different market town and also a manufacturing centre that was increasingly specialising in a commodity that had neither local roots nor local market.

Also, the rural environment in which the town is located had been changing. While in the villages the GR had been a powerful factor of change, it was by no means the only one. In 1983 agriculture was still the main activity in terms of employment. But the villages themselves were diversifying their economies. Non-farm activities were growing and were having a strong impact on agricultural employment and investment. In the villages, as well as in the town, the emerging non-farm activities were acquiring comparative advantages in the production of non-local goods, while urban consumption patterns spread.

The image of Arni coming from the first two surveys was one of a town in the middle of a process of growth and structural transformation that, starting from the introduction of new technology in agriculture, had progressively involved all social and economic aspects of the area. Yet in 1983 the changes were still in their initial phase and it was difficult to forecast the directions that it would take. It is this uncertainty that the Arni studies perceive and describe.

3 Arni's long-term change

This section explores Arni's long-term change in order to assess whether the picture emerging from the Arni Studies for the period 1973–1983 is also confirmed in the following decade. I will be using the quantitative and qualitative information coming from the three Arni surveys, which is classified and elaborated into a consistent statistical database for the first time for this book. While the quantitative information is used to examine the long-term trends of change, the qualitative information integrates the quantitative evidence, indicating the main features of Arni's economy and society in the 1990s. The background of my assessment is the analysis of the town presented in the Arni studies, together with the recent literature on the region, in particular Harriss-White (2003a) and Harriss-White and Janakarajan (2004).

3.1 On the data from the Arni surveys

The Arni surveys provide two types of data: census data and sample data. In each round, the census data – i.e. the information on the number of Arni's businesses in each sector – has been generated from a 'functional map' of business premises in the built area of the town. In the 'functional map' – which in the absence of a listing of business premises supplied by the local government represents the list of sampling units – the firms were classified on the basis of their sector and location in the town. Then, in each round, a 6 per cent random sample of firms was drawn from the sampling frame, randomly replacing the few non-cooperative firms (2–3 per cent) with similar firms. In the sampling, attempts have been made 'to represent the clustered character of the urban economic fabric' (Harriss-White, 2009: 22). In the first two rounds, samples were drawn throughout every street, while in the third round the town was first divided into five areas, and samples were drawn randomly and proportionately from each stratum. The samples were then stratified according to the sector of the firms and to the site in which they were located.

The 6 per cent sample was chosen in the first round on the basis of the availability of time and resources. Then, it became the rule for the other rounds. The statistical significance of the 6 per cent random sample over the rounds is uncertain. In 1973 the variance of key variables in the study population was unknown and, then, it was impossible to identify the right sample size – and also to assess the representativeness of the 6 per cent sampling fraction. The increasing variability of firms over time has inevitably reduced the statistical significance of the samples in the following rounds (Harriss-White, 2009: 22).

The ways in which the surveys have been carried out ensure the accuracy and completeness of the census and sample data. In the first two rounds, the main researcher was 'known' in Arni (Harriss-White, 2009: 26); in addition, an assistant helped with language and with the organisation of the interviews; and, in the third round, the research was supported by a 'key informant', P.J. Krishnamurthy, a retired and respected teacher in Arni with a profound familiarity with the town.

The firms were interviewed on several aspects of their activity: from their history, to input and output markets, to geographical and economic linkages with the rural hinterland and with other economic centres in the state and in India at large. The material coming from the surveys was integrated by interviews with local informants on the general features of the town and on its economy and society.

3.2 Arni's socio-economic transformation after the Green Revolution

I explore below the process of growth and structural transformation in Arni after the introduction of the HYVs in local agriculture. My aim is to assess to what extent the post-GR change in the town is consistent with the dynamics of Indian rural capitalism described in Chapter 3.

Some introductory information is necessary. (i) Both census and sample data are employed for the long-term analysis. (ii) The sample data comes from 119 schedules for 1973, 127 schedules for 1983 and 209 schedules for 1993. (iii) The businesses have been thematically organised by the types of products sold. They have been grouped in 10 major groups as follows: *rice and paddy* including rice mills and rice wholesale trade; *agricultural products* containing other products than rice; *foods* including all types of food items; *farm inputs* also including animal foods; *silk products* including silk factories and handloom weavers; *fuel and energy retailers* also including petrol/station services; *transport repairs and services* containing all types of transport, including taxis, cycles and buses; *other repairs and services* including a large number of activities, from canteens and hotels to barbers, doctors, lawyers and insurance; *money and financial services* including pawnbrokers, moneylenders, finance companies and banks. Finally, as a residual group, *general merchants* includes many types of retailers, ready-made clothing, jewellery, weaving machinery, pottery and construction. (iv) All monetary data are expressed in constant values (Rs 1993).[10] (v) Each sample contains a vast majority of small-size firms and few very large firms (the sample size is presented in Table 6.1). While a major increase in the number of both types of businesses is observed over the decades, the differences between the two types (particularly in size, as we will see below) are remarkable. Therefore, in elaborating the sample data, I distinguish between the two types of businesses each time it is useful to the analysis.

Growth and diversification

Since the early 1970s Arni's economy has been growing constantly at a very high rate. This growth is not fully reflected in the urban population, which was 60,815 at the end of the 1990s (data from the Census of India, 2001). Yet, this should be considered an underestimate due to the fact that the municipality gains in being small (Harriss-White, 2003b: 22) and villages in the town's vicinity resist formal incorporation because that involves increases in local taxes. A more realistic estimate that takes into account the commuting workers from the

Table 6.1 Size of the Arni samples

Business	1973			1983			1993		
	(a)	(b)	Total	(a)	(b)	Total	(a)	(b)	Total
1 Rice and paddy	22	0	22	8	0	8	5	1	6
2 Agricultural products	4	0	4	2	0	2	5	2	7
3 Foods	13	1	14	22	0	22	49	1	50
4 Farm inputs	3	0	3	5	0	5	8	1	9
5 Silk products	13	0	13	23	0	23	4	1	5
6 General merchants	31	1	32	36	2	38	67	1	68
7 Fuel and energy retailers	5	0	5	4	1	5	3	1	4
8 Transport repairs and services	5	0	5	6	0	6	16	0	16
9 Other repairs and services	15	0	15	12	0	12	25	0	25
10 Money and financial services	6	0	6	5	1	6	10	0	10
Total	117	2	119	123	4	127	192	8	194

Source: Arni surveys (1973, 1983, 1993).

Notes
a = small businesses.
b = big businesses.

villages and the migrant labour force would be 100,000 people (Harriss-White, 2003b: 22).

The growth and diversification of Arni's economy emerges very clearly from the surveys. The census data shows that the overall number of firms has more than trebled in the two decades and that the increase is unevenly distributed among the activities (Table 6.2).

The growth in the number of businesses over the two decades (198.3 per cent) is observed for all sectors. As measured by the number of businesses, *agricultural products, rice and paddy, money and financial services*, and *farm inputs* show the lowest rate of growth. *Silk products* show a marked increase over the period, which results from a very high increase in the first decade, followed by a marked slow-down in the second one. Conversely, *general merchants* have showed a steady increase over the period, and a notable rate of growth is observed for *foods, fuel and energy retailers*, and for *other repairs and services* in the second decade.

The sample data broadly confirms the growth of Arni's businesses. Table 6.3 shows the increase of the gross output in the sample (with an average annual rate of growth of about 9 per cent in the first decade and nearly 20 per cent in the second decade). The growth is the outcome of different sectoral performances. The growth of *agricultural products* is notable, as it is – but to a lesser extent – the one of *transport repairs and services*. Also *farm inputs, general merchants*, and *other repairs and services* show a significant increase. By contrast, *rice and paddy* substantially stagnate over the two decades, while *foods* and *silk products* show a decrease in their annual rate of growth in the second decade.

The different performance leads to a major change in the relative importance of sectors. While in 1973 *rice and paddy* covered over 40 per cent of the total

Table 6.2 Private firms in Arni

Business	1973	1983	1993	1973–1983	1983–1993	1973–1993	1973–1983	1983–1993	1973–1993
	(a)	(a)	(a)	(b)	(b)	(b)	(c)	(c)	(c)
1 Rice and paddy	62	121	159	95.2	31.4	156.5	6.9	2.8	4.8
2 Agricultural products	96	139	254	44.8	82.7	164.6	3.8	6.2	5.0
3 Foods	439	564	1,371	28.5	143.1	212.3	2.5	9.3	5.9
4 Farm inputs	13	28	32	115.4	14.3	146.2	8.0	1.3	4.6
5 Silk products*	62	243	345	291.9	42.0	456.5	14.6	3.6	9.0
6 General merchants	150	232	373	54.7	60.8	148.7	4.5	4.9	4.7
7 Fuel and energy retailers	12	18	59	50.0	227.8	391.7	4.1	12.6	8.3
8 Transport repairs and services	82	136	194	65.9	42.6	136.6	5.2	3.6	4.4
9 Other repairs and services	191	321	623	68.1	94.1	226.2	5.3	6.9	6.1
10 Money and financial services	87	121	152	39.1	25.6	74.7	3.4	2.3	2.8
Total	1,194	1,923	3,562	61.1	85.2	198.3	4.9	6.4	5.6

Source: Census of Arni's business economy (Arni surveys – 1973, 1983, 1993).

Notes
a No of units.
b Rate of growth over the period (%).
c Average annual rate of growth (%).
* In 1993 1,141 weavers were censused in addition to 345 silk businesses. For reason of comparability of the data across the years, the 1,141 weavers have not been considered in computing the rate of growth.

Table 6.3 Total gross output in the Armi samples

Business	1973		1983		1993		1973/1983	1983/1993	1973/1993
	(a)	(b)	(a)	(b)	(a)	(b)	(c)	(c)	(c)
1 Rice and paddy	53,284	40.2	99,880	31.4	57,324	3.0	6.5	-5.4	0.4
2 Agricultural products	3,678	2.8	227	0.1	1,348,802	70.0	-24.3	138.4	34.3
3 Foods	17,515	13.2	23,702	7.5	43,328	2.2	3.1	6.2	4.6
4 Farm inputs	5,101	3.9	9,267	2.9	37,733	2.0	6.2	15.1	10.5
5 Silk products	23,803	18.0	83,338	26.2	196,510	10.2	13.3	9.0	11.1
6 General merchants	22,005	16.6	44,962	14.1	144,109	7.5	7.4	12.4	9.9
7 Fuel and energy retailers	2,639	2.0	29,601	9.3	34,971	1.8	27.3	1.7	13.8
8 Transport repairs and services	227	0.2	619	0.2	35,570	1.8	10.5	50.0	28.7
9 Other repairs and services	3,086	2.3	4,195	1.3	16,652	0.9	3.1	14.8	8.8
10 Money and financial services	1,062	0.8	22,346	7.0	12,584	0.7	35.6	-5.6	13.2
Total	132,400	100.0	318,137	100.0	1,927,583	100.0	9.2	19.7	14.3

Source: Sample data (Armi surveys – 1993, 1983, 1973).

Notes
a Thousand Rs (prices 1993).
b Distribution over total (%).
c Average annual rate of growth (%).

gross output in the sample, and *silk products* and *general merchants* were below 20 per cent, the situation significantly modifies in 1983, when *rice and paddy* fell to 30 per cent and *silk products* increased to 27 per cent. Another change is observed again in 1993, when *agricultural products* dominate the sample's economy (mainly due to a very large firm), while *silk products* fell well below their 1973 level.

The change in the economic performance of sectors over the decades is also confirmed by the increase of the sample average gross output. Table 6.4 shows that, while the increase is widespread, its size significantly differs amongst sectors, both for small and big businesses. In the case of small businesses, it is worth noting the peak of *rice and paddy* and *foods* in 1983, the sharp decrease of *farm inputs* in 1993, and the reduction of *agricultural products* in 1983. The evidence on the increase in size for the big businesses is inconclusive for the vast majority of the sectors owing to the lack of information on 1973 and 1983 (which might also imply that in the two first reference years the number of big enterprises in the town was rather limited). It is interesting to note the huge difference between the average sizes of the two types of businesses, especially in relation to 1993, the year in which big businesses belonging to seven different sectors have been included in the sample. However, without knowing the statistical significance of the sampling fraction, it is difficult to say whether or not a process of concentration has been going on in Arni's business economy over the two decades.

Both census data and sample data are employed in Figure 6.1 to extrapolate the pattern of change in the business economy for the town as a whole between 1973 and 1993. The average annual rate of growth of the number of units on the hori-

Table 6.4 Total sample average gross output (prices 1993 – '000 Rs)

Business	1973		1983		1993	
	(a)	*(b)*	*(a)*	*(b)*	*(a)*	*(b)*
1 Rice and paddy	2,804	...	11,098	...	4,690	33,875
2 Agricultural products	1,226	...	114	...	3,672	665,220
3 Foods	430	5,964	1,077	...	576	15,100
4 Farm inputs	1,700	...	1,853	...	873	30,753
5 Silk products	1,984	...	3,623	...	19,127	120,000
6 General merchants	331	11,729	488	13,695	1,106	70,000
7 Fuel and energy retailers	527	...	1,020	25,520	1,657	30,000
8 Transport repairs and services	45	...	1,031	...	2,223	...
9 Other repairs and services	206	...	350	...	793	...
10 Money and financial services	177	...	245	21,120	1,258	...
Total	1,015	8,846	1,969	18,507	2,037	203,770

Source: Sample data (Arni surveys – 1993, 1983, 1973).

Notes
a = small business.
b = big business.

zontal axis is computed from the census data, while the average annual rate of growth of the gross output in Arni's businesses is estimated from the sample data on the vertical axis. This has to be taken only as a very *tentative* representation of Arni's long-term change, as, owing to the uncertainty on the statistical significance of the samples, one cannot be sure that the estimate on Arni's gross output is unbiased. However, this exercise confirms the main traits emerging from the previous analysis. It also shows that, while all sectors grow over the period, both in terms of number of units and gross value, *silk products* and *fuel and energy retailers* appear the most dynamic ones. Other high performance sectors are *other repairs and services* and *agricultural products*. Significant also is the performance of *transport repairs and services*, for which the output increases much more than the number of businesses. A similar performance is also shown by the new sector of *money and financial services*, while *farm inputs* confirm a (relatively) poor performance, both in relation to the number of businesses and to gross output.

A major conclusion can be drawn from the previous analysis that, while Arni's economy has been constantly growing from 1973 to 1993, its pattern of growth is not uniform over decades and sectors, and the economic physiognomy of the town has changed significantly in the period. While in the 1970s and the 1980s Arni is largely dominated by *rice and paddy, silk products*, and *general merchants*, new leading sectors – such as *money and financial services, agricultural products*, and *transport repairs and services* – emerge in the 1990s. Moreover, despite the fact that, in each reference year, Arni seems to 'specialise' in a single sector, its 'specialisation' varies over the years, while the town's economy continues to be deeply diversified.

Arni's businesses are diversified not only in relation to sector but also for their position in the division of labour in the production chain.

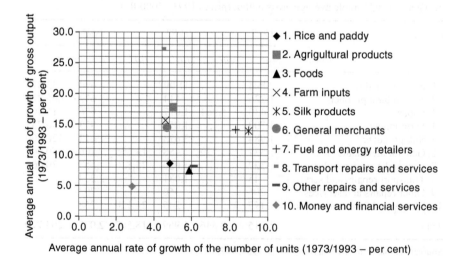

Figure 6.1 Growth and change in Arni's business economy, 1973–1993 (source: Census and sample data (Arni surveys – 1993, 1983, 1973)).

Table 6.5 classifies the town's firms both according to the sectors and to their type. Two main indications can be drawn: (i) different types of activities co-exist, in production, service, retail and wholesale trade; (ii) the mix of activities varies over the decades. The increase in the number of businesses in retail trade in the 1990s is worth emphasising.

Economic diversification is the outcome of the consolidated behaviour of Arni's capitalist entrepreneurs. Table 6.6 shows that a significant proportion of firms in the samples diversify their economic activity, investing both within their sector – but in a different sub-sector – and outside their sector. It is interesting to note that while the patterns are complex, varying over the period, nevertheless economic diversification is a basic trait over the decades, being more extensive in trade and services than in manufacturing. Moreover, in broad terms, diversification increases over the years.

Summarising, the Arni surveys provide evidence of a process of economic diversification in the making that has been going on since the 1970s. Diversification is a structural trait of the town and its pattern is mobile over time. The increase in number of businesses and the significant change in their types are the two faces of the same process of growth: Arni has progressively enlarged and renewed its economic basis over two decades, with the emergence of new activities that take the place of the traditional ones (Harriss-White, 2003a: 179). The outcome is a business economy in which firms with activities in production and trade, in agriculture and manufacturing, and in retail trade and wholesale trade, all co-exist. While the major increase in silk production and trade in 1983 had led the analysts (B. Harriss, 1991; J. Harriss, 1991) to talk about an ongoing process of specialisation, the second decade shows an inversion and Arni confirms a strong trend towards economic diversification over the whole period. So, while silk and retail trade continue to be key activities in the town in the 1990s, they have lost the dominant role they had in the 1980s when it seemed that Arni was about to transform into a 'silk town'.

Diversification appears, then, to be a key feature of Arni's capitalism and it has certainly been so (if to variable degree) since the introduction of the HYVs.

Economic integration

In the capitalist transformation of the economy, the urban and rural factor contributions (capital, labour and commodities) need examining. In the surveys, this was elicited through questions about the origin and destinations of inputs, raw materials, outputs and capital and the origin of the workforce.

Broadly, the sample data confirms the picture emerging from the information on growth and diversification. In relation to the origin of raw materials for small businesses (Table 6.7), the sample data shows that, in the 1990s, local sources and TN cover, respectively, 44 and 40 per cent of the total supply of raw materials. In comparison to the previous periods, this situation represents a major change: in the 1970s, the raw materials were largely provided by local sources (about 70 per cent), while TN and sources external to the state played only a

Table 6.5 Types of firm (number of firms)

	Wholesale	Retail	Workshop/ small scale mfg	Mill/factory	Agent	Service
Business 1993						
1 Rice and paddy	2	1	0	4	0	0
2 Agricultural products	4	1	0	3	1	0
3 Foods	5	47	0	1	0	1
4 Farm inputs	2	5	0	2	0	1
5 Silk products	2	0	0	5	0	1
6 General merchants	4	50	1	2	0	12
7 Fuel and energy retailers	1	3	0	0	0	0
8 Transport repairs and services	0	4	0	0	0	14
9 Other repairs and services	0	3	1	0	0	6
10 Money and financial services	0	0	0	0	0	9
Total	20	114	2	17	1	43
Business 1983						
1 Rice and paddy	2	0	0	4	2	0
2 Agricultural products	0	0	0	2	0	0
3 Foods	6	14	4	1	0	3
4 Farm inputs	2	3	2	0	1	0
5 Silk products	0	0	15	8	0	0
6 General merchants	3	27	8	0	1	7
7 Fuel and energy retailers	1	3	0	0	1	0
8 Transport repairs and services	0	1	0	0	1	4
9 Other repairs and services	0	1	1	0	1	10
10 Money and financial services	1	0	2	0	0	6
Total	15	49	32	15	7	30

Business 1973

1 Rice and paddy	10	5	0	16	4	6
2 Agricultural products	2	0	1	3	0	2
3 Foods	4	11	1	1	0	4
4 Farm inputs	0	3	0	0	0	0
5 Silk products	0	1	8	5	0	5
6 General merchants	7	21	7	0	1	5
7 Fuel and energy retailers	2	5	0	0	2	0
8 Transport repairs and services	0	1	0	0	0	4
9 Other repairs and services	0	0	2	0	0	15
10 Money and financial services	0	1	0	0	0	6
Total	25	48	19	25	7	47

Source: Sample data (Arni surveys – 1993, 1983, 1973).

Table 6.6 Diversification of economic activity (small and big businesses according to their investment behaviour, %)

	No diversification (a)	Same sector (b)	Different sector (c)	(b)/(b + c)
Business 1993				
1 Rice and paddy	16.7	66.7	16.7	80.0
2 Agricultural products	42.9	14.3	42.9	25.0
3 Foods	66.0	14.0	20.0	41.2
4 Farm inputs	77.8	11.1	11.1	50.0
5 Silk products	20.0	40.0	40.0	50.0
6 General merchants	77.9	5.9	16.2	26.7
7 Fuel and energy retailers	25.0	25.0	50.0	33.3
8 Transport repairs and services	43.8	18.8	37.5	33.3
9 Other repairs and services	72.0	12.0	16.0	42.9
10 Money and financial services	40.0	20.0	40.0	33.3
Total	64.0	14.0	22.0	38.9
Business 1983				
1 Rice and paddy	12.5	62.5	25.0	71.4
2 Agricultural products	0.0	0.0	100.0	0.0
3 Foods	59.1	0.0	40.9	0.0
4 Farm inputs	40.0	20.0	40.0	33.3
5 Silk products	52.2	4.3	43.5	9.1
6 General merchants	36.8	28.9	34.2	45.8
7 Fuel and energy retailers	40.0	20.0	40.0	33.3
8 Transport repairs and services	50.0	0.0	50.0	0.0
9 Other repairs and services	50.0	25.0	25.0	50.0
10 Money and financial services	0.0	50.0	50.0	50.0
Total	41.7	19.7	38.6	33.8

Business 1973

1 Rice and paddy	68.2	0.0	31.8	0.0
2 Agricultural products	25.0	0.0	75.0	0.0
3 Foods	35.7	7.1	57.1	11.1
4 Farm inputs	33.3	0.0	66.7	0.0
5 Silk products	69.2	7.7	23.1	25.0
6 General merchants	62.5	3.1	34.4	8.3
7 Fuel and energy retailers	0.0	0.0	100.0	0.0
8 Transport repairs and services	100.0	0.0	0.0	...
9 Other repairs and services	53.3	13.3	33.3	28.6
10 Money and financial services	50.0	16.7	33.3	33.3
Total	56.3	5.0	38.7	11.5

Source: Sample data (Arni surveys – 1993, 1983, 1973).

Table 6.7 Origin of raw materials (small businesses) (% distribution of average quantities in Rs 1993)

	Local			TN	Out of TN	Total	'000 Rs
	Total	Arni	Villages				
Business 1993							
1 Rice and paddy	77.3	37.3	20.7	22.7	0.0	100.0	3,258
2 Agricultural products	100.0	10.3	89.0	0.0	0.0	100.0	3,983
3 Foods	56.8	28.5	7.4	36.2	7.1	100.0	491
4 Farm inputs	51.9	8.9	19.1	47.9	0.2	100.0	689
5 Silk products	0.0	0.0	0.0	30.2	69.8	100.0	7,035
6 General merchants	32.1	5.4	4.2	63.2	4.7	100.0	1,002
7 Fuel and energy retailers	24.5	0.4	24.1	75.5	0.0	100.0	1,404
8 Transport repairs and services	22.3	9.3	0.0	24.7	53.0	100.0	1,115
9 Other repairs and services	52.2	25.8	4.4	47.8	0.0	100.0	826
10 Money and financial services	85.8	22.4	63.3	14.2	0.0	100.0	3,448
Average total value	44.0	13.1	16.2	40.0	16.0	100.0	1,168
Business 1983							
1 Rice and paddy	48.5	3.2	40.2	25.4	26.1	100.0	8,929
2 Agricultural products	100.0	25.7	73.3	0.0	0.0	100.0	69
3 Foods	63.1	4.5	3.7	23.5	13.4	100.0	936
4 Farm inputs	36.7	5.1	0.5	39.9	23.4	100.0	1,750
5 Silk products	10.1	4.8	3.1	29.9	60.0	100.0	2,505
6 General merchants	22.1	4.4	0.3	63.6	14.3	100.0	421
7 Fuel and energy retailers	1.9	0.0	1.9	5.4	92.6	100.0	909
8 Transport repairs and services	16.4	10.3	0.0	83.6	0.0	100.0	38
9 Other repairs and services	91.9	46.0	20.9	8.1	0.0	100.0	253
10 Money and financial services	100.0	18.7	81.0	0.0	0.0	100.0	189
Average total value	35.3	4.8	18.1	29.7	35.0	100.0	1,488
Business 1973							
1 Rice and paddy	90.6	32.6	42.3	9.4	0.0	100.0	2,565
2 Agricultural products	100.0	64.6	35.4	0.0	0.0	100.0	992
3 Foods	86.7	35.0	24.1	13.3	0.0	100.0	701
4 Farm inputs	8.7	3.9	4.0	91.3	0.0	100.0	1,578
5 Silk products	15.4	8.3	0.0	12.0	72.6	100.0	2,730
6 General merchants	99.7	47.1	42.1	0.1	0.1	100.0	326
7 Fuel and energy retailers	6.9	0.2	1.5	51.9	41.2	100.0	339
8 Transport repairs and services	100.0	52.6	0.0	0.0	0.0	100.0	26
9 Other repairs and services	92.3	28.4	0.0	7.7	0.0	100.0	166
10 Money and financial services	100.0	23.0	75.4	0.0	0.0	100.0	133
Average total value	69.5	22.9	24.2	17.3	13.2	100.0	1,062

Source: Sample data (Arni surveys – 1993, 1983, 1973).

residual role; and in the 1980s, local sources and sources external to TN were almost equivalent (35 per cent). It is interesting to note that in the 1990s *agricultural products, money and financial services,* and *rice and paddy* firms purchased their raw material from local sources, while *general merchants, farm inputs* and *other repairs and services* largely depended on non-local sources within the state, and *silk products* and *transport repairs and services* on sources located outside TN. Also the increasing role played by villages as sources of raw materials over the years is worth noting.

Turning to the destination of goods for small businesses (Table 6.8), in the 1990s over 60 per cent of the commodities were destined for the local area

Table 6.8 Destination of goods (small businesses) (% distribution of average quantities in Rs 1993)

	Local			TN	Out of TN	Total	'000 Rs
	Total	Arni	Villages				
Business 1993							
1 Rice and paddy	14.0	0.5	3.2	32.4	53.6	100.0	4,690
2 Agricultural products	25.6	5.5	9.5	60.1	14.4	100.0	3,672
3 Foods	100.0	56.3	43.4	0.0	0.0	100.0	586
4 Farm inputs	97.4	46.6	48.7	2.6	0.0	100.0	873
5 Silk products	13.1	0.0	0.0	44.0	42.9	100.0	19,128
6 General merchants	98.9	42.5	56.4	0.0	1.1	100.0	1,119
7 Fuel and energy retailers	100.0	50.1	34.8	0.0	0.0	100.0	1,657
8 Transport repairs and services	61.1	26.8	32.4	38.3	0.6	100.0	1,488
9 Other repairs and services	85.2	28.8	55.3	14.4	0.4	100.0	793
10 Money and financial services	94.6	45.0	31.0	1.3	4.2	100.0	1,445
Average total value	60.2	24.9	28.7	22.4	17.4	100.0	1,547
Business 1983							
1 Rice and paddy	15.7	13.0	0.0	63.0	21.4	100.0	11,098
2 Agricultural products	100.0	70.0	30.0	0.0	0.0	100.0	114
3 Foods	100.0	71.8	28.2	0.0	0.0	100.0	1,077
4 Farm inputs	100.0	32.8	67.2	0.0	0.0	100.0	1,853
5 Silk products	7.3	7.3	0.0	59.3	33.4	100.0	3,623
6 General merchants	100.0	33.6	66.0	0.0	0.0	100.0	488
7 Fuel and energy retailers	100.0	41.6	44.1	0.0	0.0	100.0	1,020
8 Transport repairs and services	58.4	12.3	33.0	41.6	0.0	100.0	103
9 Other repairs and services	87.5	39.6	47.8	12.5	0.0	100.0	350
10 Money and financial services	100.0	28.9	71.1	0.0	0.0	100.0	245
Average total value	22.7	15.9	5.8	52.4	24.9	100.0	2,499
Business 1973							
1 Rice and paddy	52.7	24.3	10.8	47.3	0.0	100.0	2,782
2 Agricultural products	33.1	0.0	0.0	66.9	0.0	100.0	1,226
3 Foods	100.0	55.5	44.5	0.0	0.0	100.0	416
4 Farm inputs	100.0	0.6	89.0	0.0	0.0	100.0	1,700
5 Silk products	3.1	3.1	0.0	32.3	64.6	100.0	1,831
6 General merchants	99.7	47.1	42.1	0.1	0.1	100.0	326
7 Fuel and energy retailers	100.0	59.1	12.3	0.0	0.0	100.0	528
8 Transport repairs and services	71.4	21.0	47.8	24.6	4.0	100.0	46
9 Other repairs and services	100.0	51.0	48.8	0.0	0.0	100.0	203
10 Money and financial services	100.0	23.0	75.5	0.0	0.0	100.0	177
Average total value	55.5	22.9	17.8	31.0	13.5	100.0	1,002

Source: Sample data (Arni surveys – 1993, 1983, 1973).

(about 50 per cent of which goes to the villages). In the 1970s the situation was similar, while in the 1980s other destinations were predominant. *Foods* and *fuel and energy retailers* provide interesting cases, as they continue, across the decades, to sell their products entirely locally. A similar situation is observed for *farm inputs*, *general merchants*, and *money and financial services*, which keep to local destinations for the vast majority of their products. By contrast, the case of *silk products* and *rice and paddy* is markedly different, owing to the significant percentage of goods directed towards destinations outside TN.

Despite the scarce information on big businesses, the sample data shows that significant differences among sectors exist in relation to the origin of raw materials (Table 6.9). Local sources prevail for *agricultural products* in 1993, for *money and financial services* in 1983, and for *foods* and *general merchants* in 1973. By contrast, in 1993 *silk products* and *general merchants* depend on sources outside TN, while *general merchants*, *fuel and energy retailers*, and partly also *farm inputs* depend on other sources in TN. Regarding the destination of goods (Table 6.10), in 1993 *rice and paddy, agricultural products* and partly also *silk products* sell their goods to other markets in TN, while *foods, farm inputs, general merchants, fuel and energy retailers*, and *transport repairs and services* depend entirely on local markets. It is worth noting, however, that in 1993 over 85 per cent of the value of the goods produced by big businesses is sold outside the local area. By contrast, the few data for 1983 and 1973 describe a different situation, showing that also for the big businesses the major part of the production goes to local markets and only in part to other TN markets.

Summarising, the sample data suggests an increasing distinction between small businesses and big businesses in their pattern of economic integration. While the former confirm the importance of local sources and local destinations, the latter show a more open pattern of economic integration, in which distant sources and destinations are systematically preferred, in particular in 1993. This distinction goes together with different patterns of market integration for sectors: while few sectors – for instance *silk* and *rice and paddy* – largely purchase raw materials from distant sources and produce for distant markets, the majority of the remaining sectors show a local form of market integration.

Another aspect relevant to the local/global integration of Arni's business economy is the source of capital and labour (Tables 6.11 and 6.12). The main geographical origin of the capital invested in Arni is from within the town itself, while only a small percentage comes from the surrounding district and the contribution from Tamil Nadu and from other Indian states is negligible. This situation is the result of two opposite trends: the increasing financial interactions of the town and the decreasing financial linkages with the district and with TN. In relation to socio-economic source, there is a wide diversification across the decades. The main sources of capital are from the investor's family and own savings from businesses, which also show an increasing trend over the years. Also the role of the finance sector is significant (but decreasing over the period), while less important (and decreasing) is the financing from farm and non-farm activities.

Table 6.9 Origin of raw materials (big businesses) (% distribution of average quantities in Rs 1993)

	Local			TN	Out of TN	Total	'000 Rs
	Total	Arni	Villages				
Business 1993							
1 Rice and paddy	0.0	0.0	0.0	50.1	49.9	100.0	29,952
2 Agricultural products	96.9	0.0	96.9	0.0	3.1	100.0	650,826
3 Foods	2.0	0.0	2.0	13.0	85.0	100.0	9,352,885
4 Farm inputs	31.1	0.0	28.5	68.9	0.0	100.0	29,711
5 Silk products	0.0	0.0	0.0	0.0	100.0	100.0	30,000
6 General merchants	0.0	0.0	0.0	100.0	0.0	100.0	63,800
7 Fuel and energy retailers	0.0	0.0	0.0	100.0	0.0	100.0	29,443
8 Transport repairs and services	...	...	...	...	...	...	0
9 Other repairs and services	...	...	...	...	...	...	0
10 Money and financial services	...	...	...	...	...	...	0
Average total value	85.9	0.0	85.9	8.8	5.3	100.0	184,870
Business 1983							
1 Rice and paddy	...	...	...	...	...	...	0
2 Agricultural products	...	...	...	...	...	...	0
3 Foods	...	...	...	...	...	...	0
4 Farm inputs	...	...	...	...	...	...	0
5 Silk products	...	...	...	...	...	...	0
6 General merchants	33.7	0.0	0.0	16.6	49.7	100.0	11,748
7 Fuel and energy retailers	0.0	0.0	0.0	100.0	0.0	100.0	25,109
8 Transport repairs and services	...	...	...	...	...	...	0
9 Other repairs and services	...	...	...	...	...	...	0
10 Money and financial services	100.0	100.0	0.0	0.0	0.0	100.0	17,780
Average total value	38.7	26.8	0.0	43.7	17.6	100.0	16,596
Business 1973							
1 Rice and paddy	...	...	...	...	...	...	0
2 Agricultural products	...	...	...	...	...	...	0
3 Foods	100.0	60.0	40.0	0.0	0.0	100.0	4,737
4 Farm inputs	...	...	...	...	...	...	0
5 Silk products	...	...	...	...	...	...	0
6 General merchants	75.0	5.0	0.0	25.0	0.0	100.0	10,437
7 Fuel and energy retailers	...	...	...	...	...	...	0
8 Transport repairs and services	...	...	...	...	...	...	0
9 Other repairs and services	...	...	...	...	...	...	0
10 Money and financial services	...	...	...	...	...	...	0
Average total value	82.8	22.2	12.5	17.2	0.0	100.0	7,587

Source: Sample data (Arni surveys – 1993, 1983, 1973).

The sample information on the origin of the labour force is rather limited, being focused only on regular workers, which, as we have seen in Chapter 3, are a very limited proportion of the workforce in Provincial India. There is a clear reduction of the workforce coming from the town, while the number of workers from the villages remains substantially stable over the years. The

Table 6.10 Destination of goods (big businesses) (% distribution of average quantities in Rs 1993)

	Local			TN	Out of TN	Total	'000 Rs
	Total	Arni	Villages				
1993							
1 Rice and paddy	0.0	0.0	0.0	100.0	0.0	100.0	33,875
2 Agricultural products	1.8	0.3	0.0	97.1	1.1	100.0	665,220
3 Foods	100.0	25.0	0.0	0.0	0.0	100.0	15,100
4 Farm inputs	100.0	48.0	52.0	0.0	0.0	100.0	30,753
5 Silk products	0.0	0.0	0.0	60.0	40.0	100.0	120,000
6 General merchants	100.0	10.3	69.1	0.0	0.0	100.0	68,000
7 Fuel and energy retailers	100.0	100.0	0.0	0.0	0.0	100.0	30,000
8 Transport repairs and services	...	...	...	...	...	...	0
9 Other repairs and services	...	...	...	...	...	...	0
10 Money and financial services	...	...	...	...	...	...	0
Average total value	10.3	3.6	3.9	85.9	3.9	100.0	203,521
Business 1983							
1 Rice and paddy	...	...	...	...	...	...	0
2 Agricultural products	...	...	...	...	...	...	0
3 Foods	...	...	...	...	...	...	0
4 Farm inputs	...	...	...	...	...	...	0
5 Silk products	...	...	...	...	...	...	0
6 General merchants	100.0	30.9	21.5	0.0	0.0	100.0	15,543
7 Fuel and energy retailers	90.0	60.0	20.0	10.0	0.0	100.0	25,520
8 Transport repairs and services	...	...	...	...	...	...	0
9 Other repairs and services	...	...	...	...	...	...	0
10 Money and financial services	100.0	50.0	0.0	0.0	0.0	100.0	21,120
Average total value	96.7	45.7	15.2	3.3	0.0	100.0	19,432
Business							
1 Rice and paddy	...	...	...	...	...	...	0
2 Agricultural products	...	...	...	...	...	...	0
3 Foods	100.0	100.0	0.0	0.0	0.0	100.0	5,964
4 Farm inputs	...	...	...	...	...	...	0
5 Silk products	...	...	...	...	...	...	0
6 General merchants	100.0	75.0	25.0	0.0	0.0	100.0	11,729
7 Fuel and energy retailers	...	...	...	...	...	...	0
8 Transport repairs and services	...	...	...	...	...	...	0
9 Other repairs and services	...	...	...	...	...	...	0
10 Money and financial services	...	...	...	...	...	...	0
Average total value	100.0	83.4	16.6	0.0	0.0	100.0	8,847

Source: Sample data (Arni surveys – 1993, 1983, 1973).

contribution of migrant labourers is negligible. Unfortunately, owing to the scarcity of the data (and to its uncertain quality) comments on specific sectors are hardly possible, and we are left without reliable information on the origin of the workforce.

Table 6.11 Origin of capital (% distribution of answers by locality and type of financing)

	1993	*1983*	*1973*
Geographical origin			
Arni	83.1	73.3	60.0
District	10.2	22.5	30.8
TN	3.4	1.7	7.5
Other states	3.4	2.5	1.7
Total	100.0	100.0	100.0
Types of financing			
Agricultural activities	6.6	13.1	8.8
Non-agricultural activities	4.2	9.2	8.1
Family assets	42.5	35.2	34.5
Savings	25.9	23.5	22.3
Financial sector	20.8	19.0	26.4
Total	100.0	100.0	100.0

Source: Arni surveys (1973, 1983, 1993).

Note
Agricultural activities = agriculture, agricultural trade; Non-agricultural activities = non-farm production, non-agricultural trade, artisan work; Savings = saving wage, unspecified savings, golden
handshake; Family assets = sale of property, rents, family inheritance, dowry; Financial sector =
loans, finance business, government.

Socio-economic organisation

A major aspect of the capitalist transformation is the change in the relationships
between economic structure and social structure. The surveys contained several
questions on the ownership of the firms, the control of caste groups over activities, and the nature of employment arrangements.

Table 6.13 presents the available information on the ownership of businesses.
The data seems to be quite reliable and consistent across the reference years. In
1993 the data shows a clear distribution biased towards individually and jointly/
family owned firms, while very few firms owned by companies, cooperatives,
and local branches of firms situated outside the town are reported. Virtually no
family private companies are observed. The latter is a major change in relation
to 1983 and, in particular, to 1973, when the number of individually owned firms
and family partnership was much lower in favour of a significant number of
family private companies (respectively 11 and 30).

We turn now to caste structure as it emerges from Arni's business economy.
Information on caste is presented in Tables 6.15 (a, b) for small business and
6.16 (a, b) for big businesses. Arni castes have been classified into four major
groups: forward castes (FCs), backward castes (BCs), most backward castes
(MBCs), and scheduled castes (SCs) (see Table 6.14).[11] The data on caste seems
to be very reliable and covers a high proportion of total sample gross output (see
Table 6.3).

Table 6.12 Home location of regular workers (number of workers)

	Town	Villages	Migrant
Business 1993			
1 Rice and paddy	3	1	0
2 Agricultural products	4	7	0
3 Foods	16	12	1
4 Farm inputs	6	4	0
5 Silk products	0	0	0
6 General merchants	17	16	2
7 Fuel and energy retailers	4	0	0
8 Transport repairs and services	12	4	0
9 Other repairs and services	7	10	0
10 Money and financial services	0	0	0
Total	69	54	3
Business 1983			
1 Rice and paddy	14	7	0
2 Agricultural products	2	2	0
3 Foods	24	11	0
4 Farm inputs	5	6	1
5 Silk products	34	13	0
6 General merchants	29	10	0
7 Fuel and energy retailers	9	0	0
8 Transport repairs and services	5	1	0
9 Other repairs and services	19	5	0
10 Money and financial services	1	2	0
Total	142	57	1
Business 1973			
1 Rice and paddy	30	3	0
2 Agricultural products	9	0	0
3 Foods	10	7	3
4 Farm inputs	3	2	0
5 Silk products	22	16	0
6 General merchants	27	7	3
7 Fuel and energy retailers	3	1	0
8 Transport repairs and services	5	4	0
9 Other repairs and services	13	5	4
10 Money and financial services	4	2	0
Total	126	47	10

Source: Sample data (Arni surveys – 1993, 1983, 1973).

Focusing on small businesses, in 1993 MBCs control over 50 per cent of the sample total output, while the remaining part is controlled by FCs (over 20 per cent), SCs (18 per cent) and finally by BCs for only 10 per cent. Some sectors are clearly in the hand of specific caste groups. FCs largely control *rice and paddy, silk products* and *money and financial services*; BCs control almost entirely *agricultural products*; MBCs control entirely *fuel and energy retailers* and *transport repairs and services,* and largely *foods* and *farm inputs,* and

Table 6.13 Businesses according to ownership (number)

	Individually owned	Jointly owned	Family partnership	Family private company	Private non-family company	Public company	Local branch	Coop	Other
Business 1993									
1 Rice and paddy	3		2						
2 Agricultural products	2		5						
3 Foods	37	1	11						
4 Farm inputs	7		2						
5 Silk products		3	1						
6 General merchants	47	2	15				1		
7 Fuel and energy retailers	2		1						
8 Transport repairs and services	11	1	4						
9 Other repairs and services	16	1	8				1		
10 Money and financial services	1		3						1
Total	126	8	52	0	0	0	2	0	1
Business 1983									
1 Rice and paddy	3	1	4						
2 Agricultural products	1		1						
3 Foods	13		5	3				1	
4 Farm inputs	3		2						
5 Silk products	14		2	2	2			3	
6 General merchants	24	3	7	3				1	
7 Fuel and energy retailers	4		1						
8 Transport repairs and services	3	1		2					
9 Other repairs and services	8		2	1	1				
10 Money and financial services	2	1	3						
Total	75	6	27	11	3	0	0	5	0

continued

Table 6.13 Continued

	Individually owned	Jointly owned	Family partnership	Family private company	Private non-family company	Public company	Local branch	Coop	Other
Business 1973									
1 Rice and paddy	14		4	1	2				
2 Agricultural products	3			1					
3 Foods	6			5			1	2	
4 Farm inputs	2			1					
5 Silk products	6	2	1	6					
6 General merchants	15		2	9	1		2	1	
7 Fuel and energy retailers	2		2	1					
8 Transport repairs and services	4			1					
9 Other repairs and services	11		1	3					
10 Money and financial services	4			2					
Total	67	2	10	30	3	0	3	3	0

Source: Sample data (Ami's surveys – 1993, 1983, 1973).

Table 6.14 Caste codes according to Arni caste hierarchy

Brahmin (Iyer, Iyengar, Rao)	**Forward castes**
Nair	
Marathi	
Nainar/Jain	
Viswakarma/Achari/Aachary (sometimes called Viswa Brahmin)	
Karuneekar	
Marwari	
Marathi	
Chettiyar/Veerasaiva/Kannara Veera Saiva/Channiya Chettiar	
Senai Udaiyar	
Reddiyar	**Backward castes**
Giramani	
Beri Chettiar	
Saurashtra	
Devar	
Muslim	
Udayar (cobbler)/Backward Caste	
Naidu	
Agamundaiya Mudaliar (Tvam)	
Vaaniya Chettiar	
Senguntha Vellalar/Mudaliar/Devanga Chettiar	
Yadava/Pillai	**Most backward**
Devadasi	**castes**
Naicker/Vanniya/Gounder	
Upparavar Chettiar	
Boyar (Boer)	
Nadar/Natar (fishermen and medicines)	
Pandithar/Navithar/Ammatan/Barber	
Dhobi/Vannan	
Ooddar (Oddar)	
Pandaram/Poojati	**Scheduled castes**
Kosavar/Kuzavar/Valluvar/Kanakkar/Odeyar (potter)	**and tribes**
Irular/Vettai Karan	
Christian (SC)	
SCS Adhidravidas/Harijans/Parayans	
Arundathiyar/Chakkliyan (Cobblers)	

contribute to the *rice and paddy* and *silk* economies. By contrast, SCs exert control only over the *general merchants* sector, covering over 70 per cent of the sector's gross output.

The 1993 situation is the outcome of a major process of change, which consists of a substantial contraction, both in the first and in the second decade, of the control on the sample economy by MBCs in favour of FCs and SCs. In 1973 MBCs controlled nearly 80 per cent of the total sample gross output, while both FCs and BCs were around 10 per cent and SCs were negligible. The control by MBCs was almost complete in several sectors (*rice and paddy, agricultural products, foods,* and *farm inputs*) with 100 per cent of total sector gross output,

Table 6.15a Small businesses: % distribution of gross output by caste group

	FCs	BCs	MBCs	SCs	Total	'000 Rs
Business 1993						
1 Rice and paddy	52.6	0.0	47.4	0.0	100.0	23,449
2 Agricultural products	2.7	97.3	0.0	0.0	100.0	18,362
3 Foods	3.8	13.3	74.7	8.1	100.0	28,228
4 Farm inputs	17.6	0.0	82.4	0.0	100.0	6,980
5 Silk products	47.1	0.0	52.9	0.0	100.0	76,510
6 General merchants	1.1	7.3	21.3	70.3	100.0	74,109
7 Fuel and energy retailers	0.0	0.0	100.0	0.0	100.0	4,971
8 Transport repairs and services	0.0	0.2	99.8	0.1	100.0	35,570
9 Other repairs and services	12.6	18.9	67.6	0.9	100.0	16,652
10 Money and financial services	62.2	0.0	37.8	0.0	100.0	12,524
Total	20.8	10.2	50.7	18.4	100.0	297,355
Business 1983						
1 Rice and paddy	0.0	13.2	86.8	0.0	100.0	99,880
2 Agricultural products	0.0	0.0	100.0	0.0	100.0	227
3 Foods	1.5	27.1	71.4	0.0	100.0	23,702
4 Farm inputs	0.0	3.9	96.1	0.0	100.0	9,267
5 Silk products	46.3	46.3	7.4	0.1	100.0	17,142
6 General merchants	1.0	24.2	72.8	2.0	100.0	16,228
7 Fuel and energy retailers	0.0	0.0	98.3	1.7	100.0	4,081
8 Transport repairs and services	4.7	0.0	81.3	14.0	100.0	566
9 Other repairs and services	15.8	61.6	22.6	0.0	100.0	4,195
10 Money and financial services	51.2	29.9	18.8	0.0	100.0	1,226
Total	5.5	19.7	74.5	0.3	100.0	176,513
Business 1973						
1 Rice and paddy	0.0	0.0	100.0	0.0	100.0	53,284
2 Agricultural products	0.0	0.0	100.0	0.0	100.0	3,678
3 Foods	1.5	2.8	95.6	0.0	100.0	11,551
4 Farm inputs	0.0	0.0	100.0	0.0	100.0	5,101
5 Silk products	43.6	21.9	34.5	0.0	100.0	23,803
6 General merchants	3.0	43.0	50.2	3.8	100.0	10,126
7 Fuel and energy retailers	0.0	0.0	100.0	0.0	100.0	2,639
8 Transport repairs and services	0.0	0.0	77.3	22.7	100.0	227
9 Other repairs and services	10.8	71.7	17.4	0.0	100.0	3,086
10 Money and financial services	25.3	43.7	31.1	0.0	100.0	1,062
Total	10.0	11.0	78.6	0.4	100.0	114,558

Source: Sample data (Arni's surveys – 1993, 1983, 1973).

Notes
Forward castes = FCs; backward castes = BCs; most backward castes = MBCs; scheduled castes and tribes = SCs.

and was over 75 per cent for *transport repairs and services*. In 1983 MBCs reduced their economic importance in relative terms, moving from nearly 80 per cent of the total sample gross output to 74 per cent in favour of BCs (which controlled about 20 per cent). In front of a generalised contraction for all remaining sectors, only *agricultural products* remained entirely in the hand of MBCs.

Table 6.15b Diversification of economic activities by caste (% distribution of gross output for small businesses)

	FCs	BCs	MBCs	SCs
Business 1993				
1 Rice and paddy	20.0	0.0	7.4	0.0
2 Agricultural products	0.8	59.0	0.0	0.0
3 Foods	1.7	12.4	14.0	4.2
4 Farm inputs	2.0	0.0	3.8	0.0
5 Silk products	58.2	0.0	26.9	0.0
6 General merchants	1.3	18.0	10.5	95.5
7 Fuel and energy retailers	0.0	0.0	3.3	0.0
8 Transport repairs and services	0.0	0.2	23.6	0.0
9 Other repairs and services	3.4	10.4	7.5	0.3
10 Money and financial services	12.6	0.0	3.1	0.0
Total	100.0	100.0	100.0	100.0
Gross output ('000 Rs)	61,817	31,281	150,681	50,577
Business 1983				
1 Rice and paddy	0.0	37.9	65.9	0.0
2 Agricultural products	0.0	0.0	0.2	0.0
3 Foods	3.7	18.5	12.9	0.0
4 Farm inputs	0.0	1.0	6.8	0.0
5 Silk products	81.2	22.8	1.0	2.3
6 General merchants	1.6	11.3	9.0	67.0
7 Fuel and energy retailers	0.0	0.0	3.1	14.2
8 Transport repairs and services	0.3	0.0	0.4	16.5
9 Other repairs and services	6.8	7.4	0.7	0.0
10 Money and financial services	6.4	1.1	0.2	0.0
Total	100.0	100.0	100.0	100.0
Gross output ('000 Rs)	9,772	34,757	131,505	480
Business 1973				
1 Rice and paddy	0.0	0.0	59.1	0.0
2 Agricultural products	0.0	0.0	4.1	0.0
3 Foods	1.6	2.6	12.3	0.0
4 Farm inputs	0.0	0.0	5.7	0.0
5 Silk products	90.5	41.5	9.1	0.0
6 General merchants	2.7	34.6	5.6	88.1
7 Fuel and energy retailers	0.0	0.0	2.9	0.0
8 Transport repairs and services	0.0	0.0	0.2	11.9
9 Other repairs and services	2.9	17.6	0.6	0.0
10 Money and financial services	2.3	3.7	0.4	0.0
Total	100.0	100.0	100.0	100.0
Gross output ('000 Rs)	11,452	12,583	90,090	433

Source: Sample data (Arni's surveys – 1993, 1983, 1973).

Note
See Table 6.15a.

Table 6.15b provides information on the 'specialisation' of caste groups in specific sectors. In 1993, SCs almost entirely 'specialise' in being *general merchants*, FCs and BCs are mainly involved, respectively, in *rice and paddy* and in *silk products*, and in *agricultural products*, and MBCs show a wide diversification amongst sectors. Yet, the picture is not uniform across the decades. In 1973, FCs showed a major 'specialisation' in *silk products*, which showed a slight decrease in 1983 (from 90 per cent of the gross output of the sector to 80 per cent). SCs showed a similar pattern, confirming their 'specialisation' in being *general merchants* (with a contraction from nearly 90 per cent in 1973 to nearly 70 per cent in 1983). By contrast, BCs and MBCs show a more diversified pattern. The former further reduced their limited 'specialisation' on *silk products* and *general merchants* in 1983, while the latter showed an initial process of 'specialisation' in *rice and paddy* from 1973 to 1983. However, the sample data for 1993 clearly suggest an inversion of the trend.

Owing to the scarce information, the analysis of big businesses does not add much to our knowledge about the caste structure of Arni's business economy. It can only be said that in 1993 MBCs dominate *fuel and energy retailers* and partly also *general merchants* (sharing the role with BCs), and that they exert a strong control over several sectors across the decades. However, it is worth noting how the data on big firms confirm and emphasise the dominant role of MBCs in Arni's economy in all reference years.

The Arni surveys also provide data on employment arrangements (Table 6.17). The key distinction is between regular labour (both family and non-family) and casual labour (male and female) and the average units of labour are given for respondent firms according to different types of employment arrangements.

The quality (and the reliability) of the available information on labour seems to be rather low, largely due to the small number of full answers. Moreover, there is a major discrepancy between the number of firms declaring regular labour and casual labour. Owing to the facts that in Provincial India a large proportion of labour is casual and that there are no reasons why Arni should be an exception in this respect, the data in Table 6.17 is difficult to analyse and to interpret. We can only focus on non-casual labour, observing that a widespread use of family labour is reported in all three surveys, with a reduction over time in the use of regular non-family labour in the case of *silk products*, *foods*, and *fuel and energy*. This change confirms the increase in the dimension of the businesses already pointed out.

4 On Arni's variety of capitalism

The Arni surveys provide detailed and abundant data on the town's capitalist change after the GR. In this chapter, this data has been selected and elaborated in order to assess whether the processes at work in Provincial India at large – explored in detail in Chapter 3 – have been at work also in the town.

Table 6.16a Big businesses: % distribution of gross output by caste group

	FCs	BCs	MBCs	SCs	Total	'000 Rs
Business 1993						
1 Rice and paddy	0.0	0.0	100.0	0.0	100.0	33,875
2 Agricultural products	0.0	0.0	100.0	0.0	100.0	1,280,440
3 Foods	0.0	100.0	0.0	0.0	100.0	15,100
4 Farm inputs	0.0	0.0	100.0	0.0	100.0	30,753
5 Silk products	0.0	0.0	100.0	0.0	100.0	120,000
6 General merchants	0.0	0.0	100.0	0.0	100.0	70,000
7 Fuel and energy retailers	0.0	0.0	100.0	0.0	100.0	30,000
8 Transport repairs and services	...	...	...	...	...	0
9 Other repairs and services	...	...	...	...	...	0
10 Money and financial services	...	...	...	...	...	0
Total	0.0	14.3	85.7	0.0	100.0	1,580,168
Business 1983						
1 Rice and paddy	...	...	...	...	...	0
2 Agricultural products	...	...	...	...	...	0
3 Foods	...	...	...	...	...	0
4 Farm inputs	...	...	...	...	...	0
5 Silk products	...	...	...	...	...	0
6 General merchants	0.0	50.0	50.0	0.0	100.0	27,390
7 Fuel and energy retailers	0.0	0.0	100.0	0.0	100.0	25,520
8 Transport repairs and services	...	...	...	...	...	0
9 Other repairs and services	...	...	...	...	...	0
10 Money and financial services	100.0	0.0	0.0	0.0	100.0	21,120
Total	25.0	25.0	50.0	0.0	100.0	74,030
Business 1973						
1 Rice and paddy	...	...	...	...	...	0
2 Agricultural products	...	...	...	...	...	0
3 Foods	0.0	0.0	100.0	0.0	100.0	5,964
4 Farm inputs	...	...	...	...	...	0
5 Silk products	...	...	...	...	...	0
6 General merchants	0.0	0.0	100.0	0.0	100.0	11,729
7 Fuel and energy retailers	...	...	...	...	...	0
8 Transport repairs and services	...	...	...	...	...	0
9 Other repairs and services	...	...	...	...	...	0
10 Money and financial services	...	...	...	...	...	0
Total	0.0	0.0	100.0	0.0	100.0	17,693

Source: Sample data (Arni's surveys – 1993, 1983, 1973).

Note
See Table 6.15a.

Table 6.16b Diversification of economic activities by caste (% distribution of gross output for big businesses)

	FCs	BCs	MBCs	SCs
Business 1993				
1 Rice and paddy	...	0.0	2.2	...
2 Agricultural products	...	0.0	81.8	...
3 Foods	...	100.0	0.0	...
4 Farm inputs	...	0.0	2.0	...
5 Silk products	...	0.0	7.7	...
6 General merchants	...	0.0	4.5	...
7 Fuel and energy retailers	...	0.0	1.9	...
8 Transport repairs and services	...	0.0	0.0	...
9 Other repairs and services	...	0.0	0.0	...
10 Money and financial services	...	0.0	0.0	...
Gross output ('000 Rs)	...	15,100	1,565,068	...
Total	...	100.0	100.0	...
Business 1983				
1 Rice and paddy	0.0	0.0	0.0	...
2 Agricultural products	0.0	0.0	0.0	...
3 Foods	0.0	0.0	0.0	...
4 Farm inputs	0.0	0.0	0.0	...
5 Silk products	0.0	0.0	0.0	...
6 General merchants	0.0	100.0	42.0	...
7 Fuel and energy retailers	0.0	0.0	58.0	...
8 Transport repairs and services	0.0	0.0	0.0	...
9 Other repairs and services	0.0	0.0	0.0	...
10 Money and financial services	100.0	0.0	0.0	...
Gross output ('000 Rs)	21,120	8,910	44,000	...
Total	100.0	100.0	100.0	...
Business 1973				
1 Rice and paddy	...	...	0.0	...
2 Agricultural products	...	...	0.0	...
3 Foods	...	...	33.7	...
4 Farm inputs	...	...	0.0	...
5 Silk products	...	...	0.0	...
6 General merchants	...	...	66.3	...
7 Fuel and energy retailers	...	...	0.0	...
8 Transport repairs and services	...	...	0.0	...
9 Other repairs and services	...	...	0.0	...
10 Money and financial services	...	...	0.0	...
Gross output ('000 Rs)	...	...	17,693	...
Total	...	...	100.0	...

Source: Sample data (Arni's surveys – 1993, 1983, 1973).

Note
See Table 6.15a.

Table 6.17 Average units of labour (number)

	Family labour (1)	Regular non-family labour (2)	Casual labourers (F)	Casual labourers (M)
Business 1993				
1 Rice and paddy	1.0	2.4	8.5	5.5
2 Agricultural products	2.4	2.3	14	11.0
3 Foods	3.3	3.6	1.0	1.0
4 Farm inputs	2.1	3.3		
5 Silk products	3.5	34.3	42.5	230.0
6 Other materials	3.7	6.3		2.0
7 Fuel and energy retailers	1.7	6.0		
8 Transport repairs and services	1.7	12.3		2.0
9 Other repairs and services	2.2	6.6		1.0
10 Money and financial services	1.4	2.0		
Business 1983				
1 Rice and paddy	1.8	5.3	16.8	4.0
2 Agricultural products	1.0	3.0	1.0	
3 Foods	1.7	5.1		2.8
4 Farm inputs	1.0	4.0		1.8
5 Silk products	2.5	22.3		1.0
6 Other materials	2.9	2.8		2.3
7 Fuel and energy retailers		3.5		1.0
8 Transport repairs and services	3.7	2.3		9.0
9 Other repairs and services	2.2	3.8		1.0
10 Money and financial services	1.0	1.0		
Business 1973				
1 Rice and paddy	1.1	2.8	5.6	3.2
2 Agricultural products	1.0	4.0	3.7	2.0
3 Foods	1.6	1.9		4.5
4 Farm inputs	1.0	3.5		
5 Silk products	2.3	34.0	12.0	5.0
6 Other materials	2.0	2.1		1.0
7 Fuel and energy retailers	2.3	1.0	1.0	5.7
8 Transport repairs and services	1.0	2.0		3.0
9 Other repairs and services	2.2	5.7		
10 Money and financial services	1.0	1.3		1.0

Source: Sample data (Arni's surveys – 1993, 1983, 1973).

Summarising

The growth of the town emerges very clearly from the sample and census data, which shows that Arni has been expanding in terms of both the number of businesses and their economic dimensions. Yet, the sample data also suggests that Arni's business economy is very *mobile* over time both in economic and in social terms.

The main trait of Arni's economy, as it emerges from the three surveys, is diversification. The growth in the number and size of businesses goes together with the change in the economic weight of sectors and in their mix. In each year, the town seems to 'specialise' in a single sector, however this 'specialisation' changes over the years. It is a sort of 'mobile specialisation'. This leads to a continuing change in the physiognomy of the town, which preserves diversification as its main trait. In Arni, economic diversification means not only the co-existence of different sectors, both in manufacturing and in trade, but also the co-existence of firms engaged in retail and wholesale trade. The growth of retail in particular is noteworthy. The evidence also shows that diversification is an acquired style of behaviour of entrepreneurs who systematically invest in segments of the economy different from the one of their usual activity.

While the data does not provide evidence of a process of concentration, few very big businesses are included in the sample in 1993 (much more than in the previous years). It is interesting to note that the very big firms operate in the most dynamic sectors, i.e. *silk products, other repairs and services, agricultural products, fuel and energy retailers*.

Also the pattern of economic integration of Arni's businesses is very mobile, with a notable increase and change over the years, as shown by the evidence on the origin of raw materials and the destination of goods. Some systematic changes may be observed. First, in broad terms, the importance of local sources is reduced in comparison to sources outside TN (but both TN and the villages slightly increase their role). However, there are interesting exceptions: some sectors – for instance *agricultural products, money*, and *rice and paddy* – purchase their raw materials from local sources, while others – *general merchants, farm inputs*, and *other repairs and services* – address outside sources. Finally, there are systematic differences between small and big businesses (for instance big businesses operating in *rice and paddy* buy their raw materials from distant sources). A similar situation is observed in the case of the destination of goods: some sectors – such as *foods, farm inputs, general merchants, fuel and energy retailers*, and *transport repairs and services* – sell their products to the local area, while others – such as *rice and paddy, agricultural products* and *silk products* – sell a large proportion of their goods to TN and to distant markets. We may conclude that, while the importance of the local area is well established, *different patterns* of local/global integration exist according to sectors and small/big businesses.

While the evidence on labour is largely inconclusive, the sample data shows that local sources are important also for capital: the local area is the most relevant origin of financing of Arni's businesses and it is increasing over the years, and the vast majority of financing comes from the family and from individual/family savings.

The final aspect that I have considered refers to the impact of social structure on economic structure. Here, two major trends need to be emphasised. While, again, the evidence on labour arrangements is inconclusive – owing to the employers' reluctance or inability to provide full answers on casual labour – the available data suggests a relative continuity in the forms of ownership, among which individually owned and family partnership prevail. By contrast, a strong mobility emerges in relation to caste structure. The reliable and abundant evidence suggests that the economic importance of caste groups changes notably over the decades. First, while MBCs are the major caste group in economic terms, their relative importance has decreased since 1973. Second, a process of diversification in the economic importance of caste groups is observed, with the increasing role of SCs as *general merchants*, i.e. small-size retailers, and FCs in *rice and paddy* and *silk products*. Third, while reducing their relative position, MBCs continue to control the bulk of Arni's economy in the major sectors, as shown in particular in the case of big businesses.

Two main conclusions may be drawn from the analysis of the evidence generated by the three surveys.

The importance of being local

The first is that Arni appears to be a 'local economic system', which increasingly relies on the relations occurring within the area constituted by the town itself and by the villages in its hinterland.

Arni's economy is composed of two broad segments, which are strictly integrated among them and show a different pattern of local/global integration. In the first segment production largely relies on local raw materials and sells partly to its hinterland and partly to other centres in TN. The second segment uses raw materials from distant sources and sells to distant markets. Few important sectors – in particular *rice and paddy* and *silk products*, but also *agricultural products* – are integrated into the global economy. They represent the bulk of Arni's economy in terms of gross output. The remaining sectors produce and sell for the town (and also for its local area) and in the town. Also, the sources of the capital are increasingly local.

The economic and spatial integration of Arni with its local areas is widely confirmed by the North Arcot surveys. They show that the villages have undergone a process of change that is closely connected with the one observed in Arni. A major implication has been the increasing urban/rural integration that has affected output and input markets as well as the provision of capital and labour.

As Harriss-White *et al.* (2004: 38–39) point out, economic diversification in Arni's hinterland has been extensive, involving both agriculture and non-farm activities. The development of non-farm activities in the villages has been one of the major trends since the 1980s and has influenced the structure of employment and the distribution of assets. Details of the diversification of agricultural employment for three villages in North Arcot are given by Jayaraj (2004) who estimates that in 1993–1994 around 40 per cent of male workers and 16 per cent of female workers report non-farm activities as their primary occupation (185–186, Tables 4 and 5).

The evidence of the North Arcot surveys also suggests that a part of the workforce in the non-farm economy is engaged in non-farm activities in the villages, while another part has been increasingly providing the workforce for the growth of trade and manufacturing activities in Arni, as well as in other local towns.

Also Srinivasan (2010: 125), on the basis of a detailed field-research on Arni and two villages in its hinterland, reports that a large number of workers commute between the town and the local area, being involved in several types of casual work. This evidence integrates the information on the origin of labour in Arni provided by the survey data.

Another confirmation about the linkages between the socio-economic changes in the town and in the villages – and then also about the increasing significance of local integration – comes from the trends in the demand of consumption and investment goods in the area. In relation to the first aspect, the notable increase in the number of retailers in Arni is matched by the significant increase of expenditures in the villages over the years, which, as Harriss-White *et al.* (2004: 36) show, is often in excess of income.[12] In relation to the second aspect, it is interesting to note that the change of destination of farm inputs in Arni – from destinations external to the area to local destinations – is partly accounted for by the increase in the use of fertilisers in the villages (Harriss-White *et al.*, 2004: 11).

From market town to market town

The second conclusion that may be drawn from the analysis of the sample and census data is that Arni continues to be, in its essence, a market town. Indeed, important activities have been developing in manufacturing – such as *silk products* – and in the processing of agricultural goods – such as *rice and paddy*. However, the evidence does not suggest an ongoing process of industrial specialisation over the years.

Trade continues to be a major activity in town, both as retail and wholesale trade. As we have already pointed out, the two forms of trade correspond to two distinct patterns of economic integration. On the one side, for *foods, farm inputs, general merchants, fuel* and several types of services – and through retailers – Arni is a market town for the local area. On the other side, for *silk products* and *rice and paddy*, and partly also for *agricultural products*, Arni is a market for TN and other Indian states.

While the first two surveys stress the growth of silk manufacturing as a major harbinger of change in the town, providing a longer-term analysis, the 1993 survey shows that there was a clear inversion and in the 1990s Arni was again a market town, with ever-diversifying patterns of integration. Silk sari production was still a leading activity in terms of production and of employment, but by no means the most important one, and the town grew to play a major role as a wholesale centre. This trend is not in contradiction with the importance of retail trade, which increases over time, being fed by the widespread expansion of incomes and consumption in the town and in villages.

In this chapter I have analysed the data on Arni's long-term change, showing that, as in Provincial India as a whole, a strong process of economic diversification has been going on in the town after the GR. As we have seen, the long-term data does not provide adequate information for the analysis of production relations, which is, as the Marxist/Institutionalist framework suggests, a necessary step to understand the nature and working of Arni's capitalism. Therefore, in the lack of suitable information on the town as a whole, I carry on with the assessment by focusing on the silk economy. The silk economy provides an important perspective to explore production relations in Arni: silk has been playing a key role in the town in the post-GR period and continues to be a major activity, both in terms of income and employment; moreover, Arni's silk economy has been deeply researched and remarkable amount of qualitative and quantitative information is available on it. This information will be extensively employed in Chapter 7.

7 Institutional and spatial embeddedness in Arni's silk economy

1 Introduction

This chapter presents a Marxist/Institutionalist analysis of Arni's silk economy. Silk is a privileged standpoint from which to assess the nature and working of provincial capitalism. While handloom weaving is the most important single activity in Indian cottage industry, silk handloom weaving has come to play a critical role in the post-GR period for the demand for silk saris associated with increased farm income. After the GR, the production of hand-woven silk saris has become a leading activity also in Arni, transforming the town into an important silk manufacturing centre in TN. In terms of employment and income, silk lost its primacy in the town in the 1990s; however, it maintained a prominent role, also for the spreading of handloom weaving to the surrounding villages.

Arni's silk sector has been the subject of in-depth research, and abundant evidence is available. Partly it comes from the Arni and North Arcot surveys, the published Arni studies, and the recent literature on rural North Arcot (Harriss-White, 2003a; Harriss-White and Janakarajan, 2004); and partly it comes from ad hoc studies that have documented its internal organisation, the knowledge technologies and practices, the change in the post-GR period, and the prospects in the local/global economy.

While the Arni Studies and the Arcot Studies provide the background for my analysis, I use the information on Arni's silk that comes from three major sources: (i) the study by Nagaraj et al. (1996) on silk weaving in the Arni area;[1] (ii) the unpublished MPhil dissertation and DPhil thesis by Roman (2004, 2008) on the organisational structure of Arni's silk economy;[2] and (iii) the supplement to field research by Sacratees (2004) that I have organised in order to update the information on the crisis of Arni's silk industry in the post-liberalisation period. Recent information on silk in the villages in the Arni's area is also found in Arivukkarasi and Nagaraj (2009).

For the abundant and reliable information and for the role of the sector in Provincial India and in Arni, silk provides a major key to explore Arni's change after the GR, integrating and complementing the long-term analysis carried out in Chapter 3. My aim is twofold: (i) to explore social production relations in order to assess who owns and who uses the means of production in Arni's silk economy, and (ii) to examine the socio-economic-territorial relations which explain its growth and change. The outcome is an original analysis that improves our understanding of Arni's capitalism.

The chapter is organised as follows. Section 2 introduces the production of hand-woven silk saris in Arni, exploring the linkages between the GR and Arni's silk economy, and uses evidence to establish the existence of a local system for silk that takes the form of an industrial district. Section 3 focuses on production organisation and social stratification in Arni's silk handloom sector. Section 4 comments on the factors accounting for the major role of silk in Arni's economy.

2 Arni's industrial district for silk handloom saris

As revealed by the Arni and North Arcot surveys, silk handloom weaving is an important industry in Arni and in the surrounding area. According to the census of businesses in Arni conducted in 1993, 1,486 firms were involved in the production of hand-woven silk saris, accounting for the largest number of firms in a single activity. This number includes weaving, twisting, and dyeing units, as well as silk cooperatives and the firms involved in the provision of inputs and in the sale of outputs (Table 7.1). Moreover, the North Arcot survey for 1993 estimates that 14 per cent of the male workforce and 7 per cent of the female workforce in the villages are employed in silk handloom weaving (Jayaraj, 2004, Tables 4 and 5: 185–186).

The TN Government acknowledges the primary role of silk handloom production in the Arni's area, including it among the TN industrial centres for silk handloom sari production (Government of Tamil Nadu, 2008: 33).

Table 7.1 Silk sari production in Arni town (1993) (number of firms)

Type of unit	Number
Silk handloom (weaving) units	1,141
Silk cooperatives	19
Twisting factories	83
Dyeing units	6
Units selling dye materials	3
Atchu pannai[a] makers	23
Pattu Izhaithal[b]	6
Units producing weaving tools	24
Silk merchants (both for yarn and saris)	159
Pawnbrokers who take yarn/zari as collateral	8
Powerlooms	1
Others	13
Total	1,486

Source: Nagaraj *et al.* (1996: 15), elaborated from the 1993 Arni survey.

Notes
a The reed in the loom through which the warp passes.
b Units that join the border (of gold/silver yarn) to the body of the sari.

The handloom sector in TN (as well as in India) is going through a long-lasting crisis that appears to be due mainly to internal organisation problems that – keeping the quality of the silk low – reduce the competitiveness of local silk on domestic and international markets and keep the workers in conditions of poverty. Yet, it is still a key sector in the state and the government has recently started new policies to address internal problems – in particular in relation to the supply of yarn and to the design and quality of the products – with the twofold aim of increasing the competitiveness of TN silk and improving the working and living conditions of the weavers (Niranjana and Vinayan, 2001; Tewari, 2001, 2000; Sacratees, 2004; NCAER, 2006; Government of TN, 2007, 2008).

In spite of the economic importance of the sector, data are difficult to find at district level. A rough estimate, that very likely underestimated the situation, is that in the mid-1990s about 12,000 handlooms were working in the Arni area (Nagaraj *et al.*, 1996: 14). It is reasonable to assume this a sufficiently correct estimate of the current situation as the crisis of the handloom sector of the last decade seems to have hit TN only superficially, inducing a negligible reduction in the number of the working looms (NCAER, 2006: 11–12).[3]

2.1 Two types of hand-woven silk saris

Arni town and its hinterland specialise in the production of two main types of silk handloom saris. Nagaraj *et al.* (1996) describe in detail the differences between them, also explaining their implications in terms of techniques and skill requirements (see also Roman, 2004, Chapter 4, Sections 1 and 2).

The saris produced in Arni's region are: (i) the *dhobi* sari – also known as traditional Arni sari – which is the simplest type. It has no design on the borders and on the *mundhani* (the final part of the sari to be worn over the shoulder) and has a uniform colour for both the borders and the body; and (ii) the *korvai* sari – also known as *Kancheepuram* sari, after the name of a nearby town renowned for the production of grand saris mainly employed for weddings – which is a complex sari, with solid and designed borders and *mundhani* (that are obtained by the use of a large quantity of *zari*) and with contrasting colours in the borders and in the body.[4,5]

As it has no designed borders and *mundhani* and has just one colour, the *dhobi* sari requires the use of a loom with a single shuttle that can be operated by a single weaver. By contrast, in the case of the *korvai* sari the borders are woven separately and then are joined to the body of the sari with separate shuttles.[6] All together three shuttles and two workers are needed: a 'fully-fledged' weaver and a helper (Roman, 2004: 50). In the first case, a fly-shuttle loom can be used, while in the second case a throw-shuttle loom with three shuttles is necessary. Moreover, in the case of the *korvai* sari, the production process usually requires the use of *jacquards*, i.e. mechanical devices to make the complex designs on the borders and on the *mundhani*.

The differences in the production processes imply different skills. While for the weaving of Arni traditional saris the skills of a single worker who knows how to operate a fly-shuttle loom are necessary, the weaving of *korvai* saris requires the knowledge of the working of a throw-shuttle loom, the capability to coordinate the work of the helper and also the ability to use *jacquards*. The acquisition of skills for the weaving of *korvai* saris is a long learning process that takes up to four years (Roman, 2004: 46–48).

It should be added that it is possible to reduce the difference in labour requirements in *korvai* sari production by introducing the so-called *thallu* machine, a mechanical device that would allow the weaving with only one worker. Yet, the *thallu* machine has shown to be difficult to operate and this difficulty adds to its cost, reducing the incentives to its introduction in *korvai* weaving in the Arni region (Nagaraj *et al.*, 1996: 23; Roman, 2008: 3).

The quality of the *korvai* saris produced in Arni is not quite the same as that of the *korvai* saris produced in Kancheepuram, as the latter have more 'grand' designs, and more *zari* and raw silk are used. Yet, they are currently marketed as *Kancheepuram* saris and have occupied a segment of the market that is intermediate between 'low-quality' silk saris and the high-quality genuine *Kancheepuram* saris.

According to the data from the Handloom Census (quoted by Nagaraj *et al.*, 1996, Table 6), until 1973 as much as 80 per cent of the handlooms in the Arni *taluq* were using fly-shuttle looms, and then were producing traditional Arni saris. The Arni and North Arcot 1993 surveys and the recent research on the region shows that in the 1990s and in the early years of this century very few weavers are still producing traditional Arni saris, while the vast majority of them, both in the town and in the villages, have turned to *korvai* saris.

2.2 The silk handloom sector and the Green Revolution

Silk sari production is a relatively recent activity in the Arni region and its origin dates back to the last period of the British colonisation, when fewer than 50 looms were working in the town, being operated by members of the traditional silk weaver castes.[7] After Independence, silk weaving slowly developed, involving an increasing number of weavers. In 1956 the first silk handloom weaver cooperative society was created (Sacratees, 2004).[8] Yet, as the first Arni survey shows, in 1973 only 62 silk firms were present in the town, while the large increase in silk weaving – and the shift from the traditional Arni saris to the *korvai* saris – was to occur in the 1970s and 1980s as part of the socio-economic change induced by the GR.

As the Arni and North Arcot surveys jointly show, the impact of the GR on the increase in the number of weaving units and on the changes of products and techniques can be explained both from the production and the consumption side.

We have seen that the shift from *dhobi* saris to *korvai* saris requires a major technical change that consists in use of throw-shuttle looms instead of fly-shuttle looms. From a technical viewpoint, this is a change that increases the intensity of labour, as the latter employ only one worker, while the former employ two workers. This change is possible when (i) the labour force to employ in the new activity is available, and (ii) available workers have the necessary skills to operate the looms and/or can learn them. The introduction of the HYVs in local agriculture seems to have ensured, directly and indirectly, both conditions. As Nagaraj *et al.* (1996) suggest, not only has the GR, with the 'modernisation' of agriculture, freed a surplus labour force, it has also induced an increasing distress among marginal producers and landless agricultural labour, obliging workers to search progressively for other jobs in the non-farm sector, also at the costly price of long-term apprenticeship.[9]

From the consumption side, the increased demand for silk saris is currently attributed to the rise of farm incomes following the introduction of technical change in agriculture. Nagaraj *et al.* (1996, Section III) analyse this issue in depth, explicitly linking the increased demand of silk saris to the emergence of middle classes after the GR. According to these authors, the production of *korvai* saris in Arni meets the demand from the agrarian middle classes better that the more expensive *korvai* saris produced in *Kancheepuram*. In this sense, Arni's silk sari production appears to be entering a new niche in the silk handloom sari market that only emerges in the 1970s and 1980s.

2.3 The formation of Arni's industrial district

I argue here that Arni's silk economy is a socio-economic system that takes the form of an industrial district – i.e. a geographical concentration of firms embedded in a community and in a locality, and involved in interdependent production processes, in which the labour process is flexible (Becattini, 1990; see also Becattini *et al.*, 2009) – and has its centre in the town itself. In it, important *functional* and *spatial* linkages exist among firms, the locality and the community.

In Arni's silk economy a large number of small and medium size production units is included, forming the *filière* for the production of silk handloom saris. As we see from Table 7.1, firms specialised in all phases of silk handloom weaving co-exist in the town – from the sale of raw materials (yarn and *zari*), to twisting and dyeing, to the production of weaving tools and the sale of saris. The local presence of the entire *filière* is a major source of external economies (mainly owing to the reduction of transaction costs in the provision of raw materials and other inputs and in the marketing of outputs) that can be internalised by the firms located in the area and involved in silk weaving. In turn, these external economies might be the basis for the competitive advantages of the area (i.e. of the firms located in the area) in local and global markets. Moreover, owing to the existence of the local *filière* for silk production, firms might engage in a number of interrelations that may create a favourable environment for joint action (in the marketing of outputs and, possibly, also in the training of workers) to increase collective efficiency.

The interdependence among firms in Arni's district has a spatial dimension. As we have seen in Chapter 6, the whole area has been following a common pattern of growth and change that has led to the diversification of the economy in the town and in the villages. This process has impacted on the distribution of resources among sectors and through space. Changes in the distribution of the workforce – with the villages being now a major source of workforce – provide a clear example of this increased economic and territorial interdependence. The pattern of integration is affected by the emergence of new activities: on the one hand, agricultural workers leave the sector to feed the growth of the silk economy in the town; on the other, the growth in number of weaving units in the villages extracts a labour force from agriculture to produce goods that are com-mercialised in the town.

While these changes show the increasing local/global integration of the town, they also show that the silk economy can grow employing the resources of the nearby area. It follows that the growth of Arni's silk economy has been only in part due to use of its own resources (i.e. resources located within the boundaries of the town), while the town has been relying on resources that are external to it, but internal to its district. The boundaries of the socio-economic system are defined on the basis of production relations, on the basis of the supply of the resources employed for growth – in particular of the labour force.

The North Arcot surveys show that post-GR change has strengthened con-sumption and production linkages in the area, consolidating the hierarchical rela-tions between Arni and the villages. In this hierarchical order, the town appears as the centre of the silk economy, keeping within its boundaries the marketing of the output. In this process, it extracts resources from the villages (that constitute the periphery of the socio-economic system), relying on them also for the repro-duction of the labour force.

Moreover, the post-GR change has impacted on the organisation in Arni's silk economy, and in particular on the *functional* linkages between the town and the villages. Two broad phases may be delimited. In the first phase – which largely coincides with the 1970s and part of the 1980s – Arni has gone through a process of specialisation in silk sari production that has become the main activity in terms of employment and gross output. In this phase, the centralisation of pro-duction in the town has allowed the learning process and the spreading of tech-niques that have ensured the specialisation of the district as a whole. In this phase the construction of the market for Arni's silk also occurred, with the spreading of demand for Arni's *korvai* type of silk sari.

In the second phase – from the second half of the 1980s onwards – the produc-tion of handloom silk saris of the *korvai* type has been progressively decentralised to the villages, while Arni has retained within its boundaries the organisation of production and the marketing of the output for the whole area. The decentralisa-tion of sari production has been possible due to the diversification of activities and employment, which has changed the economic structure in the villages after the introduction of the HYVs (Nagaraj *et al.*, 1996: 16; Jayaraj, 2004: 187).[10, 11]

3 Social production relations

Having established that Arni is the economic centre of the local production system specialised in silk handloom saris that includes also its rural hinterland,

I turn now to the analysis of its working in terms of organisational and class structure. I employ Marxist/Institutionalist categories with the intention of discovering the class forces leading growth and change in Arni's silk economy. I first describe the organisational structure, and then I turn to class formations. I conclude the section by exploring the caste/class interplay that appears to be of particular importance to understanding the working of Arni's silk handloom weaving industry.

3.1 *Organisational structure*

Arni's silk economy is informally organised and contains the entire typology of informal firms, from individual and family firms to enterprises that employ a large number of dependent weavers and other types of wage-workers under different informal contracts, both in the town and in the villages.

The whole district is based on a form of putting-out system that is precisely described by Nagaraj et al. (1996), on the basis of the Arni and North Arcot surveys, and by Roman in her research on skills and learning in silk weaving in the town. I summarise below the main features of Arni's putting-out system, with the intention of pointing out the main social categories involved in the process, so setting the scene for class analysis.

Intermediaries dominate Arni's silk economy, controlling all phases of the production process. Two major intermediaries are found: the master-weavers and the silk merchants that are locally called *maligais*. In principle, the two intermediaries have different roles: master-weavers are directly involved in production – with a variable scale of operation – and are usually weavers themselves, even if they might not be still weaving; by contrast, *maligais* are usually distant from the production process, being involved in trade.

In practice, the two roles often overlap in the same person, and the overlapping increases with the spreading of the putting-out system that progressively empties out the manufacturer role of the master-weavers and enlarges the role of *maligais* in production. In the basic model, *maligais* and master-weavers buy weaving tools, raw silk and the *zari*, and supply them to the weavers, together with instructions on colours and designs.[12, 13] The instructions for the colours and designs are updated on the basis of systematic explorations of the market carried out by the master-weavers and *maligais* themselves. Once woven, the saris are collected and sold.

Two basic types of master-weavers are found according to their scale of operation: (i) small-scale master-weavers – located both in the town and in the villages – who control a limited number of looms and who usually are weavers themselves; and (ii) large scale master-weavers who control a large number of looms – up to 1,000 (Nagaraj et al., 1996: 96) – and who are located in the town. A major difference between the two types is that small-scale master-weavers, in order to operate in the market, require the intermediation of large-scale master-weavers and *maligais* in Arni, other towns in TN and other states; by contrast, large-scale master-weavers do not need other intermediaries for their operations.

Several types of weavers are also found. A first category is made of independent weavers who directly buy raw materials, are in charge of the pre-
weaving operations and sell their saris to *maligais*. In Arni, only a small number
of weavers are 'independent' in this sense, and they are mainly located in the
town. The large majority of weavers are dependent on *maligais* and master-
weavers for credits, tools and equipment, and can be located in the town and in
the villages. Both independent and dependent weavers form units of production
usually located in their household premises and employing household members
as assistants. Both independent and dependent weavers own their looms. By contrast, there exists a third important category of weavers – the wage weavers –
who do not own their looms and work on looms owned by *maligais* or
master-weavers (Nagaraj *et al.*, 1996: 81 et seq.).

Finally, the fourth category of weavers operating in Arni is weavers working
in cooperative societies. As the 1993 Arni survey shows, the number of silk
weaving cooperatives is relatively low in Arni.[14] This is a trait that distinguishes
the town from other silk centres in TN, such as Kancheepuram.[15] This is an
anomaly for a state like TN in which the cooperative silk handloom sector has
been supported by the local government in several ways (Government of Tamil
Nadu, 2007, 2008).

The organisation of production in Arni's industrial district is then based on
two main social categories: weavers and master-weavers/*maligais*. In spite of the
internal differences in each category that might blur the boundaries, their roles in
silk weaving are distinctive. Independently of their appearance, the weavers are
'dependent' workers and are deprived of entrepreneurial functions, even when
entering social production relations as 'independent' agents. Entrepreneurial
activity is completely in the hands of master-weavers and *maligais* who control
the entire production process, ensuring at the same time the supply of raw materials and the marketing of the output, their knowledge of input and output markets
being a major aspect of their contractual power.

Master-weavers and *maligais* are not specialised agents who perform a single
function of organising logistics. On the contrary, they control the entire economics of silk, from the organisation of production to the marketing of the
output, also providing liquidity to the weavers. They organise the process of production according to the quality and quantity of resources, taking into account
their availability in the centre and in the periphery of the industrial district
(Nagaraj *et al.*, 1996: 85–87). Master-weavers and *maligais* perform *multiple
functions* and ensure, at the same time, that the resources of the industrial district
are used for multiple purposes. They are the agents who ensure that the district
as a whole enjoys *economies of scope*, i.e. economies that derive from the flexible and multi-task use of resources.

Master-weavers and *maligais* are crucial for the viability of Arni's silk
economy in the medium to long term, as they introduce new technologies
and types of product, and discover new market outlets. In many senses, they
are similar to the 'versatile integrators' who according to Becattini (1997)
have made a success of industrial districts in the Third Italy. Like Becattini's

'versatile integrators' acting in Prato, master-weavers and *maligais* in Arni's industrial district move from the organisation of production to the finding of new markets.[16] By allocating production to different types of producers and by marketing the output, they ensure that Arni's production structure adapts to market signals and changes, enhancing competitiveness.[17] They perform a 'plural' role that involves their class as a whole. To them is due the 'invention' of the Arni *korvai* type of sari and the spreading of an organisational structure – a particular type of putting-out system – able to produce it in a flexible way.

To perform their role as 'versatile integrators', master-weavers and *maligais* need to have full control over the working class in order to prevent capital/labour conflicts and to enforce a flexible organisation of production. In the next section we explore the ways in which this role is carried out.

3.2 Two segmented classes

Two main groups of agents are involved in Arni's silk economy: on the one side, there are master-weavers and *maligais* and, on the other, there are weavers and other dependent workers. Master-weavers and *maligais* are a component of the capitalist class, while weavers and the other dependent labour force are part of the class of subaltern workers: two segmented classes that are composed of groups of individuals differing in their origins and their trajectories of class formation, but showing internally a basic social and economic homogeneity. They represent the antagonist classes of Arni's silk capitalism and major actors in Arni's class dialectics.

As a class, capitalists are the outcome of distinct trajectories of class formation. Broadly, the *maligai* fraction derives from agricultural merchants and moneylenders who in the change induced by the GR have started to diversify their economic activity, investing in silk production. By contrast, the master-weaver component is the outcome of social differentiation among the weaving castes, leading to the emergence of a number of individuals who have been able to start the process of capital accumulation, also thanks to the injection of income generated by the GR.[18]

In spite of their different origins and trajectories of class formation, the two capitalist segments give birth to a single class of agents that share interests, values and lifestyles. Jointly, and often overlapping, they perform the function of 'versatile integrators' by which they perpetuate their economic control over Arni's silk economy. At the same time, they pursue common political interests, also by means of corruption and tax evasion.[19]

The class status of small-scale master-weavers who still weave and have only a small number of looms under them is more ambiguous. They constitute an intermediate class of Arni's silk economy, and their positions in social production relations depend on their ideological perception of their class interests and aspirations and on their linkages with the capitalist class.[20] If they accept – or are obliged to accept – interests and functions of *maligais* and large-scale master-weavers, then they should be considered part of the capitalist class. If they perceive their status to be similar to the workers, then they should be considered part of the subaltern class, together with weavers and other subaltern workers.

Weavers and other dependent workers – the subaltern segmented class – have different origins and different trajectories of class formation. As the evidence provided by Nagaraj *et al.* (1996) and Roman (2004) shows, only a small proportion of the weavers come from weaving castes, and they are mainly located in the town. The vast majority of weavers, in Arni and in the villages, come from non-weaving castes and from other sectors, in particular from agriculture. The other major segment of the subaltern class is made of helpers and assistants: they are mainly women and children who are involved in silk weaving as unpaid family workforce.

The social stratification of the class of subaltern workers in Arni's silk economy is complex and highly hierarchical.[21] Several modes of inequality interact in defining the hierarchy – class, caste and gender – while labour trajectories also depend on personal and family features.[22] The evidence seems to suggest a little permeability between the strata of weavers and helpers. As Roman shows (2004: 63 et seq.), women very rarely become fully-fledged weavers but remain in the condition of helpers indefinitely, often even after marriage. A similar situation is also observed in the case of children who often work in conditions similar to slavery with very little hope of improving their condition (Nagaraj *et al.*, 1996: 101).[23] A similar condition is also shared by wage-workers in ancillary industries, such as twisting and dyeing factories.

Subaltern workers are subjected to a process of commoditisation that involves weavers and helpers in different ways. Several forms of commoditisation are found: from wage labour of dependent weavers and wage weavers and self-employment of independent weavers, to sub-contracted wage labour, child and women wage labour, and bonded labour of helpers and assistants. Workers enter the commoditisation process in a situation of subordination that is typical of the informal economy.

Within the putting-out system, independent weavers have the formal status of self-employed, even if in actual terms they lack of autonomy in decision-making, both in relation to the type of saris they weave and the nature of inputs they use, and are dependent for the supply of raw materials and credit: indeed, they are dependent labour in disguise. By contrast, dependent weavers, helpers and the other segments of subaltern workers are by definition a 'dependent' labour force; yet, they have no formal written contracts and no provisions for social security. Altogether, the 'dependent' labour force is paid on the basis of the number of woven saris produced per year – in this way creating a favourable environment for exploitation and self-exploitation – and their wages are usually a little above the poverty line, in the town as well as in the villages. Nagaraj *et al.* (1996: 99) estimate that in the mid-1990s a monthly wage for a dependent weaver who owns their looms and has two children working outside the family as helpers was Rs.300 in Arni and Rs.198, in the villages, with a differential that is little more than 30 per cent. They also calculate that – due to the differential of cost of living – the wages in Arni and in the villages are about the same in terms of purchasing power, both being slightly above the poverty line.[24] These estimates are broadly confirmed in the first years of this century, due to the crisis of the handloom sector that has kept the wage demands of trade unions low (Sacratees, 2004).

It should be emphasised that usually weavers working in cooperative societies receive a higher wage in comparison to the wages paid in the private sector. Yet, as we have seen, in Arni there are only a few cooperative societies, and then the prevailing wage is based on the level defined in the private sector.

By contrast, *maligais* and master-weavers flourish. Nagaraj *et al.* (1996: 100, footnote) estimate, on the basis of the survey data for 1993, that the largest master-weaver in Arni – controlling 1,000 looms – would have a minimum return on capital of 40 per cent per year, after the payment of interests on circulating capital and the fixed costs.

In Arni's system of social organisation, upward mobility – from helper to master-weaver – is constrained by a number of obstacles. First, to become fully-fledged weavers it is necessary to go through a long period of apprenticeship, and it is necessary to have the 'right' personal features in terms of gender and caste (Roman, 2004: 48 et seq.). Second, once the stage of a fully-fledged weaver is reached, an individual needs to buy her/his loom in order to become an independent weaver. This is usually done with money anticipated by the *maligai* or the master-weaver, returned over a number of years during which the weaver lives on a very low wage. Third, to buy another loom, initiating the rise towards the status of master-weaver, involves other debts and repayments at high interest.

These obstacles to social mobility keep a large number of helpers and weavers in a condition of subordination. This explains why it has been possible in Arni to shift to *korvai* saris production: a type of production that requires the availability of low-cost, unskilled workforce – composed mainly of unpaid family labour and of women and children – to assist the fully-fledged weavers. Indeed, the availability of an unpaid and bonded labour force also accounts for the lack of incentives to introduce the *thallu* machine and then for the technological backwardness of the silk handloom sector.

3.3 Class and caste

The evidence shows that the social structure of Arni's silk economy is segmented not only along class lines but also along caste lines. Segmentation along caste lines in silk handloom weaving is a phenomenon that might appear difficult to explain because the sector involves a large number of weavers from 'traditional' weaving castes who have a strong 'sense of identity' of their status (Roman, 2004: 55–56; see also De Neve, 2005: 51 et seq.). It should be added that the 'sense of identity' of weavers is even stronger in the case of silk weaving by virtue of the 'purity' of silk (in comparison to other weaving materials), which places silk weavers at the top of a hierarchy of handloom weavers.

Indeed, the presence of non-weaving castes in weaving is a rather common situation in India, in particular in the south. De Neve (2005), in his research on the informal textile sector in two towns in central TN, explores the interaction among caste communities in weaving, while Roy (1993, Chapter 3) shows that the presence of several castes has been widespread in South India since the 1930s, resulting from the migrations of caste communities and of the progressive involvement in weaving of agricultural castes, in particular in rural areas.

According to a survey conducted by the Census of India (quoted by Nagaraj *et al.*, 1996: 48), in 1961 80 per cent of the weavers in TN belonged to the main weaving castes, and in particular to: Devangas (including the sub-caste of the Seniers), Sengunda Mudaliars, Saliars and Saurastras.[25] Since 1961 the situation has significantly changed and now the penetration of non-traditional weaving castes is widespread, both for cotton and silk. Kancheepuram is a remarkable exception, with a majority of weavers still coming from traditional weaving castes specialised in silk (Remesh, 2001).

A similar situation is found in Arni, in which small communities of traditional weavers exist, some of them with a recent specialisation in silk. According to the evidence provided by Roman (2004: 54), traditional silk weaving communities in contemporary Arni include Segunda Mudaliars, Veera Saiva Chettiars, and Devanga Chettiars (a caste group that has started specialising in silk only 40 years ago). They are involved in silk economy together with non-traditional weaving communities, such as Gounder and Udayar (Roman, 2004: 55) in the town and Agamudia Mudaliar, Vanniars and Yadavas in the villages (Nagaraj *et al.*, 1996: 56).[26]

While in principle the difference between weaving and non-weaving castes are important to assess caste stratification in Arni's silk economy and should not be neglected, this divide is neither the only one nor the most important one. Other caste distinctions among the weavers exist which are important to the nexus of class and caste. Caste segmentation appears to be most significant with respect to the learning process and upward mobility.

The evidence provided by Roman explains how the learning process in Arni's silk economy works (2004, Section 4.3). The knowledge about silk weaving is acquired by means of a learning process in which caste barriers are low, and to which in principle non-traditional weaving castes also have access. Yet, it would be wrong to say that caste is irrelevant to the way in which the learning process is organised. On the contrary, 'caste connections' (Roman, 2004: 57) are the key to learning opportunities.

To enter the profession it is necessary to go through a long period of apprenticeship in which the apprentice works with a fully-fledged weaver. In some cases – as for the *korvai* saris – the apprentice might be progressively involved in production as an assistant; and for the weaver it might be convenient to have an apprentice, as a helper is necessary to operate the throw-shuttle loom. In other cases – as for the *dharmavaran* saris – a helper is not needed and to have an apprentice is very costly to the weaver in terms of time because weaver and apprentice cannot work simultaneously on the loom. This explains why the weavers of *dharmavaran* saris do not usually take apprentices. Yet, in both cases, the learning process for silk handloom weaving is long and costly, and requires the explicit engagement of the weaver.

In case of traditional weaving castes, children start learning from their parents. In the case of non-traditional weaving castes it is necessary to find a way to enter into the sector. Roman shows that caste-based and neighbourhood-based relations supply the key to enter *korvai* weaving as they create the trust that is necessary to be accepted as an apprentice and to start the learning process. The lack of caste-based and neighbourhood-based relations – and then of trust – explains why the SCs members are virtually absent from the weaving profession.[27]

The other important perspective on the influence of caste on social stratification in Arni's silk economy is provided by upward mobility. I focus here on three main moments in which caste influences upward mobility in silk weaving. The first is the mobility from assistant to fully-fledged weaver. As I have said, this mobility is not always ensured depending on the features of the assistant, and only people with the 'right' personal features (in terms of caste and trust) can move to the status of fully-fledged weavers. For instance, SCs are systematically excluded, even in the cases in which they are accepted as assistants.

Upward mobility from weaver to master-weaver is also to large extent conditioned by caste. There is evidence that in Arni master-weavers are mainly from the traditional weaving castes and that the there is a larger proportion of individuals from weaving castes among master-weavers than among weavers (Nagaraj et al., 1996: 58).

Finally, caste origin influences upward mobility in the case of *maligais*. Here, the situation seems to be the opposite to the one of master-weavers, as weaving castes are not represented among *maligais*. This situation is easily explained if one takes into account the trajectory of formation of this segment of the capitalist class that usually develops from trade, rather than from weaving. Yet, as in the case of master-weavers, the case of *maligais* shows that the capitalist class is less caste-differentiated than the class of subaltern workers.

The evidence for Arni with the presence of several dominant castes in an activity that was traditionally in the hand of a small number of weaving castes shows that the link between caste and occupation in the silk sector in contemporary India is weak.[28] This conclusion is consistent with the literature on caste in contemporary India reviewed in Chapter 5 and with the findings on Arni in Chapter 6. Yet, the evidence analysed in this section also shows that castes still matter in Arni and that, as Roy (1993: 85) concludes for South India, so in Arni there is a strong intercaste mobility in the case of wage labour, while caste mobility from labour into the capitalist class is much lower.

Then, in Arni's silk economy, caste appears to be a *regulative* factor of social production relations that performs its regulatory function interacting with class. Caste affiliations influence access to the weaving profession and upward mobility within the sector. In so doing, they form a new segmentation within the two broad classes of capitalists and subaltern workers, creating new non-class hierarchies within each segment. In this sense, caste segmentation increases the non-permeability of Arni's social structure, hindering mobility from one segment to another.

4 On the performance of Arni's silk economy

Nagaraj *et al.* impute the leading role of silk in Arni's economy in the post-GR period to the putting-out system, which has been working as a transmission mechanism of the *korvai* weaving techniques allowing the occupation of a niche in the market for silk saris (1996: 84). The interpretation presented in this chapter suggests that this is only a partial explanation, which, while pointing to a major aspect, overlooks two key factors of the competitiveness of Arni's silk economy: the organisation of silk economy in an industrial district involving the town and the villages and the role of caste and class segmentations in the commoditization of the subaltern workers.

As the North Arcot and the Arni surveys show, the post-GR restructuring has involved the town and the villages, inducing a similar process of economic diversification, with the main consequences of transforming Arni into a manufacturing and wholesale market centre, and of giving birth and re-enforcing manufacturing and service activities in the hinterland. In the case of silk, this process has led to the formation of an industrial district for silk handloom saris that has a centre – Arni – and a periphery – the villages.

The relations between Arni and the villages are of interdependence: sari production has been progressively decentralised to the villages, while Arni retains the control of the silk economy concentrating the organisational, finance and marketing functions. So, the role of the putting-out system should be assessed in the context of the interdependence between the town and the villages.

Maligais and master-weavers are the main agents in Arni's putting-out system, enhancing the capability of the firms involved in silk production to react to market signals. In order to conceptualise their role – borrowing from Becattini's analysis of Prato's district for wool – I have proposed to consider *maligais* and master-weavers as the 'versatile integrators' of Arni's silk district: a class of capitalists who play multi-task functions, ranging from the organisation of production to the marketing of the output. Being in control of the organisational aspects of the silk economy, they promote the decentralisation of production to the villages and, being in charge of the supply of raw materials and of the disposal of the product, they ensure the local and global integration of Arni's silk economy.

Yet, the effectiveness of *maligais* and master-weavers in organising Arni's silk district is not enough to account for the performance of the sector in the post-GR period. As I argue here, to provide a complete explanation, it is necessary to assess the performance of Arni's silk economy from the perspective of labour.

The evidence supplied by Nagaraj *et al.* (1996) describes in detail the poor working conditions of the labour force in Arni's silk. It indicates that the Arni's putting-out system relies heavily on unpaid family labour and wage-workers: women and children and bonded labourers that are employed as helpers and assistants. Moreover, the research by Camilla Roman (2004, 2008) shows that the techniques for *korvai* weaving enhance the employment of the weakest strata of the workforce, while in turn the availability of unpaid family workforce contributes in reducing incentives for the introduction of technical change that might diminish labour-intensity in silk weaving. It also shows that helpers and assistants often have a reduced access to opportunities for upward mobility.

In relation to wages, Nagaraj *et al.* (1996: 99) show that dependent weavers live on a wage that is only a little above the poverty line, while Sacratees (2004) finds that – due to the crisis of silk in the first years of this century – wages of weavers have not been increasing. Moreover, due to the wage and price differentials between Arni and its periphery, weavers in the villages also share the same condition, living slightly above the poverty line. The decentralisation of silk production has been functional to the interests of capital but has not increased the standard of living of workers in the villages.

The social structure in Arni's silk district is segmented along caste and class lines. *Maligais* and master-weavers are the main segments of the capitalist class and keep the control of the silk economy firmly in their hands. The working class is also highly segmented and caste segmentation adds to class segmentation, creating a mosaic of subaltern social groups in poor living and working conditions.

Caste provides a form of internal regulation of Arni's silk economy in which caste segmentation is manipulated according to the needs of the dominant classes. While the link between caste and occupation is weak, caste barriers do exist, and are strong for the capitalist class and less strong for wage-workers. Castes hinder upward mobility, perpetuating the presence of the dominating caste groups among master-weavers and *maligais*. At the same time, caste barriers become weaker when the involvement of lower castes is necessary for economic growth and when it does not challenge power relations within the economy, as in the case of the participation of weavers from non-traditional weaving castes in the villages during upswings in the sector.

The conclusion of my interpretation is, then, in contrast with the one by Nagaraj *et al.* (1996): the key to the performance of Arni's silk district is not to be found only in the way in which the economy is organised by master-weavers and *maligais* – as Nagaraj *et al.* argue – but also – and primarily – in production decentralisation and in caste and class segmentations that, jointly, make possible the subordination of the working class to the needs of capital, in the town as well as in the villages, and, in doing so, re-enforce power relations rooted in Indian culture and institutions.

Focusing on the silk economy, the analysis conducted in this chapter has shown that several distinguishing traits of India's provincial economy are also found in Arni. In addition to diversification, widely pointed out in Chapter 6, the available evidence shows that a major section of Arni's economy is informally organised and is inhabited by two segmented classes that represent capital and labour. In its interplay with class, caste plays a key role, keeping a large proportion of the workers in a situation of subordination to capital, as shown by the poor living and working standards and by the very low class mobility. Building on this conclusion, I explore in the next chapter the mechanisms that have led workers to accept capital's hegemony. This analysis – which is the final step of my assessment of Arni's capitalism – focuses on the twofold role of caste as an institution and an ideology.

8 Capital's hegemony in Arni's corporatist civil society

1 Introduction

My aim in this chapter is the analysis of the forms in which the ideological and institutional framework regulating Arni's economic activity supports production relations. The focus is on caste taken as the institution and the ideology, which continues to represent a major organising principle in contemporary India.

I analyse the influence of caste by observing the organisation of civil society. Building on Chapter 5, I take civil society – the association of non-state associations – as the sphere in which particularistic interests are expressed and represented, and I assume that its organisation reveals the intertwining of class and non-class interests. Then, focusing on Arni's civil society, I explore the Gramscian proposition (see Chapter 5, Section 4) that caste – both as an ideology and an institution – influences production relations by creating an institutional framework in which capital's hegemony is negotiated and workers' 'spontaneous' consensus on it is gained. The analysis relies on the empirical evidence provided by an original survey of virtually all the associations existing in Arni's civil society in 1997–1998.

The chapter is organised as follows. Sections 2 and 3 present the survey of civil society and summarise its results, while Sections 4 and 5 explore the character of Arni's civil society, assessing also the implications of Arni's societal corporatism on growth and change. Section 6 elaborates on the significance of Arni's corporatist regime in the context of India's economic liberalisation.

2 The survey of Arni's civil society

The aim of the survey is to assess the economic impact of the organisation of Arni's civil society. The survey is based on a questionnaire to the associations existing in the town that explored their nature and function. The associations have been identified by the late P.J. Krishnamurthy, who greatly contributed to the collection and organisation of the empirical material on the town.[1]

The Gramscian analysis of civil society reviewed in Chapter 5 provides the theoretical framework for the empirical exercise. Civil society – the association of non-state associations – is the sphere in which class and non-class interests are expressed and represented, and exerts an influence on production relations which depends on the forms in which participation in associations is organised and the aims of the associations are defined. In particular, a major issue is whether or not associations play a regulatory function, being in charge of the representation *and* intermediation of interests, while a key indicator of the nature and function of associations is the degree of voluntariness of membership. In corporatist civil society – in which membership is compulsory and associations play a regulatory function – a substantial sacrifice in terms of democracy is compensated by the positive influence of interest organisation and representation on social stability and, then, on economic growth.

To translate the Gramscian framework in empirical terms, I de-construct the economic process in order to single out the vital points at which the impact of civil society's organisation is significant. I first distinguish the three phases of the production process: (i) the purchase of the means of production and labour power, (ii) the organisation of production, and (iii) the realisation process. Then, I explore the extent to which each phase is socially regulated by means of associations in which conflicting interests are negotiated. I point out four categories of relationships which indicate key political processes for growth and stability, in which conflicting interests emerge and social regulation is necessary: the relationships (i) between economy and state; (ii) between capital and labour; (iii) within capital; and (iv) between economy and society.

The survey collected information about civil society associations that govern the four groups of relationships in each one of the three phases of the economic process. The questionnaire reflects this de-construction of Arni's economic process in three phases and in four categories of socio-economic relationships. It includes a common portion, containing general questions, and four groups of questions for each category of the four relationships, and within each group it explores the influences of social organisation on the three phases of the production process.

The common portion includes questions on: the official aim of the association and the criterion for membership; its history; the range of – and changes in – action on the basis of the declared aim; financing and registration. The first group of questions refers to the relationships between State and economy with questions on the presence of the State in the economy and on the role of state agencies in relation to: disputes and litigation; fiscal pressure; the role of bureaucracy; the working of the public credit system vs. the private credit system; the provision of raw materials and inputs. The second group considers industrial relations and capital/labour conflicts, focusing on the role of formal business associations and trade unions. The third group concentrates on industrial organisation, and in particular on market structure and intersectoral relations. Finally, the fourth group contains questions on the social embeddedness of capital accumulation as far as family, religion and caste are concerned.

The questionnaire was submitted to the leaders or distinguished representatives of all the associations existing in Arni in the period 1997–1998, registered and un-registered, local or linked to regional and state networks, as long as they contributed to the associational order.

I collected 85 interviews, of which 66 relate to organisations that participate in associational life, in turn divided into four groups of associations according to their reported objective: philanthropic, business and professional, social, and political. The remaining 19 schedules contain interviews with individuals who play an important role in Arni's economic life, but who are not representatives of an association. This is often the case with the professions (especially lawyers) and with certain business activities relatively new in the town, for which the phase of structured organisation is still to come. These interviews complement the picture of the socio-economic structure of the town and provide information on emerging sectors and activities. This information has enabled me to assess the nature and working of Arni's organised civil society. A major supplement to the information coming from the interviews is provided by 17 additional schedules on specific aspects of collective life, in particular on caste associations and emerging economic activities, written by the late P.J. Krishnamurthy.

Altogether, I interviewed: (i) 32 business and professional associations, with an estimated coverage of approximately 2,000 people; (ii) 23 cultural and religious associations, of which 15 are caste associations. This category also includes a consumer association and seven philanthropic associations, and covers more than 35,000 people; (iii) 11 unions, covering fewer than 2,000 people.[2] The total number of people indirectly covered by this set of associations is of the order of 40,000–45,000, but this is a rough estimate, due to double-counting in organisations of caste and of trade.

The interviews do not supply data that can be analysed quantitatively and the aim of the survey was to provide *qualitative* information on Arni's organised civil society. Similarly, the information on the collective life in the town contained in Mr Krishnamurthy's notes is *qualitative* in nature. So, due to the nature of the empirical material, the analysis of Arni's civil society is supported by the examples and declarations made available in the interviews.

3 Arni's civil society

Tables 8.1 and 8.2 introduce Arni's civil society distinguishing associations and groups on the basis of their activity.[3]

Table 8.1 supports the description of the town's economy provided in Chapter 6: long-established activities, in particular for the production of goods – rice and silk – and personal and production services, co-exist with new activities dominated by 'modern' services, such as communication, finance and electronics. The table also stresses the role of the public sector in the town, as suggested by the presence of five unions that organise public sector workers. Table 8.2 integrates the description of organised civil society with a snapshot of Arni's social life. The table shows the significant presence of caste associations and of a heterogeneous group of associations – that I propose to call 'welfare' associations – whose aims are oriented to the entire town's corporate interests, rather than to individual or group interests.[4]

Table 8.1 Associations in Arni by sphere of action (economic activities)

	(a)	(b)	(c)	(d)	(e)	(f)
Production of goods						
Rice						
Arni Taluk Rice Mill Owners' Assn			1	1980		
Paddy And Rice Merchants' Assn	1			1970		147
Silk						
The Arni Silk Merchants' Assn	1				4,000	40,000
The Tiruvannamalai District Handloom Silk Designers' Assn	1			1996	65	
Silk Twisters' Assn	1			1972		3,000
Gold						
The Tamilnadu Jewel Workers Central Sangam	1		state	1963	450	
Tamilnadu Gold And Silver Merchants' Federation, Chennai	1			1960		50
Buildings						
The Tamilnadu Building Workers' Sangam, Arni	1		local	1974	500	
Arni Electricians' Sangam	1		local	1978	120	
Arni Brick Makers' Assn	1		local			
Quarry workers	1					3
Cement dealers		1				10
Electricity Board Union – Citu	1		nation	1970	230	400
Others						
Fertilisers and pesticides		1				13
Soda Factory Assn	1			1980	100	
Bakeries		1				13
Arni Small Scale Industries' Assn	1			1980	24	
Public sector unions						
Arni Branch of the National Federation of Postal Employees	1		nation	1919	47	62
Sanitary Workers' Sangam, Arni	1		local	1981	155	
Nursery schools		1				
Arni Elementary School Teachers' Federation	1			1957	60	
Private traditional services						
Personal services						
The Tamil Nadu Assn of Shaving Saloons	1		local	1956	100	100
The Arni Washermans' (Dhobi) Union	1					
The Assn for the Progress of Tailors	1		state	1995	300	2,500
Tea stall		1			300	
Lottery tickets		1				40
Consumer goods						
The Grocery Merchants' Assn of Arni	1			1972	50	
Arni Town Fruits Merchants' Assn	1		local	1982	71	
The Arni Town Flowers Merchant Sangam	1		state	1996	40	
Arni Greengrocers' Assn (Gandhi Market), Arni	1		local	1967	86	86
Vinayaka textiles		1				20
The Valampuri Vinayakar Rickshaws Pullers' Assn	1		state	1997	15	

Table 8.1 continued

	(a)	(b)	(c)	(d)	(e)	(f)
The Arni Auto Owners and Drivers' Welfare Union	1			1993	96	
The Arni Lorry Owners' Assn	1		nation	1990	150	
Dr Ambedkar Transport Workers' Union, Arni	1		state	1989	75	
Aringar Arni Bullock-Cart Drivers' Sangam	1		local	1997	120	
The Tiruvannamalai District Bus Owners' Assn	1		local	1989	110	
Arni Area Car and Van Drivers' Welfare Assn	1			1997	90	
Two Wheelers (Mopeds, etc.) Spare Parts Sales Assn		1				4
Peddal Bicycle Dealers (Mra Cycle Mart), Arni		1				6
Finance						
Arni Pawnbrokers' Assn	1				100	170
Others						
The Arni Chamber of Commerce	1			1989	103	
The Advocates Bar Assn	1		local	1961	30	30
Porters' Assn	1				63	
Turning Works (Lathe 'Pattarias')	1					
Pharmacists and Druggist Assn	1			1987	22	22
Two wheelers repair shops		1				
New activities						
Communication						
Assn of Telephone Subscribers	1			1992	250	800
Telephone booths		1				15
Professional couriers		1				6
Printing						
Typewriting (commercial education) institutes		1				14
Xerox		1				18
Printing press		1				16
Cinema and television						
The Arni Video Casstte Library Assn	1			1992	2	
The Cinema Theatre Owners' Assn	1		local	1988	4	
Cable TV Operators	1					
Electronics						
Computer studies		1				5
(Geetha) Electronics and Home Appliances		1				20
Finance						
Finance companies						30
Banks						3

Notes
a Registered association.
b Informal group.
c Type of network.
d Foundation year.
e Number of members of the association.
f Number of potential members.

Table 8.2 Associations in Arni by sphere of action (non-economic activities)

	(a)	(b)	(c)	(d)	(e)
Caste associations					
Saurashtra Podhu Sabha	1		1968		5,000
The Saurashtra Woman's Association, Arni	1		1977	22	
The Naidu Assn of Arni	1		1982		1,000
The Tamil Nadu Karneegar Sangam, Arni	1	state			
The Arni Town Vanniars' Assn	1		1983	7,000	
The Arni Tuluva Velalar Sangam	1	local	1953	100	14,000
The Tiruvannamalai District Vaaniar Sangam	1		1992	150	
The Tamilnadu Brahmins Sangam ('Tambras'), Arni Branch	1		1995	200	
The Tamilnadu Archakas Welfare Sangam	1	local	1980	65	95
Tamil Saiva Chettiar	1				
The Arni Kannada Veera Saiva Jaineekar Sangam	1	state	1927	300	
The Arni Town Sengunthar Sangam	1	local	1983	150	
Yaadavas	1				2,500
Ahamudaiya Mudaliars' Sangam	1			15,000	
Religious and political associations					
The Indian Republican Party	1	national	1994	25	
Communist Party of India – Marxist	1	national	1964	200	
Muslims	1				3,000
Roman Catholics	1				800
Protestant Christians	1				600
Jains	1				1,000
Welfare associations					
The Inner Wheel Club of Arni	1	intern	1995	22	
The Lions Club of Arni	1		1971	75	
The Rotary Club of Arni	1		1985	41	
All Pensioners' Assn	1		1984	500	
The Arni Town Welfare Committee	1		1992	40	
The Lioness Club	1		1977	85	

Notes
a Registered association.
b Type of network.
c Foundation year.
d Number of members of the association.
e Number of potential members.

Once a broad picture of Arni's organised civil society has been introduced, the second step of my analysis is to explore the nature and function of the associational order. For this purpose, I review the interviews focusing on the aspects of civil society organisation that exert the most significant impact on the economy.

I review the available information exploring the features pointed out by Gramsci in his analysis of the organised civil society, both in general terms and in the case of corporatism. In particular, I focus on the forms in which individual participation in civil society's associations is regulated, and on the impact of the organisation and representation of interests on economic growth and stability.

In relation to the first aspect, I classify the associations with reference to four degrees of voluntariness of membership defined as follows (see Tables 8.3 and 8.4):

1   Voluntary membership: when at least one of the following conditions is satisfied: (i) the number of participants is 'small' in comparison to the potential members; (ii) non-membership excludes a person only from the association's activity; (iii) other similar associations exist. This condition is found in associations that in principle are 'open' to wide participation. Examples are the Lions Club and the Rotary Club (even if they are elite institutions), and the Communist Party.

2   Exclusive but voluntary membership: when all the following conditions are satisfied: (i) not all the potential members are actual members; (ii) other similar associations do not exist; (iii) non-membership 'excludes' a person only from one specific segment of the relevant market or from some benefit. An example is the Arni Association for the Progress of Tailors, which controls and organises among its members the work coming on order from public sector institutions, such as uniforms for schools.

3   Quasi-voluntary membership by profession: membership is formally voluntary but the status of non-member excludes them from the profession.[5] It is identified by: (i) the absence of other similar associations; and (ii) membership spread to all the individuals in the profession. Examples are statutory associations, such as the Advocates' Bar Association, from which no advocate can remain outside, but also the Tamil Nadu Building Workers Sangam, the Arni Auto Owners and Drivers Welfare Associations, and the Paddy and Rice Merchants' Association.

4   Quasi-voluntary membership by birth: this category obviously includes caste associations, but also the professional associations that group individuals from a specific caste; examples are the Arni Washermen's Union and the Tamil Nadu Association of Shaving Saloons.

In relation to the second aspect, I classify the associations on the basis of two complementary criteria: (i) the influence on social stability and (ii) the influence on economic growth. This exercise is supported by the information coming from the interviews in which each association is asked to provide details on its involvement in the economic process, distinguishing four categories of relationship for the three phases of the production process. Then, for each association, the influence on social stability has been established by assessing its impact on the relations (and conflicts) between capital and labour, capital and state, labour and state, within capital, and between economic and social structure. Similarly, the influence on economic growth has been established on the basis of the impact on the access to the means of production, on the organisation of the production process and on the disposal/marketing of output.[6]

The information coming from the previous two classifications is presented in a compact form in Tables 8.5 and 8.6. Taking into account the triple key

Table 8.3 Associations and informal groups in Arni by membership and by influence on phases of production and typologies of socio-economic relation (economic activities)

	(a)	(b)	(c)	(d)	(e)	(f)	(g)	(h)	(i)	(l)	(m)	(n)
Production of goods												
Rice												
Arni Taluk Rice Mill Owners' Assn	1										1	
Paddy And Rice Merchants' Assn	1		1						1	1	1	
Silk												
The Arni Silk Merchants' Assn		1						1		1		1
The Tiruvannamalai District Handloom Silk Designers' Assn		1										1
Silk Twisters' Assn			1			1						
Gold												
The Tamilnadu Jewel Workers' Central Sangam			1					1			1	
Tamilnadu Gold and Silver Merchants' Federation, Chennai			1				1			1		
Buildings												
The Tamilnadu Building Workers' Sangam, Arni			1					1			1	
Arni Electricians' Sangam			1								1	
Arni Brick Makers' Assn			1									
Quarry workers												
Cement dealers												
Electricity Board Union – Citu								1			1	
Others												
Fertilisers and Pesticides			1									
Soda Factory Assn												
Bakeries												
Arni Small-Scale Industries' Assn	1											1

		1	2	3	4	5	6	7	8	9	10	11

Public Sector Unions

	1	2	3	4	5	6	7	8	9	10	11
Arni Branch of the National Federation of Postal Employees	1										
Sanitary Workers' Sangam, Arni		1					1		1		
Nursery Schools											
Arni Elementary School Teachers' Federation	1							1			

Private Traditional Services
Personal Services

	1	2	3	4	5	6	7	8	9	10	11
The Tamil Nadu Assn of Shaving Saloons		1		1		1	1	1			1
The Arni Washermans' (Dhobi) Union		1					1		1	1	
The Assn for the Progress of Tailors	1						1			1	
Tea stall											
Lottery tickets											

Consumer goods

	1	2	3	4	5	6	7	8	9	10	11
The Grocery Merchants Assn of Arni		1		1			1	1			1
Arni Town Fruits Merchants' Assn		1		1		1			1	1	
The Arni Town Flowers Merchant Sangam			1			1		1		1	
Arni Greengrocers' Assn (Gandhi Market), Arni			1			1	1	1			
Vinayaka textiles											

Transport

	1	2	3	4	5	6	7	8	9	10	11
The Valampuri Vinayakar Rickshaws Pullers' Assn		1		1			1	1			
The Arni Auto Owners and Drivers' Welfare Union		1			1	1	1			1	
The Arni Lorry Owners' Assn	1			1		1	1	1	1	1	
Dr. Ambedkar Transport Workers' Union, Arni	1				1		1		1		
Aringar Arni Bullock-Cart Drivers' Sangam 226–235		1				1				1	
The Tiruvannamalai District Bus Owners' Assn		1					1	1			
Arni Area Car and Van Drivers' Welfare Assn		1		1	1	1	1		1		
Two Wheelers (Mopeds, etc.), Spare Parts Sales Assn											
Peddal Bicycle Dealers (Mra Cycle Mart), Arni											

Finance

	1	2	3	4	5	6	7	8	9	10	11
Arni Pawnbrokers' Assn		1	1			1	1		1		

continued

Table 8.3 continued

	(a)	(b)	(c)	(d)	(e)	(f)	(g)	(h)	(i)	(l)	(m)	(n)
Others												
The Arni Chamber of Commerce	1											
The Advocates Bar Assn			1					1				
Porters' Assn			1				1		1			
Turning Works (Lathe 'Pattarias')			1				1	1	1			
Pharmacists and Druggist Assn		1						1	1	1		
New activities												
Communication												
Assn of Telephone Subscribers	1					1					1	
Telephone booths												
Professional couriers												
Printing												
Typewriting (commercial education) institutes												
Xerox												
Printing press												
Cinema and television												
The Arni Video Casstte Library Assn	1											
The Cinema Theatre Owners' Assn		1										
Cable TV operators		1				1					1	1
Electronics												
Computer studies												
(Geetha) Electronics and Home Appliances												
Finance												
Finance companies												
Banks												

Notes for Tables 8.3 and 8.4:

a Voluntary association.
b Voluntary exclusive association.
c Quasi-voluntary professional association.
d Quasi-voluntary membership by birth.
e Factors.
f Processes.
g Products.
h Capital–labour relations.
i Capital–State relations.
l Labour–State relations.
m Inter-capital relations.
n Non-economic relations.

Table 8.4 Associations and informal groups in Arni by membership and by influence on phases of production and typologies of socio-economic relations (non-economic activities)

	(a)	(d)	(c)	(f)	(g)	(h)	(i)	(l)	(m)	(n)
Caste associations										
Saurashtra Podhu Sabha		1	1		1		1		1	1
The Saurashtra Woman's Association, Arni		1								1
The Naidu Assn of Arni		1						1		1
The Tamil Nadu Karneegar Sangam, Arni		1								1
The Arni Town Vanniars' Assn		1								1
The Arni Tuluva Velalar Sangam		1							1	
The Tiruvannamalai District Vaaniar Sangam		1	1							
The Tamilnadu Brahmins Sangam ('Tambras') – Arni Branch		1								
The Tamilnadu Archakas Welfare Sangam		1								1
Tamil Saiva Chettiar						1				1
The Arni Kannada Veera Saiva Jaineekar Sangam							1			1
The Arni Town Sengunthar Sangam								1		1
Yaadavas		1								1
Ahamudaiya Mudaliars' Sangam		1								1
Religious and Political Associations										
The Indian Republican Party	1									1
Communist Party of India – Marxist	1				1					
Muslims	1									
Roman Catholics	1									
Protestant Christians	1								1	
Jains		1								
Welfare Associations										
The Inner Wheel Club of Arni	1									
The Lions Club of Arni	1									
The Rotary Club of Arni	1						1			1
All Pensioners' Assn	1								1	
The Arni Town Welfare Committee	1								1	
The Lioness Club	1								1	1

Note
See Table 8.3.

Table 8.5 Registered and unregistered associations in Ami by membership and by impact on social stability

	Impact on social stability						
	Number of schedules	*k-l relations*	*k-state relations*	*l-state relations*	*k-k relations*	*Social relations*	*Total**
Voluntary membership	21	5	6	4	5	9	29
Excluding voluntary membership	12	7	7	2	4	2	22
Quasi-voluntary membership by profession	17	1	3	3	2	15	24
Quasi-voluntary membership by birth	16	1	2	2	2	15	22
Total	66	14	18	11	13	41	97

Notes
k = capital; l = labour.
* Associations may impact on several aspects of social stability.

Table 8.6 Registered and unregistered associations by membership and impact on economic growth

	Number of schedules	Impact on phases of the production process			
		Factors	Process	Products	Total*
Voluntary membership	21	2	3	2	7
Excluding voluntary membership	12	6	2	6	14
Quasi-voluntary membership by profession	17	2	0	2	4
Quasi-voluntary membership by birth	16	2	0	1	3
Total	**66**	**12**	**5**	**11**	**28**

Note
* Associations may impact on several phases of the production process.

employed for the aggregation (i.e. voluntariness, influence on the phases of production process and influence on social stability), my comments on the evidence refer, in turn, to the relationships (i) between state and economy, (ii) among interest groups, and (iii) between economy and society.

State and economy

The survey shows the presence of the State in Arni's economy at four main levels. First, the State manages activities that are relevant for the informal economy and market-place society: it directly provides and regulates public services, such as banks and post offices, hospitals and schools, and supplies goods and infrastructural services, such as food and electricity. Moreover, it participates in the building of the economic infrastructure of the town, and it represents a major component of effective demand.[7] This aspect emerges clearly from the vast majority of reports from business, which emphasise the importance of orders from public sector institutions for items such as books, uniforms, building materials, housing, etc.[8]

Second, the State formally defines the regulative framework of certain aspects of 'informal' economic life. For example it concedes licences to trade and to use public land, and collects fiscal revenue and levies, albeit in a fashion challenged by avoidance and evasion.[9] Third, private citizens and members of the organisations frequently enter into contact with the police that may be conflicting or collusive.[10]

Fourth, the major concern of the associations is to find a way to direct their relations with the public authorities along mutually satisfactory lines. Despite the fact that the declared aim of the association might be to promote the 'welfare' or the 'interest' of the members, the actual aim is to limit the intrusiveness of the State in their field and to lobby for the interest of the associations. In other terms, their function is to enter into political exchange with the State – i.e. to bargain over state actions and state influence on the economy – in order to define the terms of the relationships between state/economy/society.[11] Corruption is a central ingredient of this political exchange.[12]

Economic interests

Turning to the analysis of the socio-economic organisation of Arni from a sec-toral perspective, it is important to notice that the core activities of the town are regulated by a strict associational order. So, the Paddy and Rice Mills' Associ-ation dominates the rice sector by regulating the relationships among members as far as problems with labour and weights are concerned.[13] Employer/employee relations are also managed within the rice firms and are controlled directly by collective agreements by the owners/entrepreneurs. This is also the case of the Silk Twisters' Association, which participates in the regulation of the silk sector, informing members about cases of misbehaviour of workers in order to organise collective punishment. By contrast, the major aim of the Tamil Nadu Gold and Silver Merchants' Federation is the internal control of the profession. This takes the form of quasi-voluntary membership: a necessary condition to enter the pro-fession is to be a member, while members are more or less obliged to accept the formal and informal rules decided by the association. In this sense, membership is a way of enforcing the association's rules.

The associational order also impacts on the phases of the production process. In relation to the access to factors of production, there are associations that dom-inate the private credit system (i.e. the Association of Pawnbrokers) and regulate the link between official and unofficial sources of financing. Some associations keep strong control over information about the channels to obtain loans from private sources – as in the case of the Barbers' Association and the Tamil Nadu Jewel Workers' Central Sangam, while in other cases – as for instance the Grocery Merchants' Association – credit systems are organised to allow members to 'purchase commodities ... without interest'. Also the Tamil Nadu Building Workers' Sangam 'in some cases gives interest-free loans' to members.

Associations also play a major role in education, training and enrollment of workers. This is particularly evident in the case of caste associations when they organise individuals working in the same profession, such as the Barbers' Asso-ciation and the Weavers' Association, but it is also common for other business associations that examine the family background of workers and their caste at the moment of enrolment. Caste associations – for instance The Tamil Nadu Karneegar Sangam – also provide the members with 'counselling for getting education', while other associations – for instance the Arni Washermen's Union (a caste-based association) – have the main aim to 'see that washermen are employed on a regular basis'.

Finally, the organisational structure defines the working times for each cat-egory of workers, and influences prices – but not the quality of the products – and wages. For instance, the Tamil Nadu Association of Shaving Saloons and the Arni Electricians' Sangam fix the rate for the services provided by the members. Similarly, the Arni Silk Merchants' Association controls the biennial revision of weavers' wages and exerts a pressure 'on government to provide insurance cover to weavers'. Likewise, the Tiruvannamalai District Handloom Silk Designer Association reports that – before the starting of the Sangam – design workers were getting unsatisfactory remuneration, a problem that the Sangam has solved. By contrast, the Grocery Merchants' Association, while not setting the prices, collects the information on the basis of which prices are determined, while the Arni Area Car and Van Drivers' Welfare Association ensures that the members are regularly paid their wages. Finally, the powerful Paddy and Rice Merchants' Association, denouncing the widespread risk of corruption and fraud, emphasises the necessity to define a common policy and practice for members in relation to the measures to be used in transactions.

Associations are usually in charge of the representation of members' interests. Yet, their regulatory function clearly emerges from the interviews. This is the case of the Association for the Progress of Tailors that (i) issues identity cards to regulate the participation of members, (ii) divides 'the work (from public orders) among the members' in order 'to benefit many families economically', (iii) provides assistance in order to get credit, and (iv) ensures the members' protection in cases of conflicts with the employers ('many tailors who are not members of the Association are removed with impunity by employers'). Similar cases include that of the Valumpuri Vinayakar Rickshaw Pullers' Association, whose main aim is to define an 'informal code of conduct' for members, and of the Arni Auto Owners and Drivers' Association, which sets the prices for the services provided by members and, at the same time, protects members in case of accidents and disputes. Another form of regulatory role is shown in the case of the Raw Silk Twisters' Association, which informs 'all factories' about workers who can create problems.

The regulatory role is also stressed by the Porters' Association (a caste-based association), which protects members' interests in the labour market. Similarly, the Soda Factory Association argues that 'a new shop has to be started only with the consent of the Association which would create otherwise problems for the person starting it'. Also, the Tamil Nadu Gold and Silver Jewellery Merchants' Federation regulates activity, warning its members about the risk of purchasing stolen jewels, while the Arni Pawnbrokers' Association aims to ensure that members are 'licence holders'. Another major example of the regulatory function is provided by the Chamber of Commerce, which explicitly aims at controlling competition in order to keep prices and profits at a reasonable level for Arni's business economy as a whole.

The role of labour unions is mainly confined to the public sector. Four main associations 'protect' the interests of public workers. This is the case, in particular, of the National Federation of Postal Employees, which aims to 'fight against the punishment imposed by the superior authorities' and for 'pay rise'. It also exerts pressure for 'the implementation of all the benefits and privileges given by the government'. The central and local state is also the counterpart of the other three public sector unions – Sanitary Workers' Sangam, Nursery School Sangam, and School Teachers' Federation – which share the common aim to protect the workers and their sectors of activity from corruption and inter-ference of state officials.

In addition to these, the Dr Ambedkar Transport Workers' Union should also be mentioned as a particular type of trade union that groups mainly (but not only) SCs workers who are employed by the Transport Service (government-owned). The aim of this union is to support the rights of SCs transport workers against any kind of negative discrimination, in particular when a worker is con-sidered 'undersirable' and there is the risk of 'dismission'. Finally, there is the Electricity Board Union, which has among its aims to ensure 'the security for workers and for society', to 'influence policy formation regarding wages' and to 'advise the government on policy'.

Economy and society

The caste structure and the social distribution of religions in Arni are shown in Figure 8.1, from which it emerges that members of 15 castes and sub-castes and people from the major religions, such as Hindus, Jains, Christians, Muslims all live together in the town and participate in civil society associations.[14]

This applies in particular (but not only) to business and professional associ-ations (other than those that are caste-based) that, by claiming to be 'open' to members from all castes, Muslims and Christians, assert a secular pluralistic identity. There are cases of important associations in which Muslim individuals occupy the top positions. This happens in the case of leading economic associ-ations, such as the Arni Chamber of Commerce, the Jewellery Association and the Clothing Merchants' association.

Yet caste representation in formal caste associations is strong. The representa-tion of SCs (about 15 per cent of Arni's population, the majority of whom are employed in rice mills and public health/sanitation services) is not entrusted to one caste association, but is segmented into a number of small business and pro-fessional associations, unions and political parties. These forms of 'organisa-tional' representation have two major aspects in common: they lobby to defend their members politically and economically, and they bargain with the State for the implementation of the Reservation Policy, i.e. for the positive discrimination in terms of employment opportunities and other benefits.

Small business associations aim to keep under control the internal level of conflicts, providing a sort of behavioural code that guides members. As reported in interview, the Arni Town Fruit Merchants' Sangam, in which more than 90 per cent of the members are SCs, has been formed in order to protect members from the police ('to fight its tyranny'). Also, the Rickshaw Pulling Association shares the aim to 'protect members from the harassment by the police'; yet, it also lobbies in order to ensure that the Municipality gives 'legal recognition to the rickshaw stand' and defines a behaviour code for community members who 'should not work when under the influence of drugs, not indulge in gambling, not speak to customers'. The Sanitary Workers' Sangam – a scheduled-caste-based trade union – declares the aim of protecting members from government's

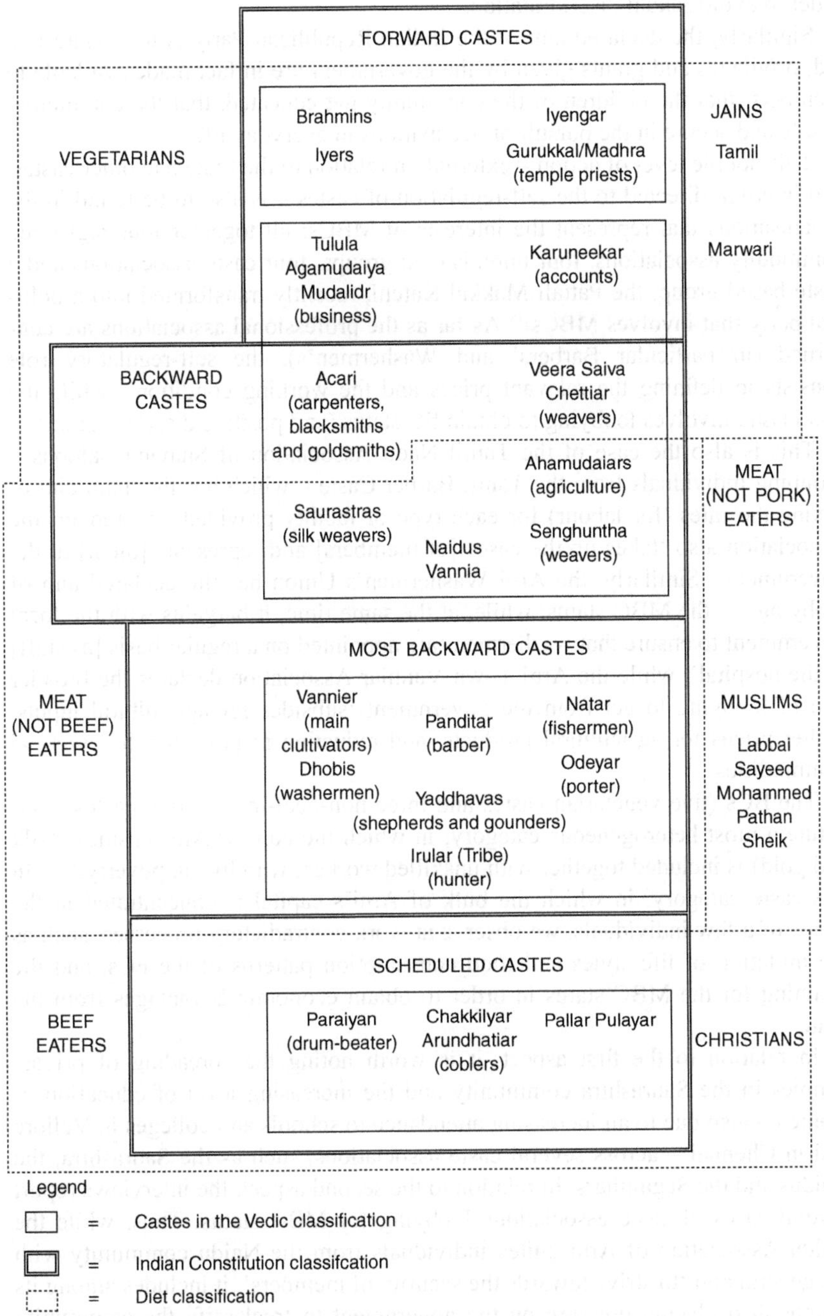

FORWARD CASTES

VEGETARIANS

Brahmins   Iyengar
Iyers   Gurukkal/Madhra
(temple priests)

JAINS
Tamil

Tulula
Agamudaiya
Mudalidr
(business)

Karuneekar
(accounts)

Marwari

BACKWARD
CASTES

Acari
(carpenters,
blacksmiths
and goldsmiths)

Veera Saiva
Chettiar
(weavers)

Ahamudaiars
(agriculture)

MEAT
(NOT PORK)
EATERS

Saurastras
(silk weavers)

Naidus
Vannia

Senghuntha
(weavers)

MOST BACKWARD CASTES

MEAT
(NOT BEEF)
EATERS

Vannier
(main
clultivators)

Panditar
(barber)

Natar
(fishermen)

Dhobis
(washermen)

Odeyar
(porter)

Yaddhavas
(shepherds and gounders)

Irular (Tribe)
(hunter)

MUSLIMS

Labbai
Sayeed
Mohammed
Pathan
Sheik

SCHEDULED CASTES

BEEF
EATERS

Paraiyan
(drum-beater)

Chakkilyar
Arundhatiar
(coblers)

Pallar Pulayar

CHRISTIANS

Legend

☐ = Castes in the Vedic classification

☐ = Indian Constitution classifcation

☐ = Diet classification

Figure 8.1 Castes hierarchies in Arni.

'scant regard to views of workers' and of monitoring the organisation of work in order to avoid sexual discrimination.

Similarly, the declared aim of the Indian Republican Party is to 'ensure that aid, privileges and grants given by the government are in fact made available to members, that the children of the community get educated, that the community is safe and secure in the pursuit of occupations in everyday life'.

This double level of action – external, in relation to the State and other castes, and internal, directed to the self-regulation of castes – is also to be found in the organisations that represent the interests of MBCs: all together four registered commodity associations, four unregistered groups, four caste associations and a caste-based group, the Pattali Makkal Katchi, recently transformed into a political party that involves MBCs.[15] As far as the professional associations are concerned (in particular Barbers' and Washermen's), the self-regulatory role consists in defining the relevant prices and the working conditions, while the main issue involves lobbying to obtain SC status (and positive discrimination).

This is also the case of the Tamil Nadu Association of Shaving Saloons – grouping individuals from the Tamil Barber Caste – which has the main aim of 'fixing the rates (for labour) for each type of facility provided'. Moreover, the Association also 'takes up the cases [of members] and represents [them] to the government'. Similarly, the Arni Washermen's Union has the declared aim of lobbying for the MBC status, while, at the same time, it bargains with the local government to ensure that washermen 'are appointed on a regular basis [as staff] in the hospital', while the Arni Town Vanniar Association declares the broader aim of lobbying to get from the government 'subsides for agricultural inputs, higher prices for agricultural products, and reduction in price for the essential commodities'.

The BCs (five vegetarian castes and three non-beef-meat-eating castes) constitute a most heterogeneous category, in which the core of Arni business (silk and gold) is included together with unskilled workers who live in poverty.[16, 17] In this caste category, in which the bulk of Arni's capital is concentrated in the hands of a few individuals, we observe at work contradictory processes, such as the imitation of life styles and food consumption patterns of the FCs, and the claiming for the MBC status in order to obtain economic advantages from the State.

In relation to the first aspect, it is worth noting the spreading of private temples in the Saurashtra community and the increasing level of education of women – also due to an increasing attendance to schools and colleges in Vellore and in Chennai – across several caste associations, such as the Saurashtra, the Naidus and the Segunthars. In relation to the second aspect, the interviews report several cases of caste associations lobbying for MBC status. Thus, while the Naidu Association of Arni unites individuals from the Naidu community with the general aim 'to strive towards the security of members', it includes among its actions also placing pressure on the government to 'reclassify the community from present BC status to the MBC category (so that they can enjoy more specific reservation quotas)'. A similar action is also reported by the Tamil Nadu

Karneegar Sangam, the Tiruvannamalai District Vanniar Sangam, the Yadavas Sangam and the Arni Kannada Veera Saiva Jainkeekar Sangam.

By contrast, other examples exist – such as that of the Tamil Nadu Jewel Workers' Central Sangam (Arni Branch), which organises goldsmiths – in which the activity is mainly aimed at the internal regulation of businesses ('to improve job security of goldsmiths') and the protection of members in trouble with the police (in the case of stolen jewels); while the Arni Town Segunthar Sangam mainly works on social welfare in order to 'improve the conditions of the community' providing 'free tuition to children' and 'aid to poor families'.

The aim of protecting the community in its relations with the local and central governments and to regulate internal relations is also observed in the case of FC civil society.[18] Here, again, the claiming of BC status is a common practice in the political exchange with local and central authorities and is an ideologically unifying aspiration for the various communities.

Caste associations exhibit two fields of action: an internal field, with the aim of self-regulation, and an external field, with the aim of lobbying and bargaining with the State to obtain advantages. So, the Tamil Nadu Brahmin's Sangam (Arni Branch) – which organises all Brahmin communities in the town – denounces the widespread feeling of 'depression and oppression' of its members due to the increasing difficulty in getting government employment, as a consequence of the Reservation Policy; this situation contrasts with the high level of education of the community in which more than 60 per cent of the members reach the level of secondary school and about 30 per cent reach the level of college education. A similar situation is denounced by the Tamil Nadu Archaka's Welfare Sangam (grouping Gurukkals – a sub-Brahmin caste), which complains about the fact that the community is not given 'due respect' by government.

From the field material it appears that caste associations perform two main roles. First, they regulate the internal relationships in two major ways: by defining a widely accepted behavioural code and by providing several forms of social support for the weakest members. Since caste associations are in some cases also occupation groups, this internal self-regulation easily becomes a major organising factor for the economy with a direct influence on capital/labour relationships, regulating the working conditions. Second, caste associations explicitly involve political exchanges with the State for the intermediation of particularistic interests. The most common attempt takes the form of lobbying to obtain a lower caste status – behaviour which is broadly found among all BC and FC associations. Other forms of political bargaining and negotiations range from requesting recognition of the public importance of specific activities – as in the case of the rickshaw pullers – to seeking protection from police harassment, as in the case of goldsmiths, and to the request of Brahmins for an improved access to public employment and more 'respectful' treatment by the State.

'Welfare' associations – i.e. the associations that claim to promote the town's interests instead of those of specific groups – complete Arni's associational order. These associations, whose spheres of action range from philanthropy to lobbying for the town's infrastructure, are significant because they contain and enhance the cross-caste idea of the town's 'unity'. Elite associations such as the Rotary Club, the Lions Club (together with its women's wing), and the Inner Wheel Club of Arni (another women's association), which are in principle open to all social classes components, actually group the well-off members of the town and legitimate the role of the elites, emphasising the importance of philanthropy.[19] These associations are involved in several forms of 'social service organisations' in the fields of health, education, and charity. They assist in the central and local government's social campaigns, organising blood and eye donations and free eye treatment. Moreover, they organise free distribution of food, books, clothes and medicines. The Rotary Club organises free shows of 'patriotic films' in Arni. In their several activities they work in strict collaboration with public institutions, such as hospitals and schools.

The action of the elite clubs is integrated by the Arni Town Welfare Committee, which has the objective of 'setting right the grievances of citizens regarding defective or deficient drainage, drinking water, environment, roads'. According to the field material, the Committee integrates the action of the elite associations, as it can enter into political exchange with the State in order to improve the welfare of the town, while the Rotary Club and the Lions Club cannot come into conflict with local government due to their philanthropic vocation. Yet, they support the action of the Committee. Together, the elite associations and the Arni Town Welfare Committee support and enhance the infrastructural and physical pre-conditions for the market economy.

We can conclude our analysis by observing that the survey has shown the existence in Arni's civil society of an associational order with a significant impact on the economy. The associations we have reviewed create the social environment for accumulation regulating individual and group interactions at two major complementary levels: first, within the associational framework (inside each association and between associations) and second between associations and the State.

4　Class relations in Arni's civil society

Arni's associational order reflects social production relations. Capital and labour are represented in a variety of forms. Yet, to identify these forms might be a challenging task because Arni, like India at large, has a complex socio-economic structure in which caste is intertwined with class. In relation to labour, the social structure operates at two levels. First, labour is aggregated in several caste associations, mainly in the SC and in MBC categories. Second, some 'professional' and 'business' associations (i.e. petty trade and small activities' associations) organise individuals who, while formally 'independent' workers, lack economic autonomy and depend on informal credit market and on merchants for the provision of inputs, and are often wage labour in disguise. Such associations should be interpreted as representing 'labour' rather than 'capital'.[20]

It should also be emphasised that non-class associations, such as caste and petty business associations, also have an ideological role as they concur in undermining the class-consciousness of the lower strata of Arni's society. The political-economic organisation of wage-labour and other types of 'dependent' labour on the basis of non-class criteria substitutes for the formal representation of workers in trade unions. Moreover, this form of aggregation – confirming that Arni's society is not only segmented by class but also by caste – provides an institutional and an ideological support to capital's hegemony.

Another feature of Arni's social structure is found in the role of 'big' business associations in the internal management of industrial relations. 'Big' business associations are overt capital associations that directly control intra-firm labour/capital relations defining behavioural codes widely recognised by members, by virtue of a low degree of voluntariness of membership.[21] Moreover, 'big' business associations are involved in the bargaining with the State in fields that are relevant for the sector as a whole, including working conditions. This role helps explaining the absence of unions in the private sector, because employers represent the interests of the employees in any context they believe to be relevant. I do not have enough information to prove the causal link between the absence of trade unions and the role of interest intermediation played by the employers. Yet, it is legitimate to believe that the inadequacy of workers' organised representation in Arni's private sector is due, in part at least, to the 'paternalistic' control of industrial relations, as it occurs in other South Indian contexts.[22]

So there is an asymmetry between the representation of labour and capital that is a major trait of Arni's associational order. While employers are widely organised by means of interest groups that shape inter-firm relations, control intra-firm relations, and bargain over the terms of state intervention, employees' organisations are weak and lack a collective dimension. This may explain why unions are missing, while the working class interests often blend with other social components, as in the cases of cultural and religious associations, or are aggregated on the basis of features other than social production relations, as in the case of caste associations. The only cases of collective workers' organisations in the contemporary meaning of the term are to be found in the trade unions of public sector workers.

The asymmetry is even more striking if we take into account that Arni shows a remarkable trend in the increase of associations, whose numbers have doubled in two decades.[23]

Two factors explain the increase in the number of associations. The first is that formal interest representation is widely recognised as a necessary condition for inter-personal and inter-group relations needed to enter political relationship with the State. This holds at an economic level, with business and professional (and in some cases also caste) associations, and at a social level, with caste and welfare associations.

The second factor is the change in the caste system. I have already stressed in Chapter 5 the new political roles of caste. While it cannot be said that economic growth has displaced the caste system in the town, caste has undergone deep processes of (political) change, adapting to the emergence of the diversified non-farm economy. While caste associations do not disappear with the development of economic associations, their role in the economy varies according to the importance and social status of the economic interests involved. In this sense, castes and economic interests mutually reinforce each other and together they support Arni's associational order.

The final remark refers to the State. The State is a central component of Arni's collective life. The actual aim of all the associations is to enter into political relationships with the State in order to negotiate particularistic interests. At the same time, it appears from the field evidence that to belong to an association is a necessary condition to enter into political relationships with the State. Moreover, in spite of liberalisation, due to its role in providing infrastructure and its contribution to effective demand in the region, the influence of the State on Arni's economy – in particular on accumulation – is still high. This explains bargaining and corruption in the multifarious attempts to privatise the benefits deriving directly or indirectly from the State.

The survey of Arni's civil society contributes to our knowledge of the town's economy and society in three major ways. First, in the town there exists an associational order that is built on economic and non-economic associations governing the production process in all phases as representatives of capital and labour's interests. Second, Arni's associational order is biased toward capital. The representation of capital is strong – owing to the joint action of 'big' business associations and locally dominant caste associations. By contrast, there is a systematic under-representation of labour, owing to lack of labour associations together with the absorption of the (disguised) labour force under non-economic and non-class associations. This bias against labour implies that decisions about recruitment of workers and about working conditions are in the hands of capital. The main responsibility for the low level of representation of workers in trade unions is due to the way caste associations and caste ideology neutralise class. Third, the State is a central institution of 'governance' and the open aim of Arni's associations is to bargain with the State in order to obtain advantages for their members. In this sense, Arni's associations appear to be intermediaries – and not only representatives – of class interests.

In ending this section, the first conclusion can be drawn that the survey evidence is largely consistent with the Gramscian proposition about the role of the organised civil society in supporting capital's hegemony. Arni's associations provide the cross-class institutional structure in which capital's hegemony is negotiated. Caste associations stand out for their twofold role: as regulating institutions for economic behaviour inside each caste group and as intermediaries in the political relationship with the State.

A notable aspect of the Gramscian argument that is not fully confirmed by the survey is the 'voluntariness' of participation in caste and non-caste associational life. Here, there is a major discrepancy between form and substance. While participation is defined in formal terms on a voluntary basis, the evidence shows that the degree of 'voluntariness' of membership is very variable, and in some significant cases participation appears to be compulsory.

This is a key aspect that should not be forgotten as it explains the role of Arni's organised civil society within the historical bloc that has been leading the industrial transformation of the town. This role is explored in the next section.

5 Arni's societal corporatism

Arni's organised civil society shows features that are typical of societal corporatism: (i) the associational order emerges under the pressure of social groups, as shown by the evidence in Section 3 (and thus is not imposed by the State); (ii) it is composed of interest associations – i.e. associations of individuals sharing social and economic interests; (iii) interest associations are involved in several types of socio-economic relations in each phase of the production process; and (iv) the underlying function of the associational order is to regulate social relationships and to create the conditions for economic growth.

Associations are at the same time *representatives* and *intermediaries* of particularistic interests, and perform their regulatory role in three major ways: by helping to determine members' interests; by negotiating agreements on members' behalf; and by enforcing such agreements to their members. In performing these roles, they assume a 'quasi-public nature'.

As usual in societal corporatism, Arni's corporatist regime is tripartite, involving state, capital and labour. Yet, the standard tripartite logic of political exchange is adapted to Arni's social structure and informal economy, in which – due to the co-existence of several forms of stratification – capital and labour are jointly represented and regulated by class and non-class associations. Caste is a major pillar of Arni's corporatism, playing a twofold role as ideology and as institution. Through caste, social constraints are transferred to the economy, determining the overlap between economy and society that is specific to corporatism.

The primary aims of Arni's associations are to enter into political exchange with the State and to provide the institutional framework for social interaction. Acting as representatives, intermediaries of members' interests and regulators, associations share behavioural codes. Membership is the necessary condition to participate in political relationships, while – in particular in cases such as 'big' business associations – non-participation implies exclusion from political exchange and often also from entry into economic activity. Accordingly, the degree of voluntariness of participation in interest associations in Arni is low and decreasing as the importance of economic interests increases.

The by-product of Arni's societal corporatism is the social stability that is obtained by controlling the level of conflicts. The field material reveals a common tendency to deny the relevance, or even the existence, of both capital/labour conflicts and inter-firm conflicts. The absence of inter-firm conflicts appears to be the result of the very existence and action of (trade and business) associations, and suggests that to limit inter-firm conflicts is their social function and that membership means accepting this. One possible implication is that the absence of inter-firm conflicts should be seen as an indicator of the efficacy of the associations in performing their function.

The situation is much more complex in the case of capital/labour conflicts. As we have seen, the survey shows that there is a major asymmetry in the representation of labour and capital, as labour is under-represented, while the larger part of the membership and the activity of business associations overtly represents capital. This asymmetry goes together with another important asymmetry that refers to the management of capital/labour relations. From the survey we understand that capital/labour relations are usually managed within individual firms and are directly controlled by employers. Associations of capitalists are in charge of all decisions concerning the enrolment of workers and working conditions. They also control the 'misbehaviour' of workers and the collective punishment of individual actions against the rules. In this sense, in Arni's corporatism, policy concertation is substantially open only to state and capital.

Caste ideology is functional to the corporatist project. Paradoxically, by undermining class-consciousness and by fracturing the unity of the working class, caste enhances social cohesion. Moreover, it provides the ideological instruments that limit the perception of the quasi-compulsory nature of the associational order, ensuring a 'voluntary' consensus in favour of the hegemony of the dominant classes, and promoting the 'voluntary' participation of subaltern classes in organised civil society.

As in societal corporatism, Arni's corporatism is meant to promote economic growth. The survey shows that the associational order enhances economic growth in three major ways. First, social stability is in itself a factor of growth as it creates a favourable environment for decision-making. This applies to all phases of the production process, from access to inputs and enrolment and training of workers, to access to output markets, to the setting of output prices and to inter-firm relations. Second, the associational order regulates the relations between Arni's economy and the State. The State is an important source of demand and associations ensure that state orders are distributed among producers without conflict. Third, the regulation of the economy reduces risk and enhances investment. This aspect is particularly important in the process of economic diversification that is an important trait of Arni's economy in the post-GR period.

6 Arni's societal corporatism and India's capitalist development

In this chapter I have explored the Gramscian proposition that caste is not only an ideology that plays an anti-class role, undermining class-consciousness and the unity of the working class; it also gives birth to an institutional structure that influences capitalist growth creating the social environment in which capital's hegemony is negotiated and workers' 'spontaneous' consensus on it is gained. The proposition has been explored by means of a survey of Arni's organised civil society that has taken into account all the organisations and associations active in the town in the period 1997–1998.

Largely confirming the proposition, the survey has shown that caste provides the ideological cement that keeps together the segments of the capitalist and subaltern classes, creating the institutional structure through which subaltern workers are led to accept the moral and intellectual leadership of capitalists. Moreover, the survey has shown that Arni's associational order contrasts with the standard Gramscian theory of hegemony for the low – and variable – degree of voluntariness of membership. I have explained this contrast, arguing that Arni is a case of societal corporatism – emerging from below under the pressure of social groups – in which the participation in associations is virtually compulsory and associations are in charge of the representation and intermediation of particularistic interests.

In concluding the chapter, my aim is to show that Arni's corporatist order is consistent with the social production relations prevailing in the town and it may be interpreted as a form of adaptation of Arni's socio-economic structure to the deregulation and informalisation associated with the liberalisation of India's economy.

The results of the survey of civil society are consistent with the evidence analysed in Chapters 6 and 7. Arni is an informal and diversified economy with low-quality employment, inhabited by small and medium-size firms. As I have shown in the case of the silk sector, class structure is dominated by the segmented classes of capitalists and subaltern workers.

The associational order is strongly biased against labour. Not only is labour under-represented; it is also excluded from the management of capital/labour relations that are directly controlled by the employers within the firms with the support of business and trade associations, which are responsible for the definition of working conditions too. Similarly, labour is under-represented in the political exchange with the State, where its interests are represented and mediated by non-class associations. The asymmetry between labour and capital is masked by the ideological support of caste and cultural associations in which the consensus on capital's hegemony is negotiated.

Jointly, social production relations and the associational order that regulates them gave birth to the corporatist historical bloc that has supported Arni's post-GR industrial transition by ensuring: (i) the control of capitalists over the means of production and subaltern workers' labour power and bodies; (ii) the ideological use of caste to fracture working class' unity; and (iii) the organised representation and intermediation of class interests in which labour is systematically under-represented and misrepresented.

Arni's corporatist historical bloc has shown to be functional to the existence and reproduction of capital's hegemony and to capitalist growth. The control over the means of production and over the labour force is the basis itself of the capitalist mode of production, while the ideological use of religion ensures the consensus in the lower strata of society over a capitalist pattern of growth that imposes indecent working conditions and that uses collective resources for class objectives.

Arni's corporatist capitalism is based on caste. Caste does not appear a 'pre-capitalist residual' to be dissolved by capitalist development. By contrast, it is a necessary 'impurity' that supports a historically specific 'variety' of capitalism in which class and non-class relations intertwine. Caste associations – the 'materialisation' of caste ideology – are necessary as non-class mediators of class interests in order to limit capital/labour and capital/capital conflicts. Caste ideology enhances the corporatist project, undermining the unity of the working class and endorsing the 'alliance' between capital and labour.

The survey only provides a snapshot of Arni's civil society and does not tell us much about the process leading to this outcome. However, useful insights might come from the contextualisation of Arni's corporatist regime within India's capitalist development in the post-GR period.

It seems to me that, analysed through a Marxist/Institutionalist lenses, Arni's societal corporatism might be interpreted as the adaptation of the local socio-economic system to the changes occurring in the global (national and international) economy.

As seen in Chapter 3, the introduction of HYVs in Indian agriculture inaugurated a season of reforms, culminating in 1991 in economic liberalisation. While initially the aim was the 'modernisation' of the economy pursued by means of technical change – as with the GR – and finalised as the reduction of instability and deprivation, since the mid-1980s the aim became economic liberalisation pursued by means of pro-market/pro-business policies. Together with deregulation and international openness, economic liberalisation brought about a marked increase of informality – already a structural trait of Indian economy – together with the consolidation of non-state forms of regulation.

At local level, economic liberalisation induced a process of socio-spatial restructuring of economic activity, which, in the case of Arni and its hinterland has been reviewed in Part II of this book. As seen, this process has enhanced the local/global integration of the town and promoted local forms of social regulation facing the retreat of the State. In front of the increasing deregulation, the associational regime revealed by the survey has provided a comprehensive regulation of Arni's economy and society, covering the major relations between the State and the economy, between capital and labour, and among firms.

Arni's social regulation by means of association is functional to economic liberalisation. While participation in associations is necessary to enter the political exchange with the State, the aim patently pursued by the associations in political exchange is to limit the intrusiveness of the State and to substitute state regulation with non-state regulation. The State is excluded from the bargaining between capital and labour over working conditions, which is again in charge of the associations. Moreover, the aim of the social regulation of capital/labour relations is to support the interests of capital. Yet, it also ensures the flexibility and informality of production organisation necessary for adapting Arni business economy to the local/global changes induced by economic liberalisation. Also, the regulation of inter-firm relations, which again is in charge of the associations, in particular as far as the source of inputs and the destination of output is concerned, has the explicit aim of creating external economies for the enterprises, enhancing the competitiveness of the town's economy in local and global (national and international) markets. Then, as a local solution to the retreat of the

State after liberalisation, the self-regulation produced by Arni's civil society associations is far-reaching, powerful and successful. It covers the major relations in the economic sphere, supporting deregulation and progressively adapting to the reduced state influence on the economy, relegating state functions to the provision and regulation of public services.

A major aspect of Arni's self-regulation is the corporatist management of capital/labour relations. The survey shows that, from the perspective of capital, this is a particularly effective form of management of capital/labour relations, owing to the fact that it keeps the level of social conflicts low, reducing workers' perception of their poor living and working conditions; and it enhances the flexibility of Arni's social structure, facilitating the adaptation to local/global changes, and the integration of Arni's economy and society in the global economy. Yet, the survey shows that the corporatist order is functional also to the existence and reproduction of Arni's diversified and informal economy in the context of post-reform Indian capitalism, for the major reason that it lowers the perception of the social costs of liberalisation, which, as we have seen in Chapter 3, are very high, especially in rural India.

This chapter concludes the assessment of Arni's capitalism. The empirical analysis on the town broadly confirms the conclusion drawn in the first part of the book for Provincial India as a whole. The evidence shows that Arni's economy is diversified and informal and that it is inhabited by two segmented classes that represent capital and labour. As it occurs in Provincial India, capitalist production relations are intertwined with relations and structures that the country has inherited from her colonial and post-colonial past. Also, the Gramscian hypothesis put forward with reference to India's economy at large is confirmed in the town, showing that caste influences production relations by creating an institutional framework in which capital's hegemony is negotiated.

Jointly, the first and the second part of this book provide evidence and analysis on the nature and working of capitalism in Provincial India. In the next chapter I review this evidence and analysis, with the twofold aim of pointing out the distinguishing traits of this variety of capitalism and of drawing the main implications in terms of working and living standards.

9   The low road of capitalism

In this book I have analysed capitalist development in Provincial India in the post-Green Revolution period. My aim was to identify its distinguishing traits and to assess its 'quality' in terms of living standards and working conditions.

The analysis has been carried out at two distinct levels. First, I have focused on Provincial India at large, which I have analysed by means of official macro data and with the support of the literature. Second, I have explored capitalist development in Arni, a market town in Northern Tamil Nadu that has been widely researched over more than four decades. The analysis has been conducted by means of an eclectic analytical framework combining Marxist and Institutionalist categories.

In concluding the book I draw conclusions from the previous analysis, commenting on the working of India's provincial capitalism.

1 The necessity of being eclectic

Two guiding principles have inspired the choice of the Marxist/Institutionalist framework for the analysis of capitalism: (i) the necessity of a theoretical background in applied socio-economic research; and (ii) the primacy of evidence over theoretical rigour. These principles follow from the belief that, while real world processes should not be adapted to fit abstract theoretical models, the identification of the forces behind socio-economic processes would not be possible without a theoretical representation of reality. Socio-economic theory is a social construction and a major task for applied analysts is to assess the interpretative power of the theory that supports empirical research and to understand when and how adaptations or improvements are needed in order to explain the evidence.

The conceptual framework chosen for my analysis is eclectic in many senses. While relying on Marxism and Institutionalism – two theories that, taken together, may account for the main features of contemporary capitalism, i.e. the variety of organisational forms and the high level of class and class conflicts – the framework includes concepts and propositions borrowed from several Marxist and Institutionalist approaches joined by their rebuff of rational/optimising behaviour. Moreover, it has been built 'empirically', selecting the theoretical contributions on the basis of their explanatory power of the evidence.

Owing to the specificities of economy and society in Provincial India, the choice of an eclectic framework was a necessity. In India, individual behaviour and social intercourse are regulated by institutions and structures deeply rooted in culture and history, giving birth to a socio-economic system that differs from the purely capitalist society owing to the persistence of non-market features. As a consequence, major segments of India's economy and society in which these features appear to be particularly strong – as in the case of rural areas – are considered 'backward' and the degree of capitalist penetration is still debated. It was necessary to support the analysis by means of a framework able to interpret the sharp contrast between India's high rate of growth and her increasing global integration and the lasting influence of non-market (non-capitalist) institutions and structures.

As discussed in previous chapters, the eclectic framework has shown to be suitable to explore the nature and working of India's provincial capitalism. It has been stressed that capitalist transition is no longer an issue in Provincial India and the distinguishing traits of provincial non-farm capitalism have been identifed, even when they are hidden behind the cultural institutions and relations that India has inherited from her colonial and post-colonial past.

2 The distinguishing traits of capitalism in Provincial India

As I have shown in Chapter 3, India's rural non-farm economy is deeply diversified and informally organised. The available micro evidence and the official data show that agriculture has lost its primacy in terms of income and employment generation and that rural diversification has shown an increasing trend. In deep contrast with the stagnation of overall employment and the decline of agricultural employment, non-farm employment shows an increasing rate of growth. In 2009–2010 more than 30 per cent of the rural workforce was engaged in non farm-activities.

Institutional embeddedness and spatial embeddedness

Different trajectories of diversification are observed. They exert a major influence on the spatial distribution of non-farm activities (in towns and villages), on their sectoral composition (production of goods and services), and on the scale of operation/structure of the firms. The activity is usually carried out in small and micro enterprises, which employ 'artisanal' technologies and are based on individual and family labour forces. Petty producers have a contradictory class location and often have an incomplete control over production, being expropriated of the bulk of their entrepreneurial functions by middlemen and subcontractors. They are 'pseudo-entrepreneurs' who employ a low-skilled labour force – mainly unpaid family labour – and use primitive technology. The 'quality' of labour arrangements for the workers of the diversified economy is also very variable – from low-paid casual work to regular well-paid work – and this variability is explained by the scale of operation but also by the degree of local/global integration of the firms, and by personal and family identities and features.

The increasing trend of rural industrialisation occurs in a context of widespread informality. The NSSO data for 2009–2010 shows that, at All India level, informality involves more than 80 per cent of the workers inside and outside the informal sector. In addition to agriculture, in which more than 90 per cent of employment is informal, informal organisation is observed in all sectors of the non-farm economy and is mainly found among self-employed workers and casual workers. While the phenomenon is spatially widespread, informality is systematically higher in rural areas than in urban areas.

While pointing out a minor contraction in informal employment since 2004–2005, the NSSO data for 2009–2010 confirms the precarious conditions in which informal workers live and work. The vast majority are engaged in very small enterprises (fewer than six employees) in which the use of electricity – a proxy to measure the development of techniques – is very low. Their pay is systematically below the pay of the workers in the formal sector, in particular in the case of rural informal workers. The data also suggests a worsening trend in working conditions. Since 2004–2005 the proportion of rural informal workers without written contracts has increased (more than 80 per cent), as has the proportion of rural informal workers not eligible for paid leave and for social benefits (again 80 per cent in both cases). Moreover, women, SC workers and ST workers are systematically segregated in low-wage and low-quality jobs. Finally, the precarious working conditions of informal workers, together with the long working hours and the lack of weekly holidays, are responsible for the high rate of occupational diseases and accidents.

While rural diversification is endemic in rural India as a cushion in agrarian crises, and informality is a structural feature of the primary sector which extends also to non-farm activities, there are few doubts that the injection of capital connected to the Green Revolution has played a key role in changing the scale of these phenomena. Together with the contraction of agricultural employment – a physiological process in a high-growing country – they have changed the organisation of Provincial India in depth. As the NSSO data suggests, with the reduction of agricultural employment below 60 per cent and the increasing process of rural industrialisation, India has entered a new phase of her structural transformation since the end of the twentieth century.

In this new phase of structural transformation, non-farm Provincial India appears to be composed of different socio-economic systems, each one with a specific mix of non-farm activities, in which production is carried out in small and micro enterprises informally organised. Besides informality and diversification, which appear as structural features, these socio-economic systems are identified by their spatial and institutional embeddedness; the vast majority of the relations and structures on which they rely occur within a delimited locality and institutions shape individual aims and choice, influencing social intercourse.

The distinctiveness of class structure

India's structural transformation goes together with a major change in class structure, which was explored in Chapter 4. With Bagchi (2002), I have argued that capital and labour need to be redefined to take into account this change.

A Marxist/Institutionalist review of the evidence available in the literature on Provincial India shows that multiple trajectories of class formation and multiple forms of labour commoditisation exist. The outcome is a class structure that is dominated by the two antagonist classes of capitalists and subaltern workers, which, while representing capital and labour, markedly differ both from the classes existing in the pre-Green Revolution period and from the classes that are specific to the purely capitalist economy.

Provincial capitalists are small-scale entrepreneurs who diversify their economic activity by employing the surplus generated by the introduction of the Green Revolution. While showing different trajectories of class formation and different patterns of capital accumulation, they are 'segments' of the same dominant class and share the control over the means of production and over labour commoditisation. Also the class of subaltern workers is made of different segments with distinct nature and origin. Yet, subaltern workers in all segments are commoditised and do not have control over the means of production, and often over their own labour power and their bodies too.

Indian capitalists are very far from the descriptions found in textbooks. They strongly differ in their behaviour as individuals and as a class, from their expensive life-styles, to the family-based dimension of their social life, to the importance given to caste, to the rent-seeking behaviour. Similarly, workers live in a condition of subordination that is a long way from the situation of 'free' workers selling their labour force for a wage. As informal workers, a large part of them do not fit under the conventional Marxist category of 'working class' and are not commoditised in the form described by Marx. Yet, they are commoditised in a plurality of forms, which reflect the plurality of employment arrangements. This plurality is a major outcome of the institutional embeddedness of India's provincial economy.

Caste as an institutions and an ideology

Moving to the superstructural sphere, and largely building on the distinctiveness of class structure, I have explored the role of caste in Chapter 5. Relying on the evidence of the secularisation of caste and of the emergence of caste politics after the Mandal Report, I have proposed an original interpretation of caste based on Marxist/Institutionalist conceptual categories. The Marxist/Institutionalist interpretation overcomes the limits of the conventional Marxist analysis, which stresses only the ideological content of caste. Caste is interpreted, at the same time, as an ideology and as institution; as an ideology, caste works as a false consciousness, fracturing the unity of the working class; as an institution, it concurs in the building of civil society organisation.

This interpretation of caste provided the theoretical support for the Gramscian hypothesis that I put forward with explicit reference to Provincial India. Relying on the evidence of the poor living and working standards in the diversified and informal non-farm economy, my hypothesis was that caste contributes in perpetuating the subordination of informal workers to capitalists – and then also ensures the survival of India's provincial capitalism – by playing a twofold role: as an ideology, caste ensures that the intellectual and moral leadership of the capitalist elites is accepted; and as an institution, caste produces a network of interclass associations in which subaltern and dominant classes negotiate the consensus over capital's hegemony.

In broad terms, the evidence of India's provincial capitalism presented and analysed in the first part of the book seems to support the Gramscian hypothesis. However, as I pointed out in concluding Chapter 5, to be explored the hypothesis requires information and data on the mechanisms through which caste impacts on socio-economic behaviour, which are available only at micro level. This explains why the hypothesis has been explored in the second part of the book, in which Arni's capitalist development has been studied empirically.

An empirical test

The empirical exercise – which has been made possible by the large amount of information available on Arni over more than four decades – has largely confirmed that the distinguishing traits of capitalism identified for Provincial India are also observed in the town (Chapters 6 and 7). The Gramscian hypothesis on the role of caste has been confirmed as well (Chapter 8).

On the basis of data on Arni's long-term change, I have shown that the town has been steadily expanding since the Green Revolution, and that Arni's business economy is *diversified* and very *mobile* over time, both in economic and in social terms. The growth in the number and size of businesses goes together with the change in the economic weight of sectors and in their mix. Not only do different sectors co-exist, both in manufacturing and in trade; firms are also simultaneously engaged in retail and wholesale trade.

As the empirical analysis has shown, Arni's economy is composed of two broad segments, which are strictly integrated among them and show different patterns of local/global integration. The first segment largely relies on local raw materials and sells, partly, to its hinterland and, partly, to other centres in Tamil Nadu. The second segment uses raw materials from distant sources and sells to distant markets. The most important sectors in the town – rice and silk – are integrated into the global economy. They represent the bulk of Arni's economy in terms of gross output. The remaining sectors produce and sell for the town (and also for its local area) and in the town. Also the sources of the capital are increasingly local.

The available evidence also suggests that Arni's capitalist economy is spatially embedded. The town is economically integrated with the villages located in its hinterland, which have undergone a process of change closely connected with the one observed in Arni. The increasing urban/rural integration has affected output and input markets, as well as the provision of capital and labour. Also, economic diversification in Arni's hinterland has been extensive, involving both agriculture and non-farm activities. The development of non-farm activities in the villages has been one of the major trends since the 1980s and has influenced the structure of employment and the distribution of assets. Symmetrically, a part of the workforce in the villages has been increasingly providing the workforce for the growth of trade and manufacturing activities in Arni, as well as in other local towns.

Another aspect showing Arni's spatial embeddedness is its function as a market town. While important activities have been developing in manufacturing – silk – and in the processing of agricultural goods – rice – the evidence does not suggest an ongoing process of industrial specialisation over the years. Arni continues to be a market town, trade continues to be a major activity in town, both as retail and wholesale trade. The two forms of trade correspond to two distinct patterns of economic integration. On the one side, for consumption goods and for services – and through retailers – Arni is a market town for the local area. On the other side, for silk and rice, Arni is a market for distant areas.

Arni's spatial embeddedness clearly emerges in relation to silk production, a sector widely researched over the last two decades, which I have analysed in order to explore production relations. Arni's silk economy provides a strong case for institutional embeddedness as well.

The available evidence on silk shows that, after the Green Revolution, both the town and the surrounding villages have been involved in a socio-spatial restructuring which has induced a wide process of economic diversification. This has transformed Arni into a manufacturing and wholesale market-centre for silk and, at the same time, has given birth to and re-enforced activities connected to silk production in the hinterland. In the process, Arni has become the centre of the local production system, while the villages have been playing the role of periphery. The relations between Arni and the villages are of interdependence: production has been progressively decentralised to the villages, while Arni retains the control of the whole local production system.

The spatial distribution of production is a major factor explaining the leading role of silk in the town. Another major factor is the putting-out system around which silk production is organised.

Arni's silk economy is dominated by a class of capitalists who play multi-task functions, ranging from the organisation of production to the marketing of the output. *Maligais* (the local term for silk merchants) and master-weavers are the main agents in Arni's putting-out system, through which they enhance the capability of the firms involved in silk production to react to market signals. They also promote the decentralisation of production to the villages and, being in charge of the supply of raw materials and of the disposal of output, ensure the local and global integration of Arni's silk economy.

The subaltern class includes weavers (both dependent and independent) and a vast group of unpaid family workers and bonded labourers who are employed as helpers and assistants. Arni's putting-out system for silk production highly relies on unpaid family labour and wage-workers, and the evidence shows that the availability of unpaid family workforce largely contributes in reducing incentives for the introduction of technical change, perpetuating the use of artisanal technologies. Helpers and assistants have a reduced access to opportunities for upward mobility.

There is evidence that dependent weavers live on a wage that is only a little above the poverty line, and that, due to the crisis of silk in the first years of this century, the wages of weavers have not been increasing. Also the weavers in the villages share a similar condition, living slightly above the poverty line. As it appears, the decentralisation of silk production has been functional to the interests of capital but has not increased the standard of living of workers in the villages.

There is strong evidence that social structure in Arni's silk economy is segmented along caste and class lines. *Maligais* and master-weavers are the main segments of the capitalist class and keep the control of silk economy firmly in their hands. The working class is also highly segmented and caste segmentation adds to class segmentation, creating a mosaic of subaltern social groups in poor living and working conditions.

Caste provides a form of internal regulation of Arni's silk economy in which caste segmentation is manipulated according to the needs of the dominant classes. While the link between caste and occupation is weak, caste barriers do exist, and are strong for the capitalist class and less strong for wage-workers. Castes hinder upward mobility, perpetuating the presence of the dominating caste groups among master-weavers and *maligais*. At the same time, caste barriers become weaker when the involvement of lower castes is necessary for economic growth and when it does not challenge power relations within the silk economy, as in the case of the participation of weavers from non-traditional weaving castes in the villages during upswings in the sector.

More evidence on the regulative role of caste has come from the survey of Arni's civil society, which has provided the empirical support to explore the Gramscian hypothesis.

Largely confirming the Gramscian proposition, the survey has shown that in the town there exists an associational order that is built on economic and non-economic associations, which, as representatives of capital and labour's interests, govern the production process in all phases. It has also shown that Arni's associational order is biased toward capital. While the representation of capital is strong – owing to the joint action of 'big' business associations and locally dominant caste associations – there is a systematic under-representation of labour. This is due to the lack of labour associations, but also to the absorption of the (disguised) labour force under non-economic and non-class associations. The bias against labour implies that decisions about recruitment of workers and about working conditions are in the hands of capital. Also, the representation of workers in trade unions is remarkably low as a consequence of the action of caste, which neutralises class by means of associations and ideologies. Finally, the survey shows that the State is a central institution of 'governance' and the open aim of Arni's associations is to bargain with the State in order to obtain advantages for their members. In this sense, Arni's associations appear to be intermediaries – and not only representatives – of class interests.

So there is an asymmetry between the representation of labour and capital that is a major trait of Arni's associational order. While employers are widely organised by means of interest groups that shape inter-firm relations, control intra-firm relations, and bargain over the terms of state intervention, employees' organisations are weak and lack a collective dimension. Associations provide the cross-class institutional structure in which capital's hegemony is negotiated. Caste associations stand out for their twofold role: as regulating institutions for economic behaviour inside each caste group and as intermediaries in the political relationship with the State.

A notable aspect of the Gramscian argument that is not fully confirmed by the survey is the 'voluntariness' of participation in caste and non-caste associational life. Here, there is a major discrepancy between form and substance. While participation is defined in formal terms on a voluntary basis, the evidence shows that the degree of 'voluntariness' of membership is very variable, and in significant cases participation appears to be compulsory. I have interpreted this contradictory situation by suggesting that Arni's organised civil society shows features that are typical of societal corporatism. I have come to this conclusion on the evidence which shows that Arni's organised civil society is composed of interest associations involved in several types of socio-economic relations in each phase of the production process; the function of the associations is to regulate social relationships and to create the conditions for economic growth; and the associational order emerges under the pressure of social groups (and not of the State).

Caste is a major pillar of Arni's corporatism, playing the twofold role of ideology and of institution. Caste ideology is functional to the corporatist project. Paradoxically, by undermining class-consciousness and by fracturing the unity of the working class, caste enhances social cohesion. Moreover, it provides the ideological instruments that limit the perception of the quasi-compulsory nature of the associational order, ensuring a 'voluntary' consensus in favour of the hegemony of the dominant classes, and promoting the 'voluntary' participation of subaltern classes in organised civil society. Caste associations – the 'materialisation' of caste ideology – are necessary as non-class mediators of class interests in order to limit capital/labour and capital/capital conflicts.

The conclusion of my analysis has been that caste does not appear a 'precapitalist residual' to be dissolved by capitalist development. By contrast, it is a necessary 'impurity' that supports a historically specific 'variety' of capitalism in which class and non-class relations intertwine.

3 Social downgrading

The analysis conducted in this book shows that the idea of Provincial India as a static society and economy is wrong and misleading. A major process of change has being going on since the Green Revolution, which has deeply impacted on the organisation of production, on class structure, on the mode of regulation of the economy and society. The injection of capital associated with the new agricultural technology and economic liberalisation have concurred in leading Provincial India to a new phase in her structural transformation. This phase is clearly marked by the contraction of agricultural employment and by the growth of rural non-farm employment.

The nature of this change has been documented in the previous chapters in which we have analysed the nature and working of capitalism in Provincial India by means of an eclectic framework. Without a Marxist/Institutionalist analysis, some of the traits we have pointed out would have been missed or misinterpreted. This is the case of class segmentation and of the twofold role of caste, but also of the institutional embeddedness of rural capitalist change. By means of Marxist/Institutionalist conceptual categories we have shown that the working of India's provincial economy, its organisation and its class structure are deeply shaped by institutions and culture. Yet, we have also shown that this influence does not mask the capitalist nature of production relations. Indeed, the traits we have pointed out identify a specific variety of capitalism.

Capitalist development in Provincial India appears to be markedly biased against labour. As we have seen, it has not created the condition for an upgrading of the living and working standards of subaltern workers. Instead, the quality of the rural non-farm jobs available for the increasing number of workers who have been leaving agriculture is very low and, as several indicators suggest, also decreasing.

India's rural non-farm economy is widely informalised and the vast majority of rural non-farm workers are employed within informal employment arrangements that perpetuate their subordination to capital. The official data suggests that the structural transformation has not changed their life. The empirical evidence of Arni has largely confirmed this situation as well. Imprisoned in informal employment arrangements – in agriculture and in rural non-farm activities – rural workers live a precarious life and cannot avoid a fate of indecent working conditions. Far from improving living and working standards, capitalist development in Provincial India is leading to a widespread downgrading of the rural labour force.

This social downgrading is largely a consequence of informality. Increasing the flexibility of economic organisation and cutting the costs that the enterprises have to face to move resources among activities on the basis of market signals, informal organisation is functional to the needs of capital worldwide. Yet, in the case of Provincial India, the impact of informality on the economy and society is enhanced and widened by the nature of production organisation and by the features of class structure. Informality is an endemic trait of economic organisation in India's rural non-farm capitalism, a feature of agriculture that transfers to non-farm activities through the use of local (agricultural) resources. As we have seen, this transfer is a major consequence of the spatial and institutional embeddedness of India's provincial economy. Reducing the constraints of sectoral specialisation, rural diversification also enhances the informality – and then also the flexibility – of the rural non-farm economy. Also, the segmentation of class structure and the ideological use of caste have an analogous impact, as they weaken class-consciousness and class action and lead subaltern workers to accept values and beliefs of the hegemonic classes. Indeed, the way in which India's provincial capitalism is organised and works produces a favourable environment for flexibility, so enhancing the interests of capital against the interest of labour.

India's provincial economy is moving along the low road of capitalism. Its socio-economic organisation prevents the upgrading of workers, perpetuating precarious working and living standards. Deprived of any form of labour protection and with unsecure employment, India's rural workers in Provincial India are at the bottom of the international precariat, which, as Guy Standing (2011) points out, inhabits the global economy in an enduring condition of subordination to capital, without any hope of social and economic improvements.

Notes

1 The complexity of capitalist development in Provincial India

1 The estimate of the dimension of Provincial India in terms of population depends on how the rather vague concept of 'small town' is defined. If the reasonable threshold of 100,000 people is accepted, then a straightforward estimate can be obtained from Census data. According to the provisional data for 2011, over a total population of 1.210 billion, 68.8 per cent (833 million) live in rural areas, while 31.2 per cent (377 million) live in urban areas. Out of the population living in urban areas, 112 million live in urban centres and towns with a population of less than 100,000, which added to the rural population gives an estimate of 945 million of people (about 78.1 per cent of India's population). If the threshold of 100,000 is considered too low and towns with 200,000 inhabitants or more are included, then also the size of the population living in Provincial India increases. However, there is an upper limit that cannot be overcome, as Provincial India – by definition – does not include large urban centres with more than 1 million people. The 2011 Census data estimates this upper limit in 1.049 billion people (86.7 per cent of total Indian population), resulting from the sum of the rural population and the population living in urban centres with less than one million people. Therefore, 78.1 per cent and 86.7 per cent delimit the interval within which the dimension of population in Provincial India can vary, according to the adopted definition of 'small towns'.

2 In India rural poverty is still remarkably higher than urban poverty. The World Bank estimates that 29.8 per cent of the urban population and 33.8 per cent of the rural population were below the (national) poverty lines in 2010 (World Development Indicators website). Moreover, there is evidence that poverty in small and medium-sized towns located in remote areas often exceeds rural poverty. A 'metropolitan bias' is found to exist in poverty, which is attributed to the gaps between small towns and large towns and metropolises in the availability of infrastructures (World Bank, 2011: 85 et seq.).

3 The term 'Green Revolution' refers to the technology transfer occurred since the mid-1960s, which had the aim of increasing food production. It was based on the introduction of high-yielding varieties, the expansion of irrigation and several types of incentives to increase the use of fertilisers and pesticides (Planning Commission, 1970).

4 According to the World Bank's Development Indicators, 51 per cent of India's workforce was employed in agriculture in 2010, while the contribution of the primary sector to GDP was 18 per cent.

2 A Marxist/Institutionalist framework for the analysis of contemporary capitalism

1 Quotations from Marx (1859: 3–4).
2 Assuming that capital takes a double form – constant capital (machinery and raw materials) and variable capital (the money for wages) – Marx defines the organic composition of capital as the ratio between the two parts (Marx, 1894, Part 1: 189).
3 The term '*Capital*' in the title of the article refers to Marx's work.
4 The '"spontaneous" consensus … is "historically" caused by the prestige (and consequent confidence) which the dominant group enjoys because of its position and function in the world of production' (Gramsci, 1975: 1519).
5 Using the category of exploitation, we can say that middle classes are made of individuals who are at the same time exploiters and exploited and/or are neither exploiters nor exploited.
6 Examples are highly skilled workers, such as professionals, self-employed producers, managers (Wright, 1985; see also Ossowski, 1966: 85–89).
7 A major example of methodological individualism is neoclassical economics.

3 Introducing non-farm capitalism in Provincial India

1 The estimates of growth rates come from the Planning Commission website, 'Macroeconomic Summary' (http://planningcommission.nic.in). The growth rates are computed at factor cost.
2 The Agreement on Agriculture was signed in 1994 at the conclusion of the Uruguay Round of the GATT, and then was extended to the WTO in 1995. With the Agreement, India committed herself to improve market access, to cut non-tariff barriers, export subsidies and domestic support to agricultural producers (Bhalla, 2007: 222).
3 Also Deaton and Drèze (2009) point out the decline in per capita calorie intake after economic liberalisation. However, they challenge Patnaik's analysis, arguing that: (i) calorie intake is not a sufficient nutrition indicator of food deprivation and other indicators, such as vitamin and mineral intakes, need to be taken into account; and (ii) the decline in calorie intake is observed in particular (but not exclusively) among high-income consumers, and so it is difficult to attribute it to the decline of per capita income. They suggest that alternative explanations might be found in the change of lifestyles that impact on consumption patterns (Engel law). In turn, Patnaik (2010a, 2010b) reacts to Deaton and Drèze's analysis, questioning their 'uncritical' application of conventional methodologies for the estimates of consumption and expenditures.
4 See Chapter 1, Note 2 for details.
5 Indeed, the impact of rural diversification on poverty is controversial as, due to their lack of education and resources, the poor only have access to low-return RNFAs. However, while not enough to lift the poor out of poverty, low-return RNFAs might protect them from further decline in entitlements (Lanjouw, 2007: 79).
6 Also the Economic Census of India supplies data on employment in non-farm enterprises operating in rural areas. However, this data systematically underestimates the phenomenon as it only includes the surveyed enterprises. Economic Census data is currently available only up to 2005; the Sixth Economic Census, conducted from September 2012, is not yet available.
7 The NSSO surveys on employment and unemployment collect information on 'usual status' workers and their sector and locality of employment. The term 'usual status' (henceforth u.s.) refers to the activity status of workers during the year preceding the date of the survey; it might include both the principal activity' and the 'subsidiary activity', i.e. an additional activity carried out for a period not less than 30 days (NSSO, 2012: 13–14).

8 1972–1973 is the first year in which the NSSO data is available.
9 Papola and Sahu (2012: 11) also estimate that in 2004–2005 the rural non-farm sector contributed over 60 per cent to rural national domestic product (it was less than 30 per cent in 1971).
10 Alagh (2005: 105–106) places the beginning of India's structural transformation at the end of the 1990s when, for the first time in history, the percentage of agricultural employment over total employment fell below 60 per cent.
11 See, among others, Hazell and Haggblade (1991), S. Bhalla (1997), Dev (1990) and Unni (1991, 1998). For a review of the research methodologies and results, see Unni (1998: A-39 et seq.). See also Coppard (2001) and Nayyar and Sharma (2005).
12 Recently the 'residual sector hypothesis' has been resumed by Himanshu (2011), who has pointed out agricultural distress as a factor leading marginal categories of rural workers into the RNF sector (see also Himanshu *et al.*, 2011). By contrast, Papola and Sahu (2012), focusing on the remarkable increase of productivity per worker in RNFAs, have suggested that the growth of RNFL over the last decade should be attributed to the employment opportunities emerging in the RNFE rather than to agricultural 'distress'.
13 The high-share group includes activities such as cotton textile, pottery, repairs, construction and transport; the high-growth group includes, among others, silk textiles and diamonds, but also some types of repairs, and business and communication services; and finally the emergent group includes food processing and chemicals, but also rural tourism and some types of business and communication services (Fisher *et al.*, 1997: 79).
14 I am using Wright's terminology introduced in this book on page 17.
15 These are the conditions for exploitation according to Wright's class theory (see pages 17 and 18).
16 Incidentally, the new, and increasingly important, phenomenon of business product outsourcing (BPO) in rural India provides significant examples of the working of value chains. Consisting of the decentralisation of industrial and service activities from foreign countries to rural towns and villages in India, the rural BPO generates RNFL in manufacturing and service firms that are included in global networks (outsourceportfolio.com/tag/india/).
17 According to the recent ILO update on employment in the informal sector (ILO, 2012), India is the country with the highest percentage of workers in informal employment among 47 low- and medium-income countries with a high degree of informalisation.
18 The Committee on Unorganised Sector Statistics has recently been established, with the mission of suggesting 'ways and means' for developing a consistent database on the informal sector (2012: *Preface*).
19 For details on the concept of 'usual status', see Footnote 7 in this chapter.
20 Created by the Government of India in 2004 with the aim of monitoring the condition of informal workers, the NCEUS was dissolved in 2009.
21 An indirect estimate of the size of informal employment can be obtained through the Worker Population Ratio, which is, in the same year, 41 per cent in rural areas and 35 per in urban areas (NSSO, 2012: 35).
22 SCs and STs represent the communities outside the Hindu caste system, which have been subject to extensive social disadvantage and discrimination. For details, see Chapter 5 (in particular Note 7) in this book.
23 The methodology adapts the one elaborated by the Central Statistical Organisation to the NCEUS approach (see NCEUS, 2008: 51 et seq.).
24 The NCEUS also stresses a difference within the informal sector between agricultural and non-agricultural workers (with the former having 1.8 fewer years of schooling than the latter), between men and women (2.4 fewer years), and among socio-religious groups.

25 The relations of informal workers with contractors (and entrepreneurs) often are deeply exploitative and give rise to new forms of bondage widely analysed in literature (Lerche, 2010; Kapadia, 2010; De Neve, 2010; Breman *et al.*, 2009). I explore this issue in Chapter 4 (Section 3.2), where I focus on labour commoditisation.

4 Exploring class structure in Provincial India

1 The first transition debate is collected in Sweezy *et al.* (1976).
2 The Brenner debate is collected in Aston and Philpin (1985). For a critique, see Hilton (1985) and Meiksins Wood (2002).
3 Major reviews of the debate are found in A. Thorner (1982a, 1982b, 1982c), J. Harriss (1982b), and Patnaik (1990).
4 On this point see also A. Thorner (1982c: 2064).
5 Keeping into account both class status and social and political interests, the concept of contradictory class location allows overcoming the distinction between intermediate classes – a classification that refers to the means of production – and middle classes – a classification that refers to income and lifestyle. See McCartney (2010: 149).
6 On this point, see McCartney and Harriss-White (2000) and Toye (1993).
7 Chari's exercise seems to me not fully convincing from a theoretical standpoint. The concept of 'toil' is suggestive as it recalls the hard working conditions of agrarian classes; yet it does not explain the entrepreneurial transformation of the Gounder caste from agriculturists to small-scale industrialists. Chari's exercise reminds me of similar attempts to find a link between agriculture and industrial accumulation in Italian industrial districts (Forni, 1987). For this literature, the reason why industrial districts developed in agricultural areas where the *mezzadria* has been the dominant arrangement was that share tenants easily transformed themselves into successful small-scale industrialists since they could employ in industry the entrepreneurial skills acquired in agriculture. In turn, the entrepreneurial skills of the erstwhile share tenants were due to the fact that *mezzadria* required a market exposition of producers much higher than the agricultural arrangements existing in other parts of the country. In the case of Tiruppur, Chari does not explain why a caste of agriculturists becomes a class of capitalists. He does not say what changes occur in their attitude and behaviour, and how and why they learn how to accumulate. He does not say what is the origin of their capital. He points to toil as explicatory variable. Yet, while toil might be felt to be as important as capital, it is not capital.
8 For Saith (2001: 103) the only certain link between agriculture and the growth of small-scale industrial clusters occurs *via* the labour market, as migrant agricultural workers look for jobs in small and medium urban centres, where industrial clusters are located.
9 See Rutten (1995, 2002) for a discussion.
10 The regulative role of caste is confirmed also by Prakash (2010) who shows the persistence of 'discriminatory attitudes and behaviour' by upper castes against Dalits when they enter the market as entrepreneurs.
11 For a discussion of the concept of 'class segments', see Zeitlin and Ratcliff (1988: 5, 8fn, and 187).
12 The segmentation of rural labour market is also stressed by Lerche (2010: 72–73), who focuses on caste and ethnicity.
13 For Marx the capitalist is the 'modern penitent of Vishnu' who constantly resists 'the temptation' of consuming his/her capital (Marx, 1890, Part 3: 43).
14 The same conclusion is reached by Sanyal (2007) (see also Chatterjee, 2008a and Sanyal and Bhattacharyya, 2009). However, they rebut the transition narrative on different grounds. For Sanyal – and for Chatterjee who builds on Sanyal (2007) – capitalist change in this historical phase cannot be seen as a process of transition because

exclusion and marginalisation are integral – and permanent – aspects of post-colonial capital. This is due to the fact that growth is increasingly capital-intensive and the individuals who are systematically dispossessed by primitive accumulation of their means of production do not have any serious possibility to be included in the circuit of capital, and then to improve their condition.

5 Caste-based interest representation and the hegemony of capital in India's civil society

1 '[T]he unity of the family is ... the feeling of love' (Hegel, 1821 [2001]: 138).

2 'Corporatism can be defined as a system of interest representation in which the constituents units are organised into a limited number of singular, compulsory, noncompetitive, hierarchically ordered and functionally differentiated categories, recognised or licensed (if not created) by the state and granted a deliberate representational monopoly within their respective categories in exchange for observing certain controls on their selection of leaders and articulation of demands and supports' (Schmitter, 1974: 93–94).

3 'Pluralism can be defined as a system of interest representation in which the constituents units are organised into an unspecified number of multiple, voluntary, competitive, nonhierarchically ordered and self-determined (as to the type or scope of interest) categories which are not specifically licensed, recognised, subsidized, created, otherwise controlled in leadership selection or interest articulation by the state and which do not exercise a monopoly of representational activity within their respective categories' (Schmitter, 1974: 96).

4 See also Cawson (1985) and O'Sullivan (1988). Streeck and Kenworthy (2005) provide an historical review of the theory and practice of corporatism.

5 Marx himself believed that caste would be removed by capitalism and saw British rule as an instrument to lay 'the material foundations of Western society' in India (1853: 217).

6 A major contrasting voice was Gandhi's, who supported caste as an instrument to foster community interests over individual interests, cooperation over conflict, duties over rights (Béteille, 1996b).

7 The Mandal Commission was set up in 1979 in order to actuate the constitutional provisions for reservation: a 'package of protective, preferential and developmental practices' in favour of the less advanced groups of Indian society. The Mandal Report was submitted in December 1980, suggesting a number of reservation measures for the backward and most-backward castes and classes, including Scheduled Castes (SCs) and Tribes (STs) – the communities outside the Hindu caste system, which have been subject to extensive social disadvantage and discrimination – and the Other Backward Castes (OBCs) – i.e. the lower Hindu castes. The implementation of the measures suggested by the Mandal Report started only in August 1990 (Radhakrishnan, 1996: 203).

8 Caste mobility refers to the movement of castes along the local caste hierarchy, according to the economic performance of their members and more or less independently of their ritual state. It takes two basic forms: 'upward mobility and embourgeoisement' – observed in the upper stratum of intermediate agricultural castes after the GR and in the emerging elites from SCs and STs; and 'downward mobility and proletarisation' – a process observed in segments of the upper castes and for the majority of SCs and STs, which remain at the bottom of the social pyramid (Sharma, 1994: 7). In-caste class differentiation is a consequence of the differences among individuals of the same caste in terms of income and social opportunities. This is observed in upper castes – which differentiate according to occupation – and in a minority of SCs and STs, owing to their access to administrative jobs. Examples of in-caste class differentiation are found both in urban and rural elites (Corbridge and Harriss, 2000: 123 and 228–229).

9 These associations (called *sangam*) are clusters of *jatis* with similar religious status.

10 For an analysis of the reasons *pro* and *contra* caste enumeration, see the debate on EPW following the Editorial of 22 May 2010.

11 Using a Marxist terminology, caste prevents class-in-itself changes in order to avoid class-for-itself actions.

12 See, for instance, Baviskar and Sundar (2008); John and Deshpande (2008); Shah (2008); Basu and Das (2009); Sen (2010).

6 Long-term change in Arni's economy

1 At the time the region produced 10 per cent of TN rice (Harriss-White *et al.*, 2004: 5).

2 In 1991 North Arcot was split in the Tiruvannamalai district and Ambdedkar (now Vellore) district, Arni being included in the first.

3 In this and in the following chapters I refer to the surveys on Arni as 'Arni surveys' and to the surveys on the surrounding villages as 'North Arcot surveys'.

4 For details on the studies on Arni see Harriss-White (2003b).

5 In 2011 Arni's population was estimated around 69,000 (see Arni's municipal website, http://municipality.tn.gov.in/arni/).

6 According to the 2001 Population Census, in TN there were 191 urban centres, of which 157 had fewer than 50,000 people and 15 between 50,000 and 99,000.

7 See for instance Griffin (1974).

8 See also Harriss and Harriss (1984).

9 This conclusion has given birth to the already mentioned debate on the notion of locality in Mellor's growth linkages (see Chapter 3, Section 3.2).

10 The 'Wholesale Price Index' (1961–2005), published by the Office of Economic Adviser, Ministry of Commerce and Industry (GoI), has been used.

11 The hierarchy of castes in Arni has been defined by the late P.J. Krishnamurthy. For details, see Table 8.7.

12 Harriss-White *et al.* (2004: 37) estimate an increase of average real expenditure over the period 1973–1994 by a factor of 6 for elite producers, 4.5 for poor producers and 2.8 for landless producers.

7 Institutional and spatial embeddedness in Arni's silk economy

1 The research by Nagaraj *et al.* (1996) explores the changes in silk weaving in Arni's region in the context of the agrarian change induced by the GR. As part of the Arni and North Arcot surveys, the research is based on a survey of the firms involved in silk weaving in Arni and in three surrounding villages. Weaving units and other units involved in silk sari production have been surveyed and detailed interviews with weavers and merchants have been conducted in Arni and in the villages, focusing on the organisational structure and on silk-weaving techniques, and on the socio-economic factors explaining the changes in silk sari demand.

2 In her 2004 dissertation, Camilla Roman analyses the notion of skill and the process of learning among Arni's weavers who she takes as examples of informal workers. Camilla explores the learning process of Arni's weavers, pointing out the features of the labour process, caste norms, religious and gender identities that shape learning trajectories. Her aim is to show the variety and complexity of skills and skill processes in the informal economy. In her 2008 thesis, Camilla focuses on the Indian handloom industry comparing the technological system in Arni's production system to other industrial areas.

3 It is interesting to note that the large increase in the number of handlooms, for all India, is found in the period after Independence. By contrast, since the 1960s the number of handlooms has remained almost stationary (Roy, 1993: 189).

4 The *zari* is the gold or silver thread that is used in the production of sari borders.

5 Also the *dharmavaran* sari is produced in the area: a more complex variety with soph-
   isticated design on the borders and on the *mundhani* (Roman, 2004: 44).
6 In this case, the sari can have up to three colours, one for the body and two more for
   the borders and *mundhani*.
7 In the Arni region the number of individuals from the traditional silk weaving castes
   is rather limited and silk weaving is mainly done by cotton weaving castes and by
   other caste communities. As Nagaraj *et al.* (1996: 51) suggest, this is a specificity of
   the area, while in other silk centres of North TN, such as *Kancheepuram*, a percentage
   as high as 80 per cent of weavers come from traditional silk weaver castes.
8 In his historical analysis of the change in handloom weaving in India since the beginning of last century and of the impact of industrialisation on weavers, Roy (1993: 135
   et seq.) shows that in 1950 Arni was already one of the small towns in TN in which
   silk weaving was concentrated with the number of handlooms around 500.
9 To learn the silk-weaving techniques, workers from Arni town and from the villages
   often go to Kancheepuran to work as assistants to fully fledged weavers from traditional silk weaving castes, who are supposed to be the keepers of the techniques
   (Nagaraj *et al.*, 1996; Roman, 2004).
10 It should be emphasised that the decentralisation observed for Arni's industrial district
   is not an isolated case in Tamil Nadu. Other important examples exist in which traditional weaving centres have progressively decentralised production to their rural hin-
   terlands. Particularly important is the case of Tiruvannamalai town in which no
   handlooms have been left, while the nearest is 10km from away from the town itself
   (Government of Tamil Nadu, 2007).
11 Focusing only on three villages in Arni's hinterland, Arivukkarasi and Nagaraj (2009)
   show a change in the pattern of localisation of silk weaving, with a reduction in the
   remote villages and a concentration in semi-urban localities near to Arni.
12 Before being given to producers, the raw silk is twisted, warped and dyed in work-
   shops that are often owned by the *maligais* and master-weavers themselves (Roman,
   2004: 42).
13 The role of master-weavers/*maligais* as moneylenders, who anticipate the money to
   weavers in the course of the production process, should also be emphasised. This
   function accounts for the spreading of bonded labour in the sector (Roy, 1993: 7).
14 According the Census of Handlooms (1987–1988), the national average is that 20 per
   cent of the overall full-time weavers in India work in the co-operative sector, 54 per
   cent are 'independent' weavers and 15 per cent 'dependent' weavers. The remaining
   11 per cent work in factories (Roy, 1993: 193–195).
15 The prominent role of cooperatives in Kancheepuram's silk weaving is stressed by
   Remesh (2001: 16–17) in a survey aimed at exploring labour relations under different
   production structures in silk industry.
16 According to Becattini and Rullani (1993: 30 et seq.), versatile integrators in Prato
   performed the following functions: the organisation of the production process, the
   linking of the different phases; the provision of information on the requirements of
   the market in terms of designs and colours; the direction of single firms toward
   specialisation in specific phases of production according to market signals.
17 On the role of the knowledge of market trends of Arni's *maligais* and on their ability
   to respond with product changes, see Roman (2008, Chapter 11).
18 For a similar analysis of class stratification in handloom weaving, see Roy (1993: 91
   et seq.). Roy imputes the historical origin of the segmentation of the capitalist class
   and of the subaltern weaving class in South India to the migrations of caste groups
   and to the involvement of peasant weavers. I will elaborate on this point in the next
   section.
19 On the widespread use of corruption and fraud in pursuing class interests in Arni, see
   Harriss-White (2003a: 64, 90).
20 It should be noted that small-scale master weavers are often involved in subaltern

relations with large-scale master-weavers and *maligais* in terms of raw materials' provision and for the marketing of the products. On this point, see Roy (1993, Chapter 3) who analyses similar situations in other Indian states.

21 According to Roy (1993: 7), inequality among weavers has been always particularly strong in rural areas in South India due to the influx of migrant (low caste) workers with a low access to resources and markets. More on this point below.

22 The use of bonded labour in the silk handloom industry in general is analysed in depth by Human Right Watch (2003). See also Remesh (2001) for an analysis on Kanchepuram's silk weaving. On women's working conditions in the handloom sector, see Ministry of Textiles (2005). Since the 1950s, the Indian central government has designed several interventions to improve the living and working conditions of workers in the handloom sector in India. The main fields are: the provision of yarn, subsidies on particular products, and differential levies and taxes. Moreover, in order to empower the weavers, attempts to eliminate the intermediaries have been made and also to enhance the participation of weavers to cooperatives (Roy, 1993: 197–204).

23 According to Arivukkarasi and Nagaraj (2009: 14), child labour has been decreasing in the Arni area in recent years owing to the improvement in literacy rates.

24 It appears that the monthly wages of weavers in Arni are a little below the average estimate of Rs.300/400 provided by the Census of Handlooms (1987–1988) for mid-1980s, as quoted by Roy (1993: 191); vice versa, the estimate for the villages of Rs.198 is decidedly below the average wage and is explained by the widespread inequality in weavers' wages in India. As Roy argues (1993: 191), the major divide in weavers' wage is the urban/rural location: at the end of the 1980s a weaver in a large and prosperous city might earn up to Rs.900, which would place her/him among the elite of the working class in the informal economy.

25 They were involved mainly in cotton weaving (with over 75 per cent of the weavers). By contrast, silk weaving was a residual sector. The only exception was the Saurastras community who was specialised in silk (with about one-quarter of the caste group engaged in silk weaving).

26 Arivukkarasi and Nagaraj (2009: 30) observe a decline in silk weaving among the non-weaving castes who started the activity in the 1980s, a phenomenon that may be largely imputed to the contraction of employment due to the silk crisis at the beginning of the new century (Sacratees, 2004).

27 Roman explains the barriers to the entry of SCs into the weaving professions also with personal traits and with the necessity to avoid close intercourse with the family of the weavers due to the fact that looms are usually located in the household premises (2004: 57–58).

28 De Neve (2005: 300 et seq.) reaches a similar conclusion in the handloom and powerloom industries in two towns in central TN.

8 Capital's hegemony in Arni's corporatist civil society

1 P.J. Krishnamurthy was also a key informant for the third Arni survey in 1993–1994.

2 This group of associations requires attention. While they all presented themselves as 'unions', significant differences exist. One of them is a caste association (Arni Washermen Union). Two are professional associations (the Association for the Progress of Tailors and the Rickshaw Pullers' Association) and two are business associations (the Arni Auto-Owners and Drivers' Association and the Arni Lorry Owners' Union). Of the remaining, four are public sector unions and two are labour unions in government-owned companies (the Dr Ambedkar Transport Workers' Union and the Electricity Board Union).

3 Here all the available empirical material has been used (interviews and notes).

4 Here I have included also the Pensioners' Association on the basis of its declared purpose.

5 This implies that the association has the means, formal and informal, legal or illegal, to oblige a non-member to become member in order to enter the profession.

6 A single association might exert an impact on several phases of the production process and on several types of socio-economic relations.

7 As shown by the Arni Silk Merchants Association, which reports having been able to obtain from government a long-distance fast bus services between the town and Chennai, Bangalore and Tiruchirapalli.

8 As in the case of the Association for the Progress of Tailors: 'the association (as a body) is able to approach institutions such as the Municipality, schools, hostels etc. where uniforms are prescribed for the staff or students and get bulk orders for stitching uniforms. The work is then divided among the members'.

9 This is the case of the Arni Lorry Owners' Association, which emphasises the role of the State in conceding the licences, and then in controlling the possibility of work of the members.

10 From the field material we observe that all individuals who work 'on the streets' (from petty traders to lorry drivers) emphasise widespread antipathy against the police. This is the case for instance with the Arni Grocery Associations, which complain about harassment by officials for selling low-quality goods. Bribes to policemen are the common response to the problem, as reported by the Arni Lorry Owners' Association about attempts of members to avoid unjustified fines.

11 This occurs in the case of the Arni Silk Merchants' Association, which has been opposing state tax on silk yarn and silk saris, while at the same time has asked the government to assist in the procurement of silk yarn from Karnataka. Also, the Tiruvannamalai District Bus Owners' Association is completely explicit on this point, arguing that the 'politicians have to be pleased' and that this is 'in fact the prime motive for starting the Sangam'. The bargaining with the state for the reduction of taxes is also the aim of the Chamber of Commerce, which complains strongly about the corruption of the lower public officials.

12 Several associations complain about the widespread corruption of public officials. This is the case of the Grocery Merchants' Association, which denounces the payment of bribes in order to renew the licences, arguing that 'a country without bribes is rare'. Similarly, the Arni Lorry Owners' Association complains about the necessity to pay a bribe to the police in order to work without 'trouble' at night and to 'overlook a fault', while the Association of Telephone Subscribers informs us about the necessity to pay a bribe to get a new connection.

13 As the representative reports: 'problems with labour or with weights and measures are (somehow) settled by the mill-owners/traders themselves'.

14 The scheme in Figure 8.1 was prepared by the late P.J. Krishnanamurthy, a secularised Brahmin, and contains a hierarchy of castes according to the Vedic order, state classification and food habits. This scheme is presented here only to suggest the complexity of Arni caste structure and is not commented on. Here I confine my analysis to the aspects related to my argument. Detailed information on castes in Arni is found in Basile and Harriss-White (2000).

15 The interests of MBCs are represented by: 'Vanniars, Barbers, Dhobis potters (Odeyars), (Yadavas do not have yet a registered association); car and van drivers, porters, auto-owners and drivers, lorry owners; flower merchants and quarry workers' (Basile and Harriss-White, 2000: 23, footnote).

16 Veera Saiva Chettiars, Acaris, and Karuneekars, in the first group; Senguntha Mudaliars, Saurashtrians, Naidus, Ahadudaiyan Mudaliars and Vanniars Chettiars in the second; for details, see Basile and Harriss-White (2000: 27).

17 The cases of the Saurashtra Podu Sabha and the Naidu Association are particular interesting in relation to this aspect. The Saurashtra Podu Sabha (that originally grouped silk weavers) includes among its members also 'Graduates and Officers' who organise the assistance of poor students within the community and are in charge of the

charity for poor members (also supported in this task by the Saurashtra Women's Association). The cross-class composition is also observed in the Naidu Association in which 20 landowners and 60 house-owners participate together with a larger number of individuals without property. Again in this case, charity interventions in support of poor families and children are organised within the community.

18 Which contain: Tuluva Vellalar Agamudaiyan Mudaliars, Jains, Brahmins (Iyer, Iyengar, Gurukkal/Madhra).

19 According to the interviews, the Lions Club is more exclusive than the Rotary Club, with 90 per cent of the members coming from the highest strata of Arni's population, against 50 per cent of the Rotary Club.

20 This is the case of petty trade associations, such as the Fruit and Vegetable Traders, and small business associations, such as the Rickshaw Pullers' Association and the Car and Van Drivers' Association.

21 As it occurs in relation to the treatment of workers that create trouble and when credit channels and inputs provisions are set for members.

22 See Chari (2004) and De Neve (2005).

23 The increase in time of the number of associations has been also confirmed in a supplementary of empirical analysis that I organised in 2004 (Sacratees, 2004).

References

Aglietta, M. (1979) *A Theory of Capitalist Regulation: The US Experience*, London and New York: New Left Books (translated from the French edition, 1976).

Ahluwalia, M.S. (1999) 'Infrastructure Development in India's Reforms', in I.J. Ahluwalia and I.M.D. Little (eds) *India's Economic Reforms and Development. Essays for Manmohan Singh*, New Delhi: Oxford India Paperbacks, Oxford University Press: 86–121.

Ahmed, S. and Varshney, A. (2008) 'Battles Half Won: The Political Economy of India Policy since Independence', Commission on Growth and Development, Working Paper No. 15, The World Bank.

Alagh, Y.K. (2005) 'Economic Structural Change and Occupational Diversification', in R. Nayyar and A.N. Sharma (eds) *Rural Transformation in India: The Role of Non-farm Sector*. New Delhi: Manohar Publishers for Institute for Human Development: 105–120.

Alavi, H. (1975) 'India and the Colonial Mode of Production', *Economic and Political Weekly*, August, Special Number: 1235–1262.

Alessandrini, M. (2009) *Jobless Growth in Indian Manufacturing: A Kaldorian Approach*, SOAS, Centre For Financial and Management Studies, Discussion Paper No. 99.

Althusser, L. (1970) 'The Object of Capital', in L. Althusser and E. Balibar (eds) *Reading Capital, Part 2*, London: NLB: 71–198 (translated from the French edition, 1965).

Archer, S.M. (1995) *Realist Social Theory: The Morphogenetic Approach*, Cambridge: Cambridge University Press.

Archer, S.M. (2000) *Being Human: The Problem of Agency*, Cambridge: Cambridge University Press.

Arivukkarasi, N.A. and Nagaraj, K. (2009) 'Some Aspects of Socio-Economic Change in Rural Arani with Special Reference to Silk Weaving Industry', paper for the International Conference on *Market Town, Market Society, Informal Economy*, Contemporary South Asian Studies Programme, Oxford University, June.

Ashton, T.H. and Philpin, C.H.E. (eds) (1985) *The Brenner Debate: Agrarian Class Structure and Economic Development in Pre-Industrial Europe*, Cambridge: Cambridge University Press.

Aswasthi, D. (2007) 'Entrepreneurship, Technology and Rural Non-Farm Sector: Field Experiences and Policy Imperatives', in R. Nayyar and A.N. Sharma (eds) *Rural Transformation in India: The Role of Non-farm Sector*, New Delhi: Manohar Publishers for the Institute for Human Development: 474–488.

Bagchi, A.K. (2002) *Capital and Labour Redefined: India and the Third World*, London: Anthem South Asian Studies.

Bandyopadhyaya, J. (2002) 'Class Struggle and Caste Oppression: Integral Strategy of the Left', *The Marxist*, Vol. 18, No. 03–04: 1–7. Available at: www.cpim.org/marxist/200203_marxist_caste&class_jbando.htm (accessed 7 August 2008).

Bardhan, A.B. (1994) 'Caste-Class Situation in India', in K.L. Sharma (ed.) *Caste and Class in India*, Jaipur and New Delhi: Rawat Publications: 405–419.

Bardhan, P. (2009) 'Notes on the Political Economy of India's Tortuous Transition', *Economic and Political Weekly*, 5 December: 31–36.

Baru, S. (2000) 'Economic Policy and Development of Capitalism in India: The Role of Regional Capitalists and Political Parties', in F.R. Frankel, Z. Hasan, R. Bhargava and B. Arora (eds) *Transforming India: Social and Political Dynamics of Democracy*, New Delhi: Oxford University Press: 207–230.

Basile, E. and Harriss-White, B. (2000) 'Corporative Capitalism: Civil Society and the Politics of Accumulation in Small Town India', QEH Working Paper Series, No. 38, QEHWPS38.

Basile, E. and Harriss-White, B. (2010) 'Introduction', 'Monographic Section on India's Informal Capitalism and its Regulation', *International Review of Sociology*, Vol. 20, No. 3: 459–473.

Basu, D. and Das, D. (2009) 'Political Economy of Contemporary India: Some Comments', *Economic and Political Weekly*, 30 May: 157–159.

Basu, K. (2008) 'India's Dilemmas: The Political Economy of Policymaking in a Globalised World', *Economic and Political Weekly*, 2 February: 53–62.

Basu, K. and Maertens, A. (2007) 'The Pattern and Causes of Economic Growth in India', *Oxford Review of Economic Policy*, Vol. 23, No. 2: 143–167.

Baumol, W.J., Litan, R.E. and Schramm, C.J. (2007) *Good Capitalism, Bad Capitalism, and the Economics of Growth and Prosperity*, New Haven and London: Yale University Press.

Baviskar, A. and Sundar, N. (2008) 'Democracy Versus Economic Transformation?', *Economic and Political Weekly*, 15 November: 87–89.

Bayly, S. (1999) *Caste, Society and Politics in India*, Cambridge: Cambridge University Press.

Becattini, G. (1990) 'The Marshallian Industrial District as a Socio-Economic Notion', in F. Pyke, G. Becattini and W. Sengenberger (eds) *Industrial Districts and Inter-Firms' Co-operation in Italy*, International Institute for Labour Studies, ILO, Geneva: 37–51.

Becattini, G. (1997) *Il bruco e la farfalla: Prato nel mondo che cambia, 1954–1993*, Firenze: Le Monnier.

Becattini, G. and Rullani, E. (1993) 'Sistema locale e mercato globale', in *Economia e politica industriale*, No. 80: 25–49.

Becattini, G., Bellandi, M. and De Propris, L. (eds) (2009) *A Handbook of Industrial Districts*, Cheltenham (UK) and Northampton (USA): Edward Eldgar.

Béteille, A. (1983) *The Idea of Natural Inequality and Other Essays*, New Delhi: Oxford University Press.

Béteille, A. (1996a) *Caste, Class and Power. Changing Patterns of Stratification in a Tanjore Village*, second edition, New Delhi: Oxford University Press.

Béteille, A. (1996b) 'Caste in Contemporary India', in C. Fuller (ed.) *Caste Today*, New Delhi: Oxford University Press.

Béteille, A. (2002) *Caste, Inequality and Affirmative Action*, Geneva: ILO.

Béteille, A. (2007) 'Classes and Communities', *Economic and Political Weekly*, 17 March: 945–952.

Béteille, A. (2012) 'The Peculiar Tenacity of Caste', *Economic and Political Weekly*, March 31: 41–48.

Bhaduri, A. (1973) 'A Study of Agricultural Backwardness under Conditions of Semi-Feudalism', *Economic Journal*, LXXXVI, 329: 120–137.

Bhagwati, J. (1999) 'The Design of Indian Development', in I.J. Ahluwalia and I.M.D. Little (eds) *India's Economic Reforms and Development: Essays for Manmohan Singh*, New Delhi: Oxford India Paperbacks, Oxford University Press: 23–39.

Bhalla, G.S. (1997) 'Structural Adjustment and the Agricultural sector in India', in G.K. Chadha and A.N. Sharma (eds) *Growth, Employment and Poverty in India: Change and Continuity in Rural India*, New Delhi: Vikas Publishing House: 21–41.

Bhalla, G.S. (2007) *Indian Agriculture Since Independence*, New Delhi: National Book Trust.

Bhalla, S. (1997) 'The Rise and Fall of Workforce Diversification Processes in Rural India', in G.K. Chadha and A.N. Sharma (eds) *Growth, Employment and Poverty in India: Change and Continuity in Rural India*, New Delhi: Vikas Publishing House: 145–183.

Bhalla, S. (2005) 'Rural Workforce Diversification and Performance of Unorganised Sector Enterprises', in R. Nayyar and A.N. Sharma (eds) *Rural Transformation in India: The Role of Non-farm Sector*, New Delhi: Manohar Publishers for the Institute for Human Development: 75–104.

Bhalla, S. (2007) 'Inclusive Growth? Focus on Employment', paper for the National Conference on *Making Growth Inclusive With Reference to Employment*, Jawaharlal Nehru University, New Delhi, June.

Bhambhri, C.P. (2005) 'Reservations and Casteism', *Economic and Political Weekly*, 26 February: 806–808.

Bhanu Mehta, P. (2004) 'Constraints on Electoral Mobilisation', *Economic and Political Weekly*, December 18: 5399–5403.

Bhaskar, V. and Gupta, B. (2007) 'India's Development in the Era of Growth', in *Oxford Review of Economic Policy*, Vol. 23, No. 2: 135–142.

Boggs, C. (2002) 'What Gramsci Means Today', in D. Dowd (ed.) *Understanding Capitalism: From Marx to Amartya Sen*, London: Pluto Press: 57–81.

Bosworth, B., Collins, S. and Virmani, A. (2007) 'Sources of Growth in Indian Economy', National Bureau of Economic Research, Working Paper No. W12901.

Bourguignon, F. and Morrisson, C. (2002) 'Inequality Among World Citizens 1820–1992', *American Economic Review*, Vol. 92, No. 4: 727–744 (reprinted in B. Milanovic (ed.) (2012) *Globalisation and Inequality*, Cheltenham: Edward Elgar).

Boyer, R. (1990) *The Regulation School: A Critical Introduction*, New York: Columbia University Press.

Boyer, R. (2005) *Coherence, Diversity and Evolution of Capitalisms: The Institutional Complementarity Hypothesis*, mimeo. Cepremap-Cnrs-Ehess. Available at: courses. wcupa.edu/rbove/eco343/050Compecon/general%20compar/050222Boyer.pdf (accessed 7 August 2008).

Breman, J. (1996) *Footloose Labour: Working in India's Informal Economy*, Cambridge: Cambridge University Press.

Breman, J. (1999a) 'The Study of Industrial Labour in Post-Colonial India – The Formal Sector: An Introductory Review', in P.J. Parry, J. Breman and K. Kapadia (eds) *The Worlds of Indian Industrial Labour*, Contributions to Indian Sociology, Occasional Studies No. 9, New Delhi: Sage Publications: 1–41.

Breman, J. (1999b) 'The Study of Industrial Labour in Post-Colonial India – The Informal

Sector: A Concluding Review', in P.J. Parry, J. Breman and K. Kapadia (eds) *The Worlds of Indian Industrial Labour*, Contributions to Indian Sociology, Occasional Studies No. 9, New Delhi: Sage Publications: 407–431.

Breman, J. (2004) *The Making and Unmaking of an Industrial Working Class: Sliding Down the Labour Hierarchy in Ahmedabad, India*, Amsterdam: Amsterdam University Press.

Breman, J. and Guérin, I. (2009) 'Introduction: On Bondage: Old and New', in J. Breman, I. Guérin, and A. Prakash (eds) *India's Unfree Workforce: Of Bondage Old and New*, New Delhi: Oxford University Press: i–xii.

Breman, J. Guérin, I. and Prakash A. (eds) (2009) *India's Unfree Workforce: Of Bondage Old and New*, New Delhi: Oxford University Press.

Brenner, R. (1976) 'Agrarian Class Structure and Economic Development in Pre-Industrial Europe', reprinted in 1985 in T.H. Ashton and C.H.E. Philpin (eds) *The Brenner Debate: Agrarian Class Structure and Economic Development in Pre-Industrial Europe*, Cambridge: Cambridge University Press: 10–63.

Burawoy, M. (1990) 'Marxism as Science: Historical Challenges and Theoretical Growth', *American Sociological Review*, Vol. 55: 775–793.

Byres, T.J. (1996) *Capitalism from Above and Capitalism from Below: An Essay in Comparative Political Economy*, Houndmills: Macmillan Press.

Byres, T.J. (1997) 'State, Class and Development Planning in India', in T.J. Byres (ed.) *The State, Development Planning and Liberalisation in India*, New Delhi: Oxford University Press: 36–81.

Cadène, Ph. (1998a) 'Network Specialists, Industrial Clusters, and the Integration of Space in India', in Ph. Cadène and M. Holmström (eds) *Decentralised Production in India: Industrial Districts, Flexible Specialization, and Employment*, Pondicherry and New Delhi: French Institute of Pondicherry and Sage Publications: 139–165.

Cadène, Ph. (1998b) 'Conclusion: A New Model for Indian Industry?', in Ph. Cadène and M. Holmström (eds) *Decentralised Production in India: Industrial Districts, Flexible Specialization, and Employment*, Pondicherry and New Delhi: French Institute of Pondicherry and Sage Publications: 393–403.

Callinicos, A. (2004), *Making History: Agency, Structure and Change in Social Theory*, Brill, Leiden-Boston.

Castells, M. and Portes, A. (1989) 'World Underneath: The Origins, Dynamics, and Effects of the Informal Economy', in A. Portes, M. Castells and L. Benton (eds) *The Informal Economies: Studies in Advanced and Less Developed Countries*, Baltimore: The Johns Hopkins University Press: 11–37.

Cawson, A. (1985) 'Varieties of Corporatism: The Importance of the Meso-Level of Interest Intermediation', in A. Cawson (ed.) *Organised Interests and the State. Studies in Meso-Corporatism*, London: Sage: 1–21.

Centeno, M.A. and Portes, A. (2003) *The Informal Economy in the Shadow of the State*, The Centre for Migration and Development, Working Paper Series – Princeton University, No. 03–06.

Chadha, G.K. (1997) 'Rural Industrialisation and its Employment Implications', in G.K. Chadha and A.N. Sharma (eds) *Growth, Employment and Poverty in India. Change and Continuity in Rural India*, New Delhi: Vikas Publishing House: 216–242.

Chadha, G.K. (2003) *Rural Industry in India: Policy Perspectives, Past Performance and Future Options*, SAAT, ILO, New Delhi.

Chakrabarti, A. and Cullenberg, S. (2003) *Transition and Development in India*, New York and London: Routledge.

Chandrasekhar, C.P. (2007) 'The "Progress" of Reform and the Retrogression of Agriculture', available at *Macroscan: An Alternative Economics Webcentre*, 15 April, www.macroscan.org (accessed 15 April 2007).

Chandrasekhar, C.P. and Ghosh, J. (2006) 'Employment Growth: The Latest Trends', Available at *Macroscan: An Alternative Economics Webcentre*, 17 November, www.macroscan.org (accessed 17 November 2006).

Chari, S. (2000) 'The Agrarian Origins of the Knitwear Industrial Cluster in Tiruppur, South India', *World Development*, Vol. 28, No. 3: 579–599.

Chari, S. (2004) *Fraternal Capital: Peasant-Workers, Self-Made Men, and Globalization in Provincial India*, Palo Alto and New Delhi: Stanford University Press and Permanent Black.

Chatterjee, P. (2001) 'On Civil and Political Society in Post-Colonial Democracies', in S. Kaviraj and S. Khilnani (eds) *Civil Society: History and Possibilities*, Cambridge: Cambridge University Press: 165–178.

Chatterjee, P. (2008a) 'Democracy and Economic Transformation in India', *Economic and Political Weekly*, 19 April: 53–62.

Chatterjee, P. (2008b) 'Classes, Capital and Indian Democracy', *Economic and Political Weekly*, 15 November: 89–93.

Chattopadhyay, P. (1972a) 'On the Question of the Mode of Production in Indian Agriculture: A Preliminary Note', *Economic and Political Weekly*, A39–A46.

Chattopadhyay, P. (1972b) 'Mode of Production in Indian Agriculture: An Anti-Kritik', *Economic and Political Weekly*, A186–A192.

Chen, M. (2005) 'The Business Environment and the Informal Economy: Creating Conditions for Poverty Reduction', paper for the Committee of Donor Agencies for Small Enterprises Development, Conference on *Reforming the Business Environment*, November, Cairo, Egypt.

Chen, M.A. (2007) 'Rethinking the Informal Economy: Linkages with the Formal Economy and the Formal Regulatory Environment', DESA Working Paper No. 46.

Chenery, H. and Syrquin, M. (1986) 'Typical Patterns of Transformation', in H. Chenery, S. Robinson and M. Syrquin (eds) *Industrialization and Growth*, New York: Oxford University Press: 37–83.

Cohen, G.A. (1978) *Karl Marx's Theory of History: A Defence*, Oxford: Clarendon Press.

Committee on Unorganised Sector Statistics (Government of India) (2012) *Report of the Committee on Unorganised Sector Statistics*, National Statistical Commission.

Commons, J.R. (1924) *The Legal Foundations of Capitalism*, New York: Macmillan Press.

Coppard, D. (2001) *The Rural Non-farm Economy in India: A Review of Literature*, NRI Report 2662, The Natural Resource Institute/DFID/The World Bank, Greenwich University.

Corbridge, S. and Harriss, J. (2000) *Reinventing India. Liberalization, Hindu Nationalism and Popular Democracy*, Cambridge: Polity Press.

Coriat, B. and Dosi, G. (2002) 'The Institutional Embeddedness of Economic Change: An Appraisal of "Evolutionary" and "Regulationist" Approaches', in G.M. Hodgson (ed.) *A Modern Reader in Institutional and Evolutionary Economics: Key Concepts*, Cheltenham: Edward Elgar: 95–123.

Cullenberg, S. (1999) 'Overdetermination, Totality, and Institutions: A Genealogy of a Marxist Institutionalist Economics', *Journal of Economic Issues*, Vol. XXXIII, No. 4: 801–815.

Cullenberg, S. (2000) 'Old Institutionalism, New Marxism', in R. Pollin (ed.) *Capitalism,*

Socialism and Radical Political Economy: Essays in Honour of Howard Sherman, Cheltenham: Edward Elgar: 81–102.

Damodaran, H. (2008a) 'Banias and Beyond: The Dynamics of Caste and Big Business in Modern India', CASI Working Paper No. 08–04.

Damodaran, H. (2008b) *India's New Capitalists: Caste, Business and Industry in a Modern Nation*, New Delhi: Permanent Black.

Das, M.D. (2003) *The Non-Farm Self-Employed in India: Who are They?*, Mimeo, Social Protection Unit, The World Bank, Washington DC.

Datt, G. and Ravallion, M. (2010) 'Shining for the Poor Too?', *Economic and Political Weekly*, 13 February: 55–60.

Davis, J.R. (2004) *The Rural Non-Farm Economy, Livelihoods and their Diversification: Issues and Options*, The Natural Resource Institute/DFID, Greenwich University.

Davis, J.R. and Bezemer, D. (2004) *The Development of the Rural Non-Farm Economy in Developing Countries and Transition Economies: Key Emerging and Conceptual Issues*, The Natural Resource Institute/DFID, Greenwich University.

De Neve, G. (2005) *The Everyday Politics of Labour: Working Lives in India's Informal Economy*, Delhi: Social Science Press.

De Neve, G. (2010) '"Contractors are the real bosses here!": Trajectories, Roles and Agency of Labour Contractors in the Tiruppur Garment Industry', paper presented at the workshop *Working for Export Markets: Labour and Livelihoods in Global Production Networks*, Sussex University, July.

Deaton, A. and Drèze, J. (2002) 'Poverty and Inequality in India: A Reexamination', *Economic and Political Weekly*, 7 September: 3729–3740.

Deaton, A. and Drèze, J. (2009) 'Food and Nutrition in India: Facts and Interpretations', *Economic and Political Weekly*, 14 February: 42–65.

Delorme, R. (1994) 'Economic Diversity as Cement and as Challenge to Evolutionary Perspectives', in R. Delorme and K. Dopfer (eds) *The Political Economy of Diversity: Evolutionary Perspectives on Economic Order and Disorder*, Cheltenham: Edward Elgar: 1–17.

Desai, S. and Dubey, A. (2011) 'Caste in 21st Century India: Competing Narratives', *Economic and Political Weekly*, 12 March: 40–49.

Deshpande, S. (2003) *Contemporary India: A Sociological View*, Delhi: Viking.

Dev, S.M. (1990) 'Non-Agricultural Employment in Rural India: Evidence at Disaggregate Level', *Economic and Political Weekly*, 14 July: 1526–1536.

Dev, S.M. (2002) 'Pro-Poor Growth in India: What Do We Know About the Employment Effects of Growth 1980–2000?' ODI Working Paper No. 161.

Dirks, N.B. (2002) *Castes of Mind*, Delhi: Permanent Black.

Dobb, M. (1962) *Studies in the Development of Capitalism*, London: Routledge & Kegan Paul (first edition 1946).

Dugger, W.M. and Sherman, H.J. (1997) 'Institutionalist and Marxist Theories of Evolution', *Journal of Economic Issues*, Vol. XXXI, No. 4: 991–1009.

Dugger, W.M. and Sherman, H.J. (2000) *Reclaiming Evolution: A Dialogue Between Marxism and Institutionalism on Social Change*, London: Routledge.

Dumont, L. (1980) *Homo Hierarchicus*, Chicago: The University of Chicago.

Edgell, S. and Townshend, J. (1993) 'Marx and Veblen on Human Nature, History, and Capitalism: Vive la Difference!', *Journal of Economic Issues*, Vol. XXVII, No. 3: 721–739.

Ellis, F. (1998) 'Survey Article: Household Strategies and Rural Livelihood Diversification', *Journal of Development Studies*, Vol. 35, No. 1: 1–38.

Elster, J. (1986) 'Further Thoughts on Marxism, Functionalism and Game Theory', in J. Roemer (ed.) *Analytical Marxism*, Cambridge: Cambridge University Press: 202–220.

Engels, F. (1894) *The Peasant Question in France and Germany*, Volume 3 of the Selected Works. Moscow: Progress Publishers. Available at: www.marxistsfr.org/archive/marx/works/download/Engles_The_Peasant_Question_in_France_and_Germany.pdf (accessed 7 August 2008).

Farmer, B.H. (ed.) (1977) *Green Revolution? Technology and Change in Rice Growing Areas of Tamil Nadu and Sri Lanka*, London: MacMillan.

Femia, J. (2001) 'Civil Society and the Marxist Tradition', in S. Kaviraj and S. Khilnani (eds) *Civil Society: History and Possibilities*, Cambridge: Cambridge University Press: 131–146.

Fisher, T., Mahajan, V. and Singha, A. (1997) *The Forgotten Sector: Non-farm Employment and Enterprises in Rural India*, London: Intermediate Technology Publications.

Forni, M. (1987) *Storie familiari e storie di proprietà. Itinerari sociali nell'agricoltura italiana del dopoguerra*, Torino: Rosenberg & Sellier.

GDP (2008) 'Caste Is Dead, Long Live Caste', *Economic and Political Weekly*, 26 January: 16–17.

Ghosh, J. (2006) 'Trade Liberalisation and Economic Restructuring: Can India Skip the Industrial Phase?', paper for the IDEAs Conference on *Post Liberalisation Constraints on Macroeconomic Policies*, January.

Gouldner, A.W. (1980) *The Two Marxisms: Contradictions and Anomalies in the Development of Theory*, London: Macmillan.

Government of India (2012) *Census of India 2011*, 'Provisional Population Total – Urban Agglomerations and Cities'. Available at: censusindia.gov.in (accessed 5 August 2012).

Government of Tamil Nadu (2007) *Policy Notes 2006–2007*, Department of Handlooms, Handicrafts, Textiles and Khadi: Handlooms and Textiles, Chennai.

Government of Tamil Nadu (2008) *Policy Notes 2007–2008*, Department of Handlooms, Handicrafts, Textiles and Khadi: Handlooms and Textiles, Chennai. Available at: www.tn.gov.in/budget/archives/budgetspeech_2007_08.htm (accessed 7 August 2008)

Gramsci, A. (1917) 'La rivoluzione contro *Il Capitale*', *Avanti!*, 24th December.

Gramsci, A. (1975) *Quaderni del carcere*, edited by V. Gerratana, 4 volumes, Torino: Einaudi.

Griffin, K. (1974) *The Political Economy of Agrarian Change: An Essay on the Green Revolution*, London: Macmillan.

Gulati, A. (1999) 'Indian Agriculture in an Open Economy: Will it Prosper?', in I.J. Ahluwalia and I.M.D. Little (eds) *India's Economic Reforms and Development. Essays for Manmohan Singh*, Delhi: Oxford India Paperbacks: 122–146.

Gupta, D. (2004) 'Introduction: The Certitudes of Caste: When Identity Trumps Hierarchy', in D. Gupta (ed.) *Caste in Question: Identity or Hierarchy?*, New Delhi: Sage: ix–xxi.

Haggblade, S. (2007a) 'Alternative Perceptions of the Rural Nonfarm Economy', in S. Haggblade, P.B.R. Hazell and T. Reardon (eds) *Transforming the Rural Non-Farm Economy: Opportunities and Threats in the Developing World*, Baltimore: IFPRI/The Johns Hopkins University Press: 25–54.

Haggblade, S. (2007b) 'Subsector Supply Chains: Operational Diagnostic for a Complex Rural Economy', in S. Haggblade, P.B.R. Hazell and T. Reardon (eds) *Transforming the Rural Non-Farm Economy. Opportunities and Threats in the Developing World*, Baltimore: IFPRI/The Johns Hopkins University Press: 352–378.

Haggblade, S., Hazell, P.B.R. and Dorosh, P.A. (2007) 'Sectoral Growth Linkages between Agriculture and the Rural Nonfarm Economy', in S. Haggblade, P.B.R. Hazell and T. Reardon (eds) *Transforming the Rural Non-Farm Economy: Opportunities and Threats in the Developing World*, Baltimore: IFPRI/The Johns Hopkins University Press: 141–182.

Haggblade, S., Hazell, P.B.R. and Reardon, T. (2007) 'Introduction', in S. Haggblade, P.B.R. Hazell and T. Reardon (eds) *Transforming the Rural Non-Farm Economy: Opportunities and Threats in the Developing World*. Baltimore: IFPRI/The Johns Hopkins University Press: 3–24.

Hall, P.A. and Soskice, D. (2001) 'An Introduction to the Varieties of Capitalism', in: P.A. Hall and D. Soskice (eds) *Varieties of Capitalism: The Institutional Foundations of Comparative Advantages*, Oxford: Oxford University Press: 1–68.

Harriss, B. (1981a) 'Agricultural Mercantile Politics and Policy: A Case Study of Tamil Nadu', *Economic and Political Weekly*, Vol. XVI, Nos 10–12, Annual Number: 441–458.

Harriss, B. (1981b) *Transitional Trade and Rural Development: The Nature and Role of Agricultural Trade in a South Indian District*, New Delhi: Vikas.

Harriss, B. (1987a) 'Regional Growth Linkages form Agriculture', *Journal of Development Studies*, Vol. 32, No. 2: 275–294.

Harriss, B. (1987b) 'Regional Growth Linkages from Agriculture and Resources Flows in Non-Farm Economy', *Economic and Political Weekly*, Vol. XXII, Nos 1–2: 31–46.

Harriss, B. (1991) 'The Arni Studies: Changes in the Private Sector of a Market Town, 1971–1983', in P. Hazell and C. Ramasamy (eds) *The Green Revolution Reconsidered: The Impact of High-Yielding Varieties in South India*, Baltimore: Johns Hopkins: 181–212.

Harriss, B. and Harriss, J. (1984) ' "Generative" or "Parasitic" Urbanism? Some Observations from the Recent History of a South Indian Market Town', *The Journal of Development Studies*, Vol. 20, No. 3: 82–101.

Harriss, J. (1982a) *Capitalism and Peasant Farming: Agrarian Structure and Ideology in Northern Tamil Nadu*, Bombay: Oxford University Press.

Harriss, J. (1982b) 'The Mode of Production Controversy: Themes and Problems of The Debate', in I. Livingstone (ed.) *Approaches to Development Studies: Essays in Honour of Athole Mackintosh*, Aldershot: Gower: 245–292.

Harriss, J. (1991) 'Agriculture/Non-agriculture Linkages and the Diversification of Rural Economic Activity: A South Indian Case Study', in J. Breman and S. Mundle (eds) *Rural Transformation in Asia*, Delhi: Oxford University Press: 449–457.

Harriss-White, B. (1996) 'Primary Accumulation, Corruption and Development Policy: Some Insights from a South Indian Case Study', *Review of Development and Change*, 1/1, January–June: 85–101.

Harriss-White, B. (2003a) *India Working: Essays on Society and Economy*, Cambridge: Cambridge University Press.

Harriss-White, B. (2003b) 'A Town in South India: Two Decades of Revisits', paper for the DPU-ODI-IBRD Conference on *Urban Longitudinal Research Methodology*, Development Policy Unit, London, 28/29 May.

Harriss-White, B. (2009) 'A Small Town in South India: Long-term Urban Studies and Three Decades of Revisits', Paper for the International Conference on *Market Town, Market Society, Informal Economy*, Contemporary South Asian Studies Programme, Oxford University, June.

Harriss-White, B. (2010a) 'Globalisation, the Financial Crisis and Petty Production in India's Informal Economy', *Global Labour Journal*, Vol. 1, No. 1: 150–177.

Harriss-White, B. (2010b) 'Taking the Part of Petty Commodity Producers', paper for the conference *Celebrating Gavin Williams*, University of Oxford, Department of Politics, Oxford, July.

Harriss-White, B. and Harriss, J. (2007) 'Green Revolution and After: The North Arcot Papers and Long-Term Studies of The Political Economy of Rural Development in South India', QEH Working Paper Series – QEHWPS146.

Harriss-White, B. and Janakarajan, S. (2004) *Rural India Facing the 21st Century: Essays on Long Term Village Change and Recent Development Policy*, London: Anthem South Asian Studies.

Harriss-White, B., Janakarajan, S. and Colatei, D. (2004) 'Introduction: Heavy Agriculture and Light Industry in South Indian Villages', in B. Harriss-White and S. Janakarajan (eds) *Rural India Facing the 21st Century: Essays on Long Term Village Change and Recent Development Policy*, London: Anthem South Asian Studies: 3–46.

Hazell, P. and Ramasamy, C. (eds) (1991a) *The Green Revolution Reconsidered*, Baltimore: IFPRI and Johns Hopkins University Press.

Hazell, P. and Ramasamy, C. (1991b) 'Conclusions and Policy Implications', in P. Hazell and C. Ramasamy (eds) *The Green Revolution Reconsidered: The Impact of High-Yielding Varieties in South India*, Baltimore: IFPRI and Johns Hopkins University Press: 238–253.

Hazell, P. and Haggblade, S. (1991) 'Rural–Urban Growth Linkages in India', *Indian Journal of Agricultural Economics*, Vol. 46, No. 4: 515–529.

Hazell, P.B.R., Hagglabade, S. and Reardon, T. (2007) 'Structural Transformation of the Rural Nonfarm Economy', in S. Haggblade, P.B.R. Hazell and T. Reardon (eds) *Transforming the Rural Non-Farm Economy: Opportunities and Threats in the Developing World*, Baltimore: IFPRI/The Johns Hopkins University Press: 83–98.

Hegel, G.W.F. (2001) *Philosophy of Right*, translated by S.W.Dyde, Kitchener (Ontario): Batoche Books (first edition in 1821).

Henry, J.F. (2001) *On the Relations between Veblen and Marx*, Mimeo, California State University.

Heyer, J. (2010) 'The Marginalisation of Dalits in a Modernising Economy', in B. Harriss-White and J. Heyer (eds) *The Comparative Political Economy of Development. Africa and South Asia*, Abingdon: Routledge: 225–247.

Hilton, R.H. (1985) 'Introduction', in T.H. Ashton and C.H.E. Philpin (eds) *The Brenner Debate: Agrarian Class Structure and Economic Development in Pre-Industrial Europe*, Cambridge: Cambridge University Press: 1–9.

Himanshu (2011) 'Employment Trends in India: A Re-examination', mimeo, *School of Social Sciences*, Jawaharlal Nehru University, New Delhi.

Himanshu, Lanjouw, P., Mukhopadhyay, A. and Murgai, R. (2011) 'Non-Farm Diversification and Rural Poverty Decline: A Perspective from Indian Sample Survey and Village Study Data', *Asia Research Centre*, Working Paper No. 44, London: LSE.

Hodgson, G.M. (1988) *Economics and Institutions: A Manifesto for a Modern Institutional Economics*, Cambridge: Polity Press.

Hodgson, G.M. (1993a) *Economics and Evolution: Bringing Life Back into Economics*, Cambridge: Polity Press.

Hodgson, G.M. (1993b) 'Introduction', in G.M. Hodgson (ed.) *The Economics of Institutions*, Aldershot: Edward Elgar: xi–xx.

Hodgson, G.M. (1998) 'The Approach of Institutional Economics', *Journal of Economic Literature*, Vol. XXXVI, March: 166–192.

Hodgson, G.M. (2000) 'What is the Essence of Institutional Economics?' *Journal of Economic Issues*, Vol. XXXIV, No. 2: 317–334.

Hodgson, G.M. (2001a) *How Economics Forgot History: The Problem of Historical Specificity in Social Science*, London: Routledge.

Hodgson, G.M. (2001b) 'The Evolution of Capitalism from the Perspective of Institutional and Evolutionary Economics', in G.M. Hodgson, M. Itoh and N. Yokokawa (eds) *Capitalism in Evolution: Global Contentions – East and West*. Cheltenham: Edward Elgar: 63–82.

Hodgson, G.M. (2003) 'Darwinism and Institutional Economics', *Journal of Economic Issues*, Vol. XXXVII, No. 1: 85–97.

Hodgson, G.M. (2004) *The Evolution of Institutional Economics: Agency, Structure and Darwinism in American Institutionalism*, London: Routledge.

Hodgson, G.M. (2007), 'Institutions and Individuals: Interaction and Evolution', in *Organization Studies*, 28(1): 95–116.

Hodgson, G.M., Itoh, M. and Yokokawa, N. (2001) 'Introduction', in G.M. Hodgson, M. Itoh and N. Yokokawa (eds) *Capitalism in Evolution: Global Contentions – East and West*, Cheltenham: Edward Elgar: 1–18.

Human Rights Watch (2003) *Small Change: Bonded Child Labor in India's Silk Industry*, Vol. 15, No. 2 (C), Children Rights Division, Human Rights Watch, New York.

Hunt, E.K. (1979) 'The Importance of Thorstein Veblen for Contemporary Marxism', *Journal of Economic Issues*, Vol. XIII, No. 1: 113–140.

ILO (1972) *Employment, Incomes and Equality: A Strategy for Increasing Productive Employment in Kenya*, Geneva: ILO.

ILO (2002) *Decent Work and the Informal Economy*, Report VI, 90th session, Geneva: ILO.

ILO (2012) *Statistical Update on Employment in the Informal Sector.* Available at: laborsta.ilo.org (accessed 3 September 2012).

ILO/WTO (2009) *Globalization and Informal Jobs in Developing Countries*, Geneva: ILO/WTO.

Islam, R. (1987) *Rural Industrialisation and Employment in Asia*, New Delhi: ILO, Asian Employment Programme.

Jackson, G. and Deeg, R. (2006) 'How Many Varieties of Capitalism? Comparing the Comparative Institutional Analyses of Capitalist Diversity', Max Plank Institute for the Study of Societies, Discussion Paper 06/02.

Jayaraj, D. (2004) 'Social Institutions and the Structural Transformation of the Non-Farm Economy', in B. Harriss-White and S. Janakarajan (eds) *Rural India Facing the 21st Century: Essays on Long Term Village Change and Recent Development Policy*, London: Anthem Press: 175–191.

Jha, P.S. (1980) *The Political Economy of Stagnation*, Delhi: Oxford University Press.

John, M.E. and Deshpande, S. (2008) 'Theorising the Present: Problems and Possibilities', *Economic and Political Weekly*, 15 November: 83–86.

Joshi, S. (2004) 'Tertiary Sector-Driven Growth in India: Impact on Employment and Poverty', *Economic and Political Weekly*, September 11: 4175–4178.

Joshi, V. and Little, I.M.D. (1998*) India: Macroeconomics and Political Economy 1964–1991*, New Delhi: Oxford India Paperbacks, Oxford University Press for the World Bank.

Kalecki, M. (1972) 'Social and Economic Aspects of Intermediate Regimes', in M. Kalecki, *Selected Essays on the Economic Growth of the Socialist and the Mixed Economy*, English translation by Z. Sadowski and others, Cambridge: Cambridge University Press: 162–169.

Kapadia, K. (2010) 'Liberalisation and Transformations in India's Informal Economy: Female Breadwinners in Working-Class Households in Chennai', in B. Harriss-White and J. Heyer (eds) *The Comparative Political Economy of Development: Africa and South Asia*, London: Routledge: 267–290.

Kar, S. and Sakthivel, S. (2007) 'Reforms and Regional Inequality in India', *Economic and Political Weekly*, February 24: 69–77.

Kattuman, P. (1998) 'The Role of History in the Transition to an Industrial District: The Case of the Indian Bicycle Industry', in Ph. Cadène and M. Holmström (eds) *Decentralised Production in India: Industrial Districts, Flexible Specialization, and Employment*, Pondicherry and New Delhi: French Institute of Pondicherry and Sage Publications: 230–250.

Kautsky, K. (1899) *La questione agraria*, Translation of *Die Agrarfrage* by G. Garritano, published in Italian with an Introduction by G. Procacci in 1959, Milano: Feltrinelli.

Kaviraj, S. (2001) 'In Search of Civil Society', in S. Kaviraj and S. Khilnani (eds) *Civil Society: History and Possibilities*, Cambridge: Cambridge University Press: 287–323.

Khalil, E.L. (1992) 'Marx's Understanding of the Essence of Capitalism', *History of Economics Review*, Vol. 17, Winter: 19–32.

Klass, M. (1980) *Caste: The Emergence of the South Asian Social System*, Institute for the Study of Human Issues, Philadelphia.

Knorringa, P. (1998) 'Barriers to Flexible Specialisation in Agra's Footwear Industry', in Ph. Cadène and M. Holmström (eds) *Decentralised Production in India: Industrial Districts, Flexible Specialization, and Employment*, Pondicherry and New Delhi: French Institute of Pondicherry and Sage Publications: 283–307.

Kolakowski, L. (2005) *Main Currents of Marxism: The Founders, The Golden Age, The Breakdown*, New York and London: W.W. Norton & Company.

Kotz, D.M. (1994), 'The Regulation Theory and the Social Structure of Accumulation Approach', in D.M. Kotz, T. McDonough and M. Reich (eds) *Social Structures of Accumulation: The Political Economy of Growth and Crisis*, Cambridge: Cambridge University Press.

Kotz, D.M., McDonough, T. and Reich, M. (eds) (1994) *Social Structures of Accumulation: The Political Economy of Growth and Crisis*, Cambridge: Cambridge University Press.

Kumar N. (2006) 'Provincialism in Modern India: The Multiple Narratives of Education and their Pain', *Modern Asian Studies*, Vol. 40, No. 2: 397–423.

Kundu, A., Sarangi, N. and Das, B.P. (2005) 'Economic Growth, Poverty and Non-farm Employment: An Analysis of Rural–Urban Linkages', in R. Nayyar and A.N. Sharma (eds) *Rural Transformation in India: The Role of Non-farm Sector*, New Delhi: Manohar Publishers for Institute for Human Development: 137–155.

Kus, B. (2006) 'State and Economic Informality in a Comparative Perspective', Working Paper CCOP, No Institute for Research on Labour and Employment, Berkeley.

Lanjouw, P. (2007) 'Does the Rural Nonfarm Economy Contribute to Poverty Reduction?', in S. Haggblade, P.B.R. Hazell and T. Reardon (eds) *Transforming the Rural Non-Farm Economy. Opportunities and Threats in the Developing World*, Baltimore: IFPRI/The Johns Hopkins University Press: 55–79.

Lenin, V.I. (1899) *The Development of Capitalism in Russia*, Volume 3 of Collected Works, fourth edition, Moscow: Progress Publishers. Available at: marx.org/archive/lenin/works//cw/volume03.htm (accessed 7 August 2008).

Lenin, V.I. (1907) 'Two Types of Bourgeois Agrarian Evolution', in *The Agrarian Programme of Social-Democracy in the First Russian Revolution, 1905–1907*, Volume 13 of Collected Works, Moscow: Progress Publishers. Available at: marx.org/archive/lenin/works//1907/agrprogr/ch01s5.htm (accessed 7 August 2008).

Lerche, J. (1995) 'Is Bonded Labour a Bound Category? Reconceptualising Agrarian Conflict in India', *The Journal of Peasant Studies*, Vol. 22, No. 3: 484–515.

Lerche, J. (2007) 'A Global Alliance Against Forced Labour? Unfree Labour, Neo-Liberal Globalization and the International Labour Organization', *Journal of Agrarian Change*, Vol. 7, No. 4: 425–452.

Lerche, J. (2010) 'From "Rural Labour" to "Classes of Labour": Class Fragmentation, Caste and Class Struggle at the Bottom of the Indian Labour Hierarchy', in B. Harriss-White and J. Heyer (eds) *The Comparative Political Economy of Development: Africa and South Asia*, Abingdon: Routledge: 64–85.

Liedholm, C. (2007) 'Enterprise Dynamics in the Rural Nonfarm Economy', in S. Haggblade, P.B.R. Hazell and T. Reardon (eds) *Transforming the Rural Non-Farm Economy: Opportunities and Threats in the Developing World*, Baltimore: IFPRI/The Johns Hopkins University Press: 99–114.

Lipietz, A. (1987) *Mirages and Miracles: The Crises of Global Fordism*, London: Verso.

Madheswaran, S. and Attewell, P. (2007) 'Caste Discrimination in the Indian Labour Market: Evidence from the National Sample Survey', *Economic and Political Weekly*, October 13: 4146–4154.

Marx, K. (1844) '*Sulla questione ebraica*', in *Un carteggio del 1843 e altri scritti*, Roma: Edizioni Rinascita, 1954: 43–86. (Italian translation of *Zur Judenfrage* first published in Deutsch-Französische Jahrbücher, Paris: 182–214.)

Marx, K. (1853) 'The Future Results of British Rule in India', New York Daily Tribune, 8 August, in K. Marx and F. Engels, *Collected Works*, Volume 12, Marx: 1853–1854, London: Lawrence and Wishart (1979): 217–222.

Marx, K. (1859) *A Contribution to the Critique of Political Economy* (Preface and Introduction), Peking: Foreign Languages Press (1976).

Marx, K. (1890) *Il capitale. Critica dell'economia politica, Libro Primo (Parts 1, 2, 3)*, Introduction by M. Dobb. Italian translation from German based on the VI edition edited by F. Engels in 1890. Edited by D. Cantimori, Roma: Editori Riuniti (1970).

Marx, K. (1893) *Il capitale. Critica dell'economia politica. Libro Secondo (Parts 1, 2)*, Italian translation from German based on the II Meissner edition in 1893. Edited by R. Panzieri, Roma: Editori Riuniti (1970).

Marx, K. (1894) *Il capitale. Critica dell'economia politica, Libro Terzo (Parts 1, 2, 3)*, Italian translation from German based on the Meissner edition in 1894, edited by M.L. Boggeri, Roma: Editori Riuniti (1970).

Marx, K. and Engels, F. (1848) *Manifesto of the Communist Party*, Peking: Foreign Languages Press, 1970.

Mavroudeas, S. (2006) 'Social Structures of Accumulation, Regulation Approach and Stages Theory', in T. McDonough, M. Reich, D.M. Kotz, and M.A. Gonzalez-Perez (eds) *Growth and Crisis: Social Structure of Accumulation Theory and Analysis*, Galway: Social Science Research Centre and Centre for Innovation & Structural Change at the National University of Ireland: 200–216.

Mayhew, A. (1987) 'The Beginnings of Institutionalism', *Journal of Economic Issues*, Vol. XXI, No. 3: 971–998.

Mayhew, A. (1989) 'Contrasting Origins of the Two Institutionalisms: The Social Science Context', *Review of Political Economy*, Vol. I, No. 3: 319–333.

McCartney, M. (2009) *India: The Political Economy of Growth, Stagnation and the State, 1951–2007*, London and New York: Routledge.

McCartney, M. (2010) *Political Economy, Growth and Liberalisation in India, 1991–2008*, London and New York: Routledge.

McCartney, M. and Harriss-White, B. (2000) 'The "Intermediate Regime" and the "Intermediate Classes" Revisited: A Critical Political Economy of Indian Economic Development from 1980 to Hindutva', Queen Elizabeth House Website, Working Paper No. 34. Available at: www.qeh.ox.ac.uk/RePEc/qeh/qehwps/qehwps34.pdf/ (accessed 7 August 2008).

Meiksins Wood, E. (2002) *The Origin of Capitalism: A Longer View*, London and New York: Verso.

Mellor, J.W. (1976) *The New Economics of Growth: A Strategy for India and Developing World*, Ithaca: Cornell University Press.

Mezzadri, A. (2010) 'Globalisation, Informalisation and the State in the Indian Garment Industry', in E. Basile and B. Harriss-White (eds) *India's Informal Capitalism and its Regulation, Monographic Section*, in *International Review of Sociology*, Vol. 20, No. 3: 491–512.

Michelutti, L. (2004) ' "We (Yadavs) are a Caste of Politicians': Caste and Modern Politics in a North Indian Town', in D. Gupta (ed.) *Caste in Question: Identity or Hierarchy?*, New Delhi: Sage: 43–72.

Milanovic, B. (2006) 'Global Income Inequality: A Review', *World Economics*, Vol. 7, No. 1: 131–157 (reprinted in B. Milanovic (ed.) (2012) *Globalisation and Inequality*, Cheltenham: Edward Elgar).

Milanovic, B. (2010) *The Haves and the Have-Nots: A Brief and Idiosyncratic History of Global Inequality*, New York: Basic Books.

Milanovic, B. (2011) 'Global Inequality: From Class to Location, From Proletarians to Migrants', Policy Research Working Paper, 5820, Development Research Group, The World Bank.

Ministry of Textiles (2005) *Working Conditions of Women in the Handloom Sector*, Committee on Empowerment of Women, Report presented at the Lok Sabha Secretariat on 5 December, New Delhi.

Mishra, S. (2007), 'Agrarian Scenario in Post-reform India: A Story of Distress, Despair and Death', Working Paper 001, Indira Gandhi Institute of Development Research, Mumbai.

Mitra, A. and Mitra, S. (2005) 'Rural Nob-farm Sector: A State Level Profile', in R. Nayyar and A.N. Sharma (eds), *Rural Transformation in India: The Role of Non-farm Sector*, New Delhi: Manohar Publishers for Institute for Human Development: 121–136.

Moser, C. (1978) 'Informal Sector and Petty Commodity Production: Dualism or Dependence in Urban Development?' *World Development*, Vol. 6, Nos 9–10: 1041–1064.

Mukherjee, R. (2000) 'Caste in Itself, Caste and Class, or Caste in Class', *Journal of World-Systems Research*, Vol. VI, No. 2: 332–339.

Murthy, C.S. (2005) 'Rural Non-Agricultural Employment in India: The Residual Sector Hypothesis Revisited', Centre for Economic and Social Studies, Working Paper No. 67, Hyderabad.

Nagaraj, K., Janakarajan, S., Jayaraj, D. and Harriss-White, B. (1996) 'Sociological Aspects of Silk Weaving in Arni and its Environs', paper for the *Workshop on Adjustment and Development*, Madras Institute of Development Studies, Chennai.

Narayan, B. (2004a) 'Inventing Caste History', in D. Gupta (ed.) *Caste in Question. Identity or Hierarchy?*, New Delhi: Sage: 193–220.

Narayan, B. (2004b) 'National Past and Political Present', *Economic and Political Weekly*, 31 July: 3533–3540.

Nath, V. (2000) 'Entrepreneurship by Regions and Castes: A Survey', *Economic and Political Weekly*, 26 August/2 September: 4207–4211.

Nayyar, R. and Sharma, A.N. (2005) 'Introduction', in R. Nayyar and A.N. Sharma (eds) *Rural Transformation in India: The Role of Non-farm Sector*, New Delhi: Institute for Human Development: 11–26.

NCAER (2006) *Examining Employment Figures in the Handloom Sector*, Study commissioned by All India Artisans and Craftworkers Welfare Association (AIACA) National Council of Applied Economic Research (NCAER), New Delhi.

NCEUS (2007) *Report on Conditions of Work and Promotion of Livelihoods in the Unorganised Sector*. Available at: www.nceus.gov.in (accessed 6 December 2008).

NCEUS (2008) *Report on Definitional and Statistical Issues Relating to Informal Economy*. Available at: www.nceus.gov.in (accessed 6 December 2008).

NCEUS (2009) *The Challenge of Employment in India: An Informal Economy Perspective*, Vols. I and II. Available at: www.nceus.gov.in (accessed 6 December 2010).

Niranjana, S. and Vinayan, S. (2001) *Report on Growth and Prospects of the Handloom Industry*, Study Commissioned by the Planning Commission, Dastkar Andhra.

NSSO (Government of India) (2006) *Employment and Unemployment Situation in India (2004–2005)* (NSS 61st Round), National Sample Survey Organisation, Ministry of Statistics and Programme Implementation.

NSSO (Government of India) (2011) *Employment and Unemployment Situation in India (2009–2010)* (NSS 66th Round), National Sample Survey Organisation, Ministry of Statistics and Programme Implementation.

NSSO (Government of India) (2012) *Informal Sector and Conditions of Employment in India (2009–2010)* (NSS 66th Round), National Sample Survey Organisation, Ministry of Statistics and Programme Implementation.

O'Hara, Ph.A. (2000) *Marx, Veblen, and Contemporary Institutional Political Economy: Principles and Unstable Dynamics of Capitalism*, Cheltenham: Edward Elgar.

O'Sullivan, N. (1988) 'The Political Theory of Neo-Corporatism', in A. Cox and N. O'Sullivan (eds) *The Corporate State: Corporatism and the State Tradition in Western Europe*, Aldershot: Edward Elgar: 3–26.

Ossowski, S. (1966) *Struttura di classe e coscienza sociale*, Torino: Einaudi (translated from the Polish edition, 1957; published in English in 1963).

Pande, M. (2011) *The Other Country: Dispaches From the Mofussil*, New Delhi: Penguin Books India.

Papola, T.S. (1992) 'Rural Non-Farm Employment: An Assessment of Recent Trends', *Indian Journal of Labour Economics*, Vol. 35, No. 3: 238–245.

Papola, T.S. and Sahu, P.P. (2012) *Growth and Structure of Employment in India: Long-Term and Post-Reform Performance and the Emerging Challenge*, New Delhi: Institute for Studies in Industrial Development.

Papola, T.S. and Sharma, A.N. (2005) 'Towards a Policy Agenda for Rural Non-farm Sector', in R. Nayyar and A.N. Sharma (eds) *Rural Transformation in India: The Role of Non-farm Sector*, New Delhi: Manohar Publishers for Institute for Human Development: 509–516.

Patnaik, U. (1971a) 'Capitalist Development in Agriculture: A Note', *Economic and Political Weekly*: A123–A130.

Patnaik, U. (1971b) 'Capitalist Development in Agriculture: Further Comment', *Economic and Political Weekly*: A190–A194.

Patnaik, U. (1972) 'On the Mode of Production in Indian Agriculture: A Reply', *Economic and Political Weekly*: A145–A151.

Patnaik, U. (1990) 'Introduction,' in *Agrarian Relations and Accumulation: The 'Mode of Production' Debate in India*, Bombay: Sameeksha Trust/Oxford University Press: 1–10.

Patnaik, U. (1997) 'India's Agricultural Development in the Light of Historical Experience', in T.J. Byres (ed.) *The State, Development Planning and Liberalisation in India*, New Delhi: Oxford University Press: 172–197.

Patnaik, U. (2004) *The Republic of Hunger*. Public Lecture on the occasion of the 50th Birthday of Safdar Hashmi, Safdar Hashmi Memoprial Trust, New Delhi, April.

Patnaik, U. (2010a) 'A Critical Look at Some Propositions on Consumption and Poverty', *Economic and Political Weekly*, 6 February: 74–80.

Patnaik, U. (2010b) 'On Some Fatal Fallacies', *Economic and Political Weekly*, 20 November: 81–87.

Perry, G.E., Maloney, W.F., Arias, O.S., Fajnzylber, P., Mason, A.D. and Saavedra-Chanduvi, J. (2007) *Informality: Exit and Exclusion*, Washington: The World Bank.

Planning Commission (Government of India) (1970) *4th Five Year Plan: 1969–74*. Available at: www.planningcommission.nic (accessed 6 July 2011).

Planning Commission (Government of India) (2008) *Eleventh Five Year Plan: 2007–12. Vol. I: Inclusive Growth*. Delhi: Oxford University Press.

Prakash, A. (2010) 'Dalit Entrepreneurs in Middle India', in B. Harriss-White and J. Heyer (eds) *The Comparative Political Economy of Development: Africa and South Asia*, Abingdon: Routledge: 291–316.

Radhakrishnan, P. (1996) 'Mandal Commission Report: A Sociological Critique', in M.N. Srinivas (ed.) *Caste: Its Twentieth Century Avatar*, Delhi: Viking: 203–220.

Raj, K.N. (1973) 'The Politics and Economics of "Intermediate Regimes"', *Economic and Political Weekly*, 7 July: 1190–1198.

Ranadive, B.T. (2002) 'Caste, Class and Property Relations', in G. Shah (ed.) *Caste and Democratic Policies in India*, Delhi: Permanent Black: 134–161.

Rani, U. and Unni, J. (2009) 'Do Economic Reforms Influence Home-Based Work? Evidence from India', *Feminist Economics*, Vol. 15, No. 3: 191–225.

Rao, J.M. (1997) 'Agricultural Development Under State Planning', in T.J. Byres (ed.) *The State, Development Planning and Liberalisation in India*, New Delhi: Oxford University Press: 126–171.

Reardon, T., Berdegué, J., Barrett, C.B. and Stamoulis, K. (2007) 'Household Income Diversification into Rural Nonfarm Activities', in S. Haggblade, P.B.R. Hazell and T. Reardon (eds) *Transforming the Rural Non-Farm Economy. Opportunities and Threats in the Developing World*, Baltimore: IFPRI/The Johns Hopkins University Press: 115–140.

Remesh, B.P. (2001) *Organisational Structure, Labour Relations and Employment in Kancheepuram Silk Weaving*, V.V. Giri National Labour Institute, NOIDA, Research Studies Series No. 021.

Renkow, M. (2007) 'Cities, Towns, and the Rural Nonfarm Economy', in S. Haggblade, P.B.R. Hazell and T. Reardon (eds) *Transforming the Rural Non-Farm Economy: Opportunities and Threats in the Developing World*, Baltimore: IFPRI/The Johns Hopkins University Press: 183–198.

Resnick, S. and Wolff, R. (1987) *Knowledge and Class*, Chicago: Chicago University Press.

Rodrik, D. and Subramanian, A. (2004a) 'From "Hindu Growth" to Productivity Surge: The Mystery of the Indian Growth Transition', IMF Working Paper, No. 77.

Rodrik, D. and Subramanian, A. (2004b) 'Why India Can Grow at 7 Percent a Year or More: Projections and Reflections', IMF Working Paper, No. 118.

Roemer, J. (1986) '"Rational Choice" Marxism: Some Issues of Method and Substance', in J. Roemer (ed.) *Analytical Marxism*, Cambridge: Cambridge University Press: 191–201.

Roman, C. (2004) 'Skills and Silks: Learning to Work in the Informal Sector', unpublished M. Phil. Thesis, Oxford University.

Roman, C. (2008) 'Learning and Innovation in Clusters: Case Studies from Indian Silk Industry', unpublished D.Phil. Thesis, Oxford University.

Roy, T. (1993) *Artisans and Industrialization: Indian Weaving in the Twentieth Century*, Delhi: Oxford University Press.

Roy, T. (1999) *Traditional Industry in the Economy of Colonial India*, Cambridge: Cambridge University Press.

Rudra, A. (1978) 'Class Relations in Indian Agriculture (part III)', *Economic and Political Weekly*, June 17: 998–1004.

Rudra, A., Majid, A. and Talib, B.D. (1969) 'Big Farmers of the Punjab: Some Preliminary Findings of a Sample Survey', *Economic and Political Weekly*: A143–A151.

Rutherford, M. (1989) 'What is Wrong with the New Institutional Economics (and What is Still Wrong with the Old)?', *Review of Political Economy*, Vol. I, No. 3: 299–318.

Ruthven, O. (2010) 'Government Inspectors and "Ethical" Buyers: Regulating Labour in Moradabad's Metalware Industry', in E. Basile and B. Harriss-White (eds) *India's Informal Capitalism and its Regulation. Monographic Section*, in *International Review of Sociology*, Vol. 20, No. 3: 473–490.

Rutten, M. (1995) *Farms and Factories: Social Profile of Large Farmers and Rural Industrialists in West India*, Delhi: Oxford University Press.

Rutten, M. (2002) 'A Historical and Comparative View on the Study of Indian Entrepreneurship', *Economic Sociology*, European Electronic Newsletter Vol. 3, No. 2: 3–16, Available at: econsoc.mpifg.de/archive/esfeb02.pdf (accessed 7 August 2008).

Sacratees, J. (2004) *Economy of Arni Silk*, Mimeo, Madras Institute of Development Studies, Chennai.

Saith, A. (1992) *The Rural Non-Farm Economy: Processes and Policies*, Geneva: ILO.

Saith, A. (2001) 'From Village Artisan to Industrial Clusters: Agendas and Policy Gaps in Indian Rural Industrialisation', *Journal of Agrarian Change*, Vol. 1, No. 1: 81–123.

Sanyal, K. (2007) *Rethinking Capitalist Development: Primitive Accumulation, Governmentality and Post-Colonial Capitalism*, London and New Delhi: Routledge.

Sanyal, K. and Bhattacharyya, R. (2009) 'Beyond the Factory: Globalisation, Informalisation of Production and the New Location of Labour' *Economic and Political Weekly*, May 30: 35–44.

Schmitter, Ph.C. (1974) 'Still the Century of Corporatism?', *Review of Politics*, Vol. 36, No. 1: 85–131.

Schmitter, Ph.C. and Lehmbruch, G. (eds) (1979) *Trends Toward Corporatist Intermediation*, London and Beverly Hills: Sage Publications.

Schumpeter, J. (1934) *The Theory of Economic Development: An Inquiry into Profits, Capital, Credit, Interest, and the Business Cycle*, Cambridge, MA: Harvard University Press.

Scoones, I. (1998) 'Sustainable Rural Livelihoods: A Framework for Analysis', IDS Working Paper No. 72.

Sen, A. (1997) 'Structural Adjustment and Rural Poverty: Variables that Really Matter', in G.K. Chadha and A.N Sharma (eds) *Growth, Employment and Poverty in India: Change and Continuity in Rural India*, New Delhi: Vikas Publishing House: 78–109.

Sen, A. (2010) 'From Rescue Measures to Fuller Democracy', *Economic and Political Weekly*, 10 April: 51–57.

Sen, A. and Himansu (2004a) 'Poverty and Inequality in India – I', *Economic and Political Weekly*, 18 September: 4247–4263.

Sen, A. and Himansu (2004b) 'Poverty and Inequality in India – II. Widening Disparities During the 1990s', *Economic and Political Weekly*, 25 September: 4361–4375.

Sen, A.K. (2005) *The Argumentative Indian*, London: Penguin Books.

Sen, A.K. (2006) *Identity and Violence*, London: Allen Lane (for Penguin Books).

Sen, A.K. and Drèze, J. (2002) *India: Development and Participation*, New Delhi: Oxford University Press.

Sen, A.K. and Drèze, J. (eds) (1997) *Indian Development: Selected Regional Perspectives*, New Delhi and Oxford: Oxford University Press.

Shah, A.M. (2007) 'Caste in the 21st Century: From System to Elements', *Economic and Political Weekly*, 3 November: 109–116.

Shah, G. (2002) 'Introduction: Caste and Democratic Politics in India', in G. Shah (ed.) *Caste and Democratic Policies in India*, Delhi: Permanent Black: 1–31.

Shah, M. (2008) 'Structures of Power in Indian Society: A Response', *Economic and Political Weekly*, November 15: 78–83.

Sharma, K.L. (1994) 'Introduction: Some Reflections on Caste and Class in India', in K.L. Sharma (ed.) *Caste and Class in India*, Jaipur and New Delhi: Rawat Publications: 1–17.

Sheth, D.L. (1999) 'Secularisation of Caste and Making of New Middle Class', *Economic and Political Weekly*, 21–28 August: 2502–2510.

Shinoda, T. (2000) 'Institutional Change and Entrepreneurial Development: SSI Sector?', *Economic and Political Weekly*, 26 August/2 September: 3205–3216.

Srinivas, M.N. (1952) *Religion and Society Among the Coorgs of South India*, Bombay: Oxford University Press.

Srinivas, M.N. (1996) 'Introduction', in M.N. Srinivas (ed.) *Caste: Its Twentieth Century Avatar*, Delhi: Viking: ix–xxxviii.

Srinivas, M.N. (2003) 'An Obituary on Caste as a System', *Economic and Political Weekly*, 1 February: 455–459.

Srinivasan, M.V. (2010) 'Segmentation of Urban Labour Markets in India: A Case Study of Arni, Tamil Nadu', unpublished Ph.D. Thesis, Jawarhalal Nehru University.

Srivastava, R. (2012) 'Changing Employment Conditions of the Indian Workforce and Implications for Decent Work', *Global Labour Journal*, Vol. 3, No. 1: 63–90.

Srivastava, R.S. (2005) 'Bonded Labour in India: Its Incidence and Pattern', ILO Working Paper No. 43.

Standing, G. (2011) *The Precariat: The New Dangerous Class*, London and New York: Bloomsbury Academic.

Start, D. and Johnson, C. (2004) 'Livelihood Options? The Political Economy of Access, Opportunity and Diversification', ODI Working Paper No. 233.

Streeck, W. and Kenworthy, L. (2005) 'Theories and Practices of Neocorporatism', in T. Janoski, R.R. Alford, A.M. Hicks and M.A. Schwartz (eds) *The Handbook of Political Sociology*, Cambridge: Cambridge University Press: 441–460.

Sweezy, P., Dobb, M. and Hill, C. (1976) *The Transition from Feudalism to Capitalism*, Introduction by R.H. Hilton, London: NLB.

Tewari, M. (2000) 'Toward a New Production Sensibility – The Impact of Economic Liberalization on Regional Industry: The Case of Tamil Nadu, India', paper prepared for the Harvard India Program, Harvard University, Cambridge, MA.

Tewari, M. (2001) *The Challenge of Reform: How Tamil Nadu's Textile and Apparel Sector is Facing the Pressures of Liberalization*, India Program, Center for International

Development, Harvard University and the Government of Tamil Nadu. Available at: www.cid.harvard.edu/archive/india/pdfs/challenge_textile_lib_tewari0101.pdf (accessed 7 August 2008).

Thorat, A. (2010) 'Ethnicity, Caste and Religion: Implications for Poverty Outcomes', *Economic and Political Weekly*, 18 December: 47–53.

Thorat, S. and Newman, K.S. (2007) 'Caste and Economic Discrimination: Causes, Consequences and Remedies', *Economic and Political Weekly*, 13 October: 4121–4124.

Thorner, A. (1982a) 'Semi-Feudalism or Capitalism? Contemporary Debate on Classes and Modes of Production in India (Part I)', *Economic and Political Weekly*, 4 December: 1961–1908.

Thorner, A. (1982b) 'Semi-Feudalism or Capitalism? Contemporary Debate on Classes and Modes of Production in India (Part II)', *Economic and Political Weekly*, 11 December: 1993–1999.

Thorner, A. (1982c) 'Semi-Feudalism or Capitalism? Contemporary Debate on Classes and Modes of Production in India (Part III)', *Economic and Political Weekly*, 18 December: 2061–2086.

Torri, M. (2000) *Storia dell'India*, Rome and Bari: Laterza.

Toye, J.F.J. (1993) *Dilemmas of Development*, second edition, London: Cass.

Unni, J. (1991) 'Regional Variations in Rural Non-Agricultural Employment: An Exploratory Analysis', *Economic and Political Weekly*, 19 January: 109–122.

Unni, J. (1998) 'Non-Agricultural Employment and Poverty in Rural India: A Review of Evidence', *Economic and Political Weekly*, 28 March: A36–A44.

Unni, J. (2000) *Sustainable Development and Social Security: The Role of the Non-farm Sector*, New Delhi: Vikas Publishing House.

Unni, J. and Rani, U. (2005) 'Gender and Non-farm Employment', in N. Nayyar and A.N. Sharma (eds) *Rural Transformation in India: The Role of the Non-farm Sector*, New Delhi: Manohar Publishers for Institute for Human Development: 156–174.

Unni, J. and Raveendran, G. (2007) 'Growth of Employment (1993–94 to 2004–05): Illusion of Inclusiveness?', in *Economic and Political Weekly*, 20 January: 196–199.

Upadhya, C. (1997) 'Culture, Class and Entrepreneurship: A Case Study of Coastal Andhra Pradesh', in M. Rutten and C. Upadhya (eds) *Small Business Entrepreneurs in Asia and Europe*, New Delhi: Sage: 47–80.

Vaid, D. (2007) 'Caste and Class in India: An Analysis', Paper for the CIQLE Workshop, September.

Vaidyanathan, A. (1986) 'Labour Use in Rural India: A Study of Spatial and Temporal Variations', *Economic and Political Weekly*, December 27: A130–A146.

van Der Linden, M. (2008) *Workers of the World: Essays Toward a Global Labor History*, Leiden-Boston Brill.

Varma, P.K. (1998) *The Great Indian Middle Class*, New Delhi: Penguin Books.

Veblen, T. (1899) *The Theory of the Leisure Class: An Economic Study of Institutions*, reprinted with a review by W.D. Howells, New York: August, M. Kelly Bookseller (1965).

Veblen, T. (1906) 'The Socialist Economics of Karl Marx and his Followers: Part I Karl Marx', *The Quarterly Journal of Economics*, Vol. 20, August. Reprinted in Veblen, T. (1919) *The Place of Science in Modern Civilisation and Other Essays*, New York: Huebsch: 409–430.

Veblen, T. (1919) *The Place of Science in Modern Civilisation and Other Essays*, New York: Huebsch.

Vijayabaskar, M. (2005) 'Governance of Flexible Accumulation in Clusters: Can it Create

'Decent Work' in Low-income Regions?', Paper for the Queen Elizabeth House's 50th Birthday Conference *New Development: Threats and Promises*, Queen Elizabeth House, Oxford University.

Vijayabaskar, M. (2010) 'Global Crises and Local Labour Response: A Case for Regional Social Regulation', paper presented at the workshop *Working for Export Markets: Labour and Livelihoods in Global Production Networks*, Sussex University, July.

Visaria, P. and Basant, R. (eds) (1994) *Rural Non-Agricultural Employment in India*, New Delhi: Sage Publications.

Wade, R. (2004) 'Is Globalization Reducing Poverty and Inequality?' *World Development*, Vol. 32, No. 4: 567–589.

Wandschneider, T. (2003) *Determinants of Access to Rural Nnon-farm Employment: Evidence from Africa, South Asia and Transition Economies*, NRI Report No. 2578.

Wankhede, H. (2008) 'The Political and Social in the Dalit Movement Today', *Economic and Political Weekly*, 9 February: 50–57.

Williamson, P.J. (1989) *Corporatism in Perspective: An Introductory Guide to Corporatist Theory*, London: Sage.

World Bank, The (2006) *World Development Report 2006: Equity and Development*, Washington and New York: The World Bank/Oxford University Press.

World Bank, The (2011) *The Perspective of Poverty in India: Stylized Facts From Survey Data*, Washington: The World Bank.

World Bank, The (n.d.) *World Development Indicators.* Available at: data.worldbank.org/data-catalog/world-development-indicators (accessed 5 August 2012).

Wright, E.O. (1985) *Classes*, London: Verso.

Wright, E.O. (2005) 'Foundations of a Neo-Marxist Class Analysis', in E.O. Wright (ed.) *Approaches to Class Analysis*, Cambridge: Cambridge University Press: 1–26.

Wright, E.O. (2006) 'Class', in J. Beckert and M. Zafirovsky (eds) *International Encyclopedia of Economic Sociology*, London: Routledge: 62–68.

Zeitlin, M. and Ratcliff, R.E. (1988) *Landlords and Capitalist:. The Dominant Class of Chile*, Princeton: Princeton University Press.

Index

agency 3–4, 16
agency and structure: Analytical Marxism
    20; Evolutionary Institutionalism 21–3;
    Marx's theory 19–20
agrarian change: in Arni 108–9; and
    capitalist transition 76; and class
    formation 81
Agreement on Agriculture 39, 199n3, 2
Althusser, Louis 16
Archer, S. Margaret 20
Arni business economy: economic
    organisation 131–8; growth and
    diversification 115–21; local/global
    integration 121–31, 143–4
Arni surveys 107–9
Arni's civil society 163–73; class relations
    180–3; economic interests 174–5:
    relationships between economy and
    society 176–80; survey 161–2
Arni's industrial district for silk saris
    147–51; formation 150–1; silk sari
    production 148–9; social production
    relations 151–9
Arni's societal corporatism 183–4; and
    India's capitalist development 184–7
autonomous commoditisation 18; in
    Provincial India 85–7

Bagchi, Amiya Kumar 3, 83–4, 88, 191
Baru, Sanjaya 3, 81
Basile, Elisabetta 2, 39, 70–1, 206n14,
    n15, n16
Basu, Kaushik 37–8
Becattini, Giacomo 150, 153, 204n16
Béteille, Andre 96–100, 202n6
Bhaduri, Amit 77
Bhalla, G.S. 37, 39, 199n3, 2
Bhalla, Sheila 39, 43, 50–1, 200n11
Breman, Jan 51, 85–7, 201n25

Burawoy, Michael 12, 15
business associations in Arni 162, 174,
    176, 180–4, 194
Byres, Terence J. 37, 76, 78

capital and labour redefined 88–9
capital/labour conflicts 14, 26–8, 33, 74,
    80–1, 183–4
capitalism: according to Evolutionary
    Institutionalism 25–6; according to
    Marx 11–14; laws of motion 12; main
    traits 11–14; unpredicted developments
    14–15
caste: a Marxist/Institutionalist analysis
    99–100
caste associations in Arni 163, 166–7,
    174–6, 178–82, 186, 194–5; and in India
    97, 99, 103
caste and civil society/political society
    102–4
caste and class: in Arni 156–8; in India 98
caste consciousness and class-
    consciousness 99
caste identity and caste politics 97–8
caste as institution and ideology 95, 191–2
Castells, Manuel 55, 57
Cawson, Alan 94, 202n4
Chadha, G.K. 40, 43, 52, 54
Chakrabarti, Anjan 3, 80, 96
Chari, Sharad 82–3, 201n7, 207n22
Chatterjee, Partha 102–3, 201n14
Chen, Martha A. 56–7
civil society: according to Gramsci 91–2;
    as association of associations 90; and
    caste 102–4; and political society
    102–4
class analysis: according to Marx 12–13;
    according to Critical Marxism 17–18
class formation in Provincial India 81–5

class segmentation 5, 7, 88, 98; in Arni's silk economy 154–6; in Arni's civil society 185–7
class structure and the transition to capitalism 75–6
class structure in India 76–9
Cohen, Gerald A. 19
contradictory class location 17
contribution of eclecticism 3–4, 6, 33, 188–9
Corbridge, Stuart 3, 97, 202n8
corporatism 92; and pluralism 93
corporatist civil society: interest representation 91–2; interest intermediation 92–5
Cullenberg, Stephen 3, 28, 80, 96

De Neve, Gert 69, 86, 156, 201n25, 205n28, 207n22
Deaton, Angus 3, 199n3, 3
debates on India's class structure: Indian modes of production (IMP) 77; intermediate classes (IC) 77–8; a Marxist/Institutionalist critique 79–81
Delorme, Robert 23
distinguishing traits of capitalism: in Provincial India 189–92; in Arni 192–5
Dobb, Maurice 76
dogmatic Marxism *see* Orthodox Marxism
Drèze, Jean 3, 199n3, 3
Dugger, Sherman 28
Dugger, William M. 28
Dumont, Louis 96

eclectic framework *see* Marxist-Institutionalist framework
economic diversification: in Arni 115–20; factors and trajectories 45–50; in Provincial India 42–50, 84; the role of agricultural resources 41, 73, 196; theoretical analysis 40–2
economic reforms 37–8
economic theory versus empirical analysis 2–3, 188
Edgell, Stephen 27
Elster, Jon 20
embeddedness of capitalist change 5–6, 23–4, 33; in Arni 159–60; in Provincial India 73; in Provincial India and in Arni 189–95
Engels, Friedrich 12, 76
Evolutionary Institutionalism 4, 20–6

family labour in Arni 111, 138, 155–6, 159; in Provincial India 53–4, 69–70
family: and entrepreneurship 84, 131, 142, 152; and inequality 26; and labour commoditisation 86–9; and the recruitment in the informal economy 69; as regulating institution 24, 84
Farmer, Ben H. 108

Ghosh, Jayati 39
Gouldner, Alvin W. 15
Gramsci, Antonio 15, 16, 20, 91–2, 95, 165, 199n2, 4
Gramsci's theory of hegemony 15–16; the role of ideology 16
Gramscian hypothesis on the role of caste 100–2, 187, 192, 194
green revolution (GR) 37–8; and Arni's silk economy 149–50; and capitalist development in Arni 107–10, 112–15, 138, 145; and capitalist development in Provincial India 2, 7, 36–40, 45, 72, 81–2, 88; and silk handloom production in India 146

Harriss-White, Barbara 2, 3, 69, 71, 79, 85–7, 97, 99, 108–12, 114–21, 143–4, 146, 201n6, 203n6, 1, n6, 4, n6, 12, 204n19, 206n14, n15, n16
Harriss, Barbara 50, 51, 52, 53
Harriss, John 3, 41, 53, 97, 202n8
Henry, John F. 27–8
heteronomous commoditisation 18; in Provincial India 85–7
Heyer, Judith 99
High Yielding Varieties (HYVs) 36: and change in Arni 108–10, 115, 121, 150–1, 186; and change in Provincial India 37; *see also* green revolution
Himanshu 38, 200n12
historical bloc 16; in Arni 183, 185
Hodgson, Geoffrey 2, 14, 19, 20–5, 29, 30, 32
Hunt, Emery Kay 27

ILO 55–8, 200n17
Indira Gandhi *see* economic reforms
inequality in India's economy 38–9; in Provincial India 39–40
informal employment 58; poor quality 68–71
informal sector in Provincial India 58–68; contribution to GDP 67; gender bias 66; regulation 70–1

informal sector: theoretical analysis 54–7
institution 6; and habits 21–3
institutional embeddedness *see*
    embeddedness of capitalist change

Janakarajan, S. 108, 110, 114
Jayaraj, D. 51, 52, 143, 147, 151
Jha, P.S. 78
jobless growth in India 39

Kalecki, Michail 77, 78
Kaviraj, Sudipta 102
Kolakowski, Leszek 14

labour commoditisation: in Critical
    Marxism 18–19; in Marx 13–14; in
    Provincial India 85–6
Lerche, Jens 54, 69, 85–7, 98, 201n25, n12

McCartney, Matthew 37–8, 79, 201n5, n6
Maertens, Annemie 37, 38
Mandal Commission and Mandal Report
    90, 96–8, 202n7
Marx, Karl 3, 4, 11–15, 17–18, 26–9, 76,
    85–6, 88, 91, 191, 199n2, 1, n2, 2, n2, 3,
    201n13, 202n5
Marxist-Institutionalist dialogue 26–8;
    Veblen's critique 27
Marxist-Institutionalist framework: the
    analysis of capitalism 33–4; the analysis
    of capitalism in Provincial India 34–5;
    propositions 29–33
Mayhew, Anne 22, 24, 27
Mellor, John W. 45, 50, 110, 112, 113,
    203n6, 9
Mellor's growth linkages 45; critical
    analysis and tests 50
methodological collectivism 20
methodological individualism 20
Michelutti, Lucia 97
Milanovic, Branco 2
Mofussil India *see* Provincial India

Nagaraj, K. 108, 146, 148–53, 155–60,
    203n7, 1, 204n7, n9, 205n23, n26
Nayyar, Rohini 53–4, 200n11
necessary impurities 24, 32; in Arni 185,
    195
neo-corporatism *see* societal corporatism
North Arcot surveys 109–10

O'Hara, Philip Anthony 28
Orthodox Marxism 11–14; and Critical
    Marxism 15–19

Papola, T.S. 39, 42–3, 51–3, 200n9
Patnaik, Utsa 37, 39, 77, 199n3, 3, 201n3
Portes, Alejandro 55, 57
postulates of historical materialism 12
Provincial India: a Marxist-Institutionalist
    conceptualisation 72–4; poor-quality
    employment 72; poor economic
    performance 72; as a variety of
    capitalism 1–2; variety of organisational
    forms 71

Rajiv Gandhi *see* economic reforms
Rani, Uma 3, 54
Resnick, Stephen 15
Rodrik, Dani 37–88
Roemer, John 20
Roman, Camilla 146, 148–9, 152, 155–9,
    203n7, 2, 204n5, n9; n12, n17, 205n27
Roy, Tirthankar 40, 157, 158, 203n7, 3,
    204n8, n13, n18, 205n20, n21, n22, n24
rural industry 51; and Mahatma Gandhi
    51–2
rural non-farm activities (RNFAs) 3;
    localisation 52–3; *see also* economic
    diversification
rural non-farm economy (RNFE):
    definition 40; as a residual sector in
    India 50
rural non-farm employment (RNFL) in
    India: empirical analysis 42–54; long-
    term expansion 42; uneven distribution
    44
rural subaltern workers in India 51–2;
    contradictory class locations 53–4
Rutheford, Malcolm 24
Rutten, Mario 81–5, 201n9

Sanyal, Kalyan 103, 201n14
Scheduled Castes (SCs) 66, 68, 72,
    200n22, 202n7, n8; in Arni's business
    economy 131–2, 135, 138, 143; in
    Arni's civil society 176; in Arni's silk
    economy 158, 205n27
Scheduled Tribes (STs) 66, 68, 72,
    200n22, 202n7, n8; in Arni's business
    economy 131–2, 135, 138, 143; in
    Arni's civil society 176; in Arni's silk
    economy 158, 205n27
segmented classes *see* class segmentation
self-employed workers 69–70
Sen, Amartya Kumar 3, 26
Shah, Ghanshyam 96–9
Sharma, Alakh N. 52, 53, 54, 200n11

Sharma, K.L. 1994 96, 97, 99, 202n8
Sherman, Howard J. 28
social downgrading 195–7
societal corporatism: macro-economic
    impact 95; and state corporatism 94
spatial embeddedness *see* embeddedness
    of capitalist change
Srinivas, M.N. 96–8
Srinivasan, M.V. 144
Srivastava, Ravi S. 39, 87
Standing, Guy 197
structure/superstructure: according to Marx
    12–13; according to Gramsci 15–16
Subramanian, Arvind 37, 38

Torri, Michelguglielmo 37–8
Townshend, Jules 27
trade unions in Arni 162, 181–2, 194

Unni, Jeemol 3, 39, 45, 51, 52–4, 200n11
Upadhya, Carol 82, 84
urban/rural relations 3; in Arni 108,
    110–13, 143, 193; in Provincial India
    40–1, 51–3, 97

van der Linden 18, 19, 29, 87
variety of capitalism: concept 1–2; Arni's
    capitalism 138–45
Veblen, Thorstein 21, 24–5, 26–8
Veblen's critique of rational optimising
    behaviour 21
Vijayabaskar, M. 69

welfare associations in Arni 163, 166–7,
    179, 181
Wolff, Richard 15
Wright, Erik Olin 17, 29, 199n2, 6

For Product Safety Concerns and Information please contact our
EU representative GPSR@taylorandfrancis.com Taylor & Francis
Verlag GmbH, Kaufingerstraße 24, 80331 München, Germany